Abc

Thomas E. Morimoto was born in Edmonton, Alberta, in 1918 and grew up in Fort McMurray, one of seven brothers. As a young man he hoed vegetables in his father's garden, worked on a scow on the Athabasca River, with the International Bitumen Company at Bitumount, Alberta, as a gold miner in the Northwest Territories, and under Wop May at Canadian Airways, where he became a radio operator. After serving as a signalman during the Second World War, Tom returned to Canada and studied at the University of Alberta, where he earned his MSc in chemical engineering. He worked in the burgeoning oil industry of Alberta and travelled the world on trade missions before moving to Dubai in 1978 and becoming a part of its oil and gas industry for nine years. Retired since 1987, Tom is an avid golfer, having regularly shot his age. Tom also maintains an interest in mining and oil and gas stocks, which he trades via the Internet. He lives in Kelowna and Arizona with his wife of sixty years, Kim, and has two granddaughters, Ariel and Danielle, in Edmonton. ∎

Cover and interior design by Dean Pickup
Cover images: Footprints along a dune, Jeremy Woodhouse / Getty Images; Tom Morimoto; Boreal forest, DesignPics
Edited by Kirsten Craven
Copyedited by Geri Rowlatt
Proofread by Lesley Reynolds
Scans by ABL Imaging

The type in this book is set in Sabon.

The publisher gratefully acknowledges the support of The Canada Council for the Arts and the Department of Canadian Heritage.

The publisher also acknowledges the support of the Alberta Historical Resources Foundation.

**Canada Council
for the Arts**

**Conseil des Arts
du Canada**

We acknowledge the financial support of the Government of Canada through the Book Publishing Industry Development Program (BPIDP) for our publishing activities.

Printed in Canada

2007 / 1

First published in the United States in 2007 by
Fitzhenry & Whiteside
311 Washington Street
Brighton, Massachusetts 02135

National Library of Canada Cataloguing in Publication Data

Morimoto, Tom, 1918-
Breaking trail : from Canada's northern frontier to the oil fields of
Dubai / a memoir by Tom Morimoto.

Includes bibliographical references.
ISBN 978-1-897252-17-8

1. Morimoto, Tom, 1918-. 2. Canada, Northern—Biography. 3. Dubayy (United Arab Emirates : Emirate)—Biography. 4. Chemical engineers— Canada—Biography. 5. Japanese Canadians—Biography. I. Title.

TP140.M67A3 2007   660'.092   C2007-900919-0

Fifth House Ltd.
A Fitzhenry & Whiteside Company
1511, 1800-4 St. SW
Calgary, Alberta T2S 2S5

1-800-387-9776
www.fitzhenry.ca

BREAKING TRAIL

From Canada's Northern Frontier
to the Oil Fields of Dubai

a memoir, a history by Tom Morimoto

FIFTH
HOUSE

Acknowledgements

I wish to thank all the people who have helped me in putting this volume together. There are probably some names that I will miss, but some of those who have been of great assistance are: Rick Pilger of the University of Alberta, for the great job of structuring my story into this book's various chapters; Dr. Doug Owram, for his critical review and valuable suggestions; Ken Hill, the son of Fort McMurray pioneer Walter Hill, for the use of his father's northern photographs; Mrs. Irene Shandly, the niece of R. C. Fitzsimmons, for her permission to use photographs of Bitumount; D. J. Comfort for permission to quote from *Ribbons of Water and Steamboats North*; Denny May, the son of the great aviator Wop May, for permission to include photographs of his father and airplanes in the North. I would also like to thank editor Kirsten Craven, copyeditor Geri Rowlatt, and managing editor Meaghan Craven, for their work on the text. ■

Tom Morimoto, 2007

For my wife, Kim, and my two
granddaughters, Ariel and Danielle,
and in memory of my son, Dana.

Contents

Foreword

R. N. Mannix

What you are about to read is the absolutely remarkable and true life story of an incredible man, an engineer, and a truly great Canadian: Mr. Tom Morimoto.

It is a history of northern Canada, particularly the Fort McMurray and Yellowknife areas, and of how these two frontier communities went from boom times to bust, from rocks, trees, and frozen lakes and rivers to the mining cities of today. Morimoto's story is also about the initial development of the world famous oil sands of Alberta (Tom worked with both Bob Fitzsimmons and Karl Clark), as well as building the pipelines and gas plants of western Canada. Having grown up in Fort McMurray, Tom Morimoto was part of the North and its industries right from the start and was a true pioneer in its development.

But Tom's memoir is more than a recounting of Alberta's industrial development—it flows deeper than that. Read on and you will find the story of one man's incredibly lucky and yet horrific wartime experience. Tommy (as he is fondly known by his friends) spent sixty-two months of his life in Europe during the Second World War. He lived to tell what it was like to sail to and from Britain, go over the mines and beaches of Normandy, establish a military presence in Europe, and continue the fight until victory in 1945. He returned home to Canada physically unscathed by the war but significantly impressed by it and all the other aspects Europe had to offer.

Upon his return from the war effort, Tommy went back to school under the Veterans' Act, earning a degree in chemical engineering and then his master's degree, which set him up perfectly for the oil and gas boom in western Canada in the 1950s and 1960s.

Mr. Morimoto was the man in whom my father, Mr. Fred C. Mannix, had the faith, trust, and confidence to build our organization's engineering activities in a company called Mon-Max (Montreal Engineering/Mannix). My father always spoke very highly of Tommy and involved him in many projects as our organization helped build the infrastructure of Canada after the war. Tommy built Mon-Max into one of the finest and largest gas-plant, pipeline, and chemical-plant engineering firms in Canada. He was always a fighter, taking on the big American engineering construction companies and showing them how to construct world-scale gas-plant facilities.

He was a product of the Depression and the ruggedness of the North Country, and it was out of his experiences that his determination and work ethic developed. He was highly respected by those he worked with, and throughout his career he was in great demand for his engineering, technical design, and management skills.

It was through Tommy's entrepreneurial and inquisitive spirit (and a bit of good luck) that he eventually went on to manage a world-scale gas project in Dubai, using the flared gas from their oil fields in the Middle East to create usable gas products. He lived in Dubai for nearly a decade and was involved in the start-up of the gas business in that region, just as he had pioneered the industry here in Alberta.

Tommy is a true gentleman, loved and respected by those who have known him. At the same time he is a colourful and competitive person, with his sporting activities ranging from championship boxing to skiing, baseball, hockey, table tennis, horse racing and golf. Despite his busy life, hobnobbing with royalty in England or skiing with his old friend Brock Montgomery at Sunshine Village, Tom has always been a quiet and family-oriented individual. He enjoyed incredible support and love from his wife, Kim, and he in turn cared for her, their only son, Dana, and a niece, while balancing all of his other responsibilities.

Breaking Trail is an engaging memoir of a remarkable and humble leader, rich in personal details; people's names; stories and insights about the development of Canada's oil, gas, and tar sands sector; gold mining in the North; exciting adventures in Europe during the Second World War; trade missions in South America and Russia; and gas developments in the Middle East. Here is a man who was always willing to learn, never giving up on his dreams and willing to risk his life and limb for his country and fellow Canadians.

Mr. Morimoto's life story provides many lessons for all of us. He was an exemplary gentleman. He worked with great dedication and loyalty to family, friends, and his country of birth. Finally, his characteristics of honesty, integrity, foresight, and entrepreneurial spirit, all of which are continually needed in our society, are a tremendous example for us to follow.

We sincerely hope readers will enjoy the true life story of Mr. Tom Morimoto, a highly respected and truly remarkable Canadian. ∎

Introduction

Dr. Doug Owram

Deputy Vice-Chancellor, University of British Columbia, Kelowna, BC

First let me admit to a conflict of interest. I met Tom Morimoto, an alumnus of the University of Alberta, when we played in (and won) a university-based golf tournament a few years ago. Since then I have had the opportunity to meet Tom and his charming wife, Kim, several times. They are kind, intelligent, and thoughtful people, and it is thus with some bias that I took up the opportunity to write an introduction to Tom's memoir. I knew enough about the story to know it would be interesting and, like Tom himself, lively. I was not disappointed.

Two things struck me in reading this story. The first is how Tom Morimoto, in an unassuming way, witnessed or participated in many of the main historical themes of an era. The second is how the book reveals the way in which an individual's life opens up to new possibilities when there is the right combination of willingness, lack of presumption, and a sense of adventure.

To say that this book helps us understand our history might seem an overstatement. Tom was undoubtedly a very successful individual, but he was never a general, an elected politician, or an international diplomat. Yet, as the following pages reveal, his experiences capture much of Canada—from life in a northern frontier town, through a soldier's experience in World War II, to post-war opportunity and prosperity.

This is a story with distinct stages. The first stage occurs in northern Alberta, which, as Tom notes, was an unlikely destination for his parents—first-generation Japanese Canadians. Yet the sense of adventure that brought his parents north foreshadowed the same sense of adventure that marks Tom's own life. Certainly early life in the frontier town of Fort McMurray was an essential ingredient in his development. There was both a rough edge to life and a spontaneity that was at times innovative and at others chaotic. The social order of the community as it appears in these pages seems to be a paradox. Many of those attracted to this small outpost more than fulfilled the tradition that frontiers attract both eccentrics and adventurers. Events could verge on the chaotic and seem, to the reader, to appear somewhat threatening. At the same time Tom nicely depicts the intimacy and stabilizing forces binding this small frontier community. When everybody knew everybody there were a series of connections that would have been impossible in larger communities. Typical of this theme is Tom's description of the midnight mass at the Roman Catholic Church. First, there is the simple fact that Tom thought nothing of attending mass even though he was not Catholic and, indeed, his father was Shinto. Second, once there they could hear "Father Letreste give his sermon in four languages—French, English, Cree, and Chipewyan."

The second phase of the story, and Tom's life, came with the beginning of World War II. When the blitzkrieg began Tom headed off—all 5 feet, 2 inches and 116 pounds of him—to join the army. Though he didn't even come close to army size requirements he was a trained radio operator and that, apparently, was worth some height and weight! By 1941 he was in England. While there Tom (remember his weight!) joined the boxing team and made it to the army finals, winning the silver medal. Then, in 1944 everything changed. Tom landed with the thousands of other Canadians on D-Day and was with his unit through France and into Germany through 1944–45.

The war experience is interesting in itself but there are two reasons historically that make his World War II years important. First, as a Japanese Canadian the very fact he served in the army was unusual. Had he tried to enlist after December 1941 it is extremely unlikely he would have been accepted. Even as it was there were questions from headquarters about his loyalty and talk about recalling him to Canada. He was fortunate, however, in having supportive officers locally and thus was able, as he puts it, to resist the demands from back home. Overall, he concludes that he suffered little prejudice during the war: "I think this illustrates the fairness of the men who were my comrades and justifies my pride in having served with them."

The second reason that the World War II section stands out is that Tom is representative of many thousands of Canadians for whom the war is a great divide in their lives and their expectations. The war took him out of the north, exposed him to the United Kingdom, which he returned to many times thereafter. The Veteran's Charter also gave him the opportunity to attend the University of Alberta, graduating from Engineering in 1949. The importance of university education and the opportunity created by the charter is something I have heard over and over again from Tom's generation. Those who took university as a natural event, a continuation always expected of us, cannot fully appreciate just how important the charter was to Tom's generation

The same talents that Tom had shown earlier in life were now combined with his degree and a post-war boom. Tom quickly moved into ever more interesting roles as an engineer and businessman. In Calgary and Houston was witnessed the transformation of Alberta's economy in the wake of the Leduc discovery of 1947. The story Tom tells is a microcosm of what the economists would term "linkage" as more and more expertise devolved from Houston to Calgary and a full-fledged oil city was born.

Before long this expertise began to be re-exported and along with the expertise went Tom. Expanding work in Latin America, Northern Africa, and, most of all, the Middle East both testified to his growing presence in the industry and Canada's maturity as a country. However, such a description doesn't do justice to a story that includes knife attacks, visits to Royal Ascot, and a group of people with personalities that would have been at home among the frontier eccentrics of Fort McMurray.

So, in the end, the book tells us many things, but most of all it is an interesting story by a person who never passed up opportunities to see what came next and to do an exceptional job. This takes me back to golf. Tom's life, like his game, seems to reflect a neat intersection of opportunity, enthusiasm, and ability. It has been a joy to read the manuscript and a privilege to know Tom and his wife. ■

Preface

Tom Morimoto

I wrote this memoir mainly because my son asked me to tell him about my history and experiences, of which he knew very little. Also, I think that having been born in 1918 and having lived in northern Canada in the early 1920s and 1930s, I lived through a historic period in Canada before civilization changed the North Country forever.

Since leaving Fort McMurray, where I grew up, I have had a varied career, staking gold claims in the Northwest Territories, travelling to countries such as Algeria and Russia, and managing a large gas operation in Dubai.

Over the years I have met people from all walks of life, which has been very rewarding. I would like to pay tribute to the people who have helped me on my way. I am grateful for all the good things that have happened to me, and I hope that these recollections will go some distance to thanking my many benefactors.

I have previously told some of the stories I have set down here, and some of my listeners suggested that I write a book about my experiences. This narrative is the result. I hope it will give readers some insight into what life was like in the early days in the North Country, as well as what life was like during the war years and in Dubai when it was just emerging from its somnolent state into the modern era. ■

PART ONE

FORT MCMURRAY

Establishing Roots in Canada

*I*t is surprising to some people that someone like me, a second generation Japanese-Canadian (Nisei), should have grown up in northern Canada. As a matter of fact, many people have taken me to be a Native Indian or Inuit, presumably because it seemed so unlikely that anyone of Japanese descent would come from the North Country. It is all due to my father being an enterprising person, always willing to try something new. His name was Katsuhei, but he was known as Tommy.

My father was a tiny man, only 4 feet 10 inches (about 1.5 m) in height and weighing 92 pounds (42 kg). But, pound for pound, he was the strongest man I've ever known. He could easily carry 200 pounds (90 kg) on his back and was tireless when doing any sort of manual labour. During the Depression, people were allowed to work to pay off their provincial taxes. So, during the summer, my father would work shovelling gravel. He could shovel more gravel than any of the burliest, strongest men whom he worked alongside.

I remember once when I was fifteen and I was doing some chin-ups,

1

my father asked me what I was doing. I explained how I wanted to strengthen my arms by lifting myself by them to touch my chin on the bar. I told him how difficult it was to do twenty chin-ups. He promptly said, "Let me try that," and did forty and then said, "That was too easy." He then did forty chin-ups with one arm, then forty with the other arm. I have never seen anyone else do this! I was so disgusted at how puny my efforts seemed in comparison that I never let him know what a remarkable feat he had accomplished. I've always regretted not telling him so.

Looking back, I'm grateful to my father for the way he brought us up. He insisted that, since we were born in Canada, we had to be good Canadians, which meant adopting all the customs and mores of the country. As a result, we had to go to Sunday school and church whether we liked it or not. We had to be polite to our elders and be good citizens and contribute to our native land.

My father was born in Japan and had quite a hard life. His father died when he was nine years old, leaving only his mother and him to eke out a living. He worked as a coal miner in Japan and then immigrated, first to Hawaii in 1905 and then to Canada the following year. He used to tell me how terribly hot it was in Hawaii and didn't seem to agree with those who waxed lyrical about what a paradise it was. His recollections of the islands were not pleasant ones—only memories of hard, back-breaking work and searing heat in the sugarcane fields. After arriving in Canada in 1906, he found various jobs in British Columbia. He first worked as a houseboy in a whorehouse—or, as he called it, a "sporting girls house." Then he became a logger in a lumber camp and became an expert with an axe, cutting down cedar trees and splitting cedar shingles. When I was still quite young, he taught me how to use an axe and how to split wood, and since then I have surprised some pretty strong men by being able to split a piece of wood that they were having difficulty with because they didn't have the proper technique.

From British Columbia, my father went east to Edmonton, Alberta, in 1912 and worked as a cook in the Cecil Hotel. When the First World War broke out, he tried to join the army but was rejected because he was too small. He then went to barber college and became a barber and opened a barber shop and rooming house on 101 Street in Edmonton, near the Royal George Hotel. My mother, Mitome, came to Canada from Japan in 1917 as a picture bride. Her family knew my father's mother, and the marriage was arranged long distance. When she arrived in Edmonton, my father taught her the barbering trade and together they worked in their barber shop and rooming house. The premises included baths, and with this combination they did a great business, especially with the many servicemen returning from the Great War in 1919 and 1920.

My parents outside their rooming house in Edmonton. The Royal George Hotel towers above the rooming house on the right.

I was born in May 1918 and don't remember anything about my childhood in Edmonton except for an incident when I cut the back of my wrist on a broken bottle. It must have frightened me a great deal for me to remember that, because I was only two years old at the time. I remember my mother saying that I used to strut down the street with my hands under my suspenders and wander into the Woolworth's five-and-dime store just a few doors away. There, a salesgirl would make a big fuss over me—probably because I was the only two-year-old child in the vicinity. I was probably a spoiled brat because of all the attention.

My mother, Mitome, my father, Katsuhei, and me as a baby in Edmonton in 1918.

My parents prospered with their business, but this didn't last. Their landlord was Abe Cristall, who owned the Royal George Hotel, which was almost next door. Abe was a very astute businessman, and when he saw how well my father was doing he raised his rent by twenty-five dollars to fifty dollars each month. After a number of rent hikes, the rent became so high that my parents decided they could no longer stay in business and would have to look for something else. It was 1920 and the chief spokesman for Fort McMurray was Colonel Jim Cornwall. Cornwall was a famous northern personality of whom much has been written. When my father went to Fort McMurray to survey the situation, he met Cornwall, who persuaded him to relocate his business there. Cornwall had arranged for the area to be subdivided into lots, two of which my father purchased.

The Alberta and Great Waterways Railway (later called the Northern Alberta Railways) had just completed its railway line from Edmonton to Waterways, which was located 300 miles (480 km) north of Edmonton. With oil sands and thick beds of salt only several hundred feet underground, it looked as though Fort McMurray had a tremendous future. Unfortunately for my father, he was about fifty years too early.

Still, in 1920 Fort McMurray was booming. Buildings were going up all along Franklin Avenue, which was and still is the main street of the town. Impressed by all this activity, my father chose a site on Franklin Avenue and had a building for his rooming house and barber shop erected by Sven Swanson, a Swedish carpenter. In March 1921 my mother took the train from Edmonton to Waterways with her two little sons in tow— me just two months shy of three years of age and my brother, Bob, just a little over a year old (five more brothers—I had no sisters—would be born in Fort McMurray). Because I was so young, I remember very little of the train ride. The Alberta and Great Waterways Railway built from Edmonton to Waterways was to be extended 3 miles (5 km) farther to Fort McMurray. However, it didn't reach Fort McMurray until the Second World War, when a U.S. Army construction unit built a spur line to The Prairie, which was midway between Waterways and Fort McMurray. When we arrived, we detrained at Old Waterways, which was several miles south of the eventual location of the hamlet of Waterways.

The railway and passenger cars that we rode in were the old "colonist cars" built in the 1880s and 1890s for Canadian Pacific Railway (CPR) to carry colonists from eastern to western Canada. The cars had hard wooden seats with no cushions and an upright coal stove at one end, both for heating and cooking. Everyone had to carry his or her own food and do what cooking they could on this coal stove. It took several days to cover the distance as there was not too much concern about a schedule. In those days there was still a lot of wildlife in the country. If moose were sighted, the train crew would stop the train and bail out for a spot of moose hunting. After leaving the town of Lac La Biche, which is about 100 miles (160 km) north of Edmonton, the route traversed sections of muskeg. Since the railway had been constructed through these areas by dumping loads of gravel on top of the muskeg, the roadbed at times seemed to be almost like a floating bridge, and the train would have to slow to a crawl over these stretches.

After several days we arrived at Old Waterways, where we stayed overnight and slept on the floor of the "restaurant" dining room. I can remember my mother telling me of her horror at seeing the cook's socks drying on a line over the soup pots on the kitchen stove, the water dripping from the socks into the soups. Even years later, whenever I saw the cook, who had become a mining camp cook, I always thought of the dripping socks. We left the next morning for the 7-mile (11-km) trek to Fort McMurray on a wagon pulled by a team of horses owned by the Ryan brothers. The ride to Fort McMurray from Old Waterways is my earliest recollection of the place, probably because of the sheer terror I felt sitting on top of our household goods, which were piled high on the wagon. We were crossing Horse Creek, and it seemed to me the wagon was tilted at a forty-five-degree angle. I felt certain I was going to fall off.

After we moved to Fort McMurray, my father's business was quite good for the first couple of years. However, after the initial boom following the completion of the railway to New Waterways, 3 miles (5 km) away, business languished and Fort McMurray became a sleepy little hamlet, especially in the wintertime. Eventually affairs deteriorated so much that in 1924 my father decided to go trapping muskrats in the Athabasca River delta. The delta is a huge floating swamp with a teeming population of muskrats. At that time you were allowed to trap these animals during the winter, although trapping is now limited to the spring months. Winter travel was all by dog team. As soon as the ice on the Athabasca River was thick enough, my father went by dog team to Embarras Portage, about 150 miles (240 km) north of Fort McMurray.

As I recall it, my father made a couple of trips that winter from Fort McMurray to Embarras Portage. During one of his return trips to Fort McMurray, the temperature dropped to -65°F (-54°C). His travelling companion was a fur trader named Bill Gordon, who was very obese and had to ride in the carriole of the toboggan because he couldn't run or walk fast enough to keep up with the dog team. The second night out from Embarras, they were about to make camp when they discovered they had left their axe at the last campsite. My father was trying to find dead branches but without an axe was having difficulty getting enough wood to keep a fire going. Apparently poor Bill was almost frozen and of little help. Fortunately for them, another fur trader—Jim Darwish, who was on his way from Fort Rae in the Northwest Territories to Fort McMurray—came to the rescue. Luckily he had stopped at their previous campsite, noticed their axe, and brought it along. In a short time my father had a roaring fire going. He was very grateful to Jim Darwish[1] and often spoke of how he had saved their lives. In the harsh Canadian winter, life was sometimes held by the slenderest of threads— the loss of an axe could mean the difference between life and death.

Anyone who has never travelled by dog team in the dead of winter when the temperature drops to -40° to -60°F (-40° to -53°C) will have difficulty understanding the hardships that northern travellers endured. After a hard day on the trail they would try to find a sheltered spot near the riverbank, perhaps at the mouth of a creek, where they could find some dead trees for firewood and, if they were lucky, some birchbark with which to start a fire. They would then clear space for the fire and for a place to sleep. After lighting their fire they would cut spruce boughs to serve as a canvas for a bed on which they could arrange their blankets. (Very few early northern travellers had sleeping bags. Some of

them, like Billy Loutit, who became famous for his memorable walking feats, did not carry any sleeping gear at all.) After the fire was going, they would melt snow for water and make tea in a lard pail suspended over the fire. Then they would thaw out fish for the dogs. If they were well supplied, they would have pork and beans that had been precooked and frozen for their meal. After eating they would pile as many logs as possible onto the fire to keep it going during the night.

In 1925, following his trapping venture, my father leased land from the Hudson's Bay Company (HBC) near the location of the present bridge across the Athabasca River at Fort McMurray. This area was known as Hudson's Bay Flats and covered about 10 acres (4 ha) of very fertile soil. He grew potatoes and vegetables, which he shipped farther north, and made enough money to keep us from having to go on relief during the Depression. He even managed to send me to high school in Edmonton from 1932 to 1934 during the depths of the Depression.

My father also tried his hand at muskrat farming. In 1929 he obtained some twenty or so muskrats from Fred Olander, a Swedish trapper who trapped on a lake (either Mildred or Ruth Lake) that was on or near the present Syncrude property north of Fort McMurray.

A dog train leaving Fort McMurray, ca. 1920. (photograph by Walter Hill, courtesy Ken Hill)

These muskrats he transported 30 miles (50 km) or so south of Fort McMurray to Kinosis Lake. About 3 miles (5 km) long and marshy around its shores, Kinosis Lake was an ideal place for muskrats. My father obtained a lease on the lake and began his muskrat farm. Billy Gregoire, a local Métis who lived at Willow Lake (now Gregoire Lake), began building a log cabin at Kinosis for my father in 1929. However, Gregoire was not available to finish the work. My father probably couldn't afford to hire anyone else, so he completed the building himself. People wondered how he had managed to hoist the large logs to the upper levels by himself; he did it by using an improvised tripod and a long pole attached to the tripod as a lever. My father had a great practical engineering mind and often came up with ingenious solutions to such problems. When the walls of the log house were completed, the roof was constructed of logs overlain by dirt. Here again he used levers to hoist the dirt to the roof. The cracks in the walls of the house were chinked with moss. During the summer my father kept working at his potato and vegetable farm in Fort McMurray while my mother and my younger brothers and I went to live at Kinosis during the school holiday months of July and August. This was in 1929 when I was eleven.

The Alberta and Great Waterways Railway had a water tank on the railroad near Kinosis, where their trains always stopped to fill up with water on their weekly runs between Edmonton and Fort McMurray. This stop was about 3 miles (5 km) from our cabin. My father would send groceries for our family via the railway, and the baggage man would throw them off at the water tank. This meant that each week my brother and I had to make the walk to the railway and back, 6 miles (10 km) in all. My brother Bob, who was nine, had burned his leg in an accident, so my little brother Harry, who was only seven, had to accompany me to bring back the load of groceries. I can remember encouraging him by saying, "It's only a little way now to the big tree," and then, "It's not far now to the creek." The trail wound through the bush, and the path was quite well defined. It had probably been used for years, as had so many of the bush trails. At any rate there was not much chance of us getting lost as long as there was daylight. We would finally arrive back at our cabin, exhausted from carrying our 40 pounds (18 kg) or so of supplies, to be greeted by our relieved mother.

There were a lot of pike, or jackfish as we called them, in Kinosis Lake, but it was too reedy to fish from shore. Since we didn't have a boat, we weren't able to fish. The lake was a beautiful pristine body of water still unspoiled by civilization. To this day I still remember hearing the haunting cries of the loons and watching the ducks with their little offspring swimming about near the shore. I also recall now with wonder how we ran barefoot and how the soles of our feet toughened up so we could walk on twigs or roots without noticing them. At the time we didn't give it a thought.

During the summer of 1929, the only summer we spent at Kinosis Lake, we had unremitting rain for a week. The little creek running into the lake near our log cabin grew from a meandering brook to a deep raging torrent. Worst of all, our sod roof leaked, so we had to move out of the house, set up a tent, and move into it. (Eventually, with more dirt and the passage of time, the cabin's roof became waterproof.) As a result of the flooding, the log bridge that spanned the creek near our cabin was almost torn away. When we crossed it on our weekly trek to the railway to pick up our groceries, it was canted at a precarious angle and we had to gingerly pick our way across. When my father came to see us a week later, he was horrified to learn that we had crossed on the bridge and said we were lucky that the bridge had not collapsed.

Another memory of that summer is our struggle to keep the mice away from our provisions. To foil them we would hang our hams and other food items from the ceiling, suspended by a piece of twine. However, we discovered they were nimble enough to even come down the piece of cord to get at the ham. One of my favourite games was to listen at night for the mice, then creep up in the dark and grab an unsuspecting mouse by the tail from his perch on the ham. It took quick reflexes to catch the mouse, but I caught quite a few.

Finally, when September came my brother Harry and I returned to Fort McMurray and went back to school. My mother and other brothers stayed in Kinosis for two weeks longer, and my father went out there as well. This meant that I, at the age of twelve, and my brother, aged eight, lived by ourselves for two weeks, cooking our own meals and going to school each day. Nowadays, this would probably be considered child neglect, but it seemed perfectly natural to us.

Eventually, in 1932, after a few years of trying to breed enough muskrats so that he could harvest some of them for their fur, my father had to give up the project. The Natives kept trapping the muskrats, so there weren't enough left to make a go of it. We only spent the one summer there in 1929, but I have often thought nostalgically of what an idyllic place it was. About five years ago, I went to visit my Métis friend Bill Woodward at Gregoire Lake (formerly known as Willow Lake). He offered to take me the few miles to Lake Kinosis but we discovered the road was flooded, so we had to abandon the idea. ■

Fort McMurray in the 1920s

*L*ooking at the modern city of Fort McMurray, it is difficult to imagine that up until the Second World War began it was a sleepy little village, or rather two small villages—Fort McMurray and Waterways—which were about 3 miles (5 km) apart, with a total permanent population of perhaps two or three hundred. I say permanent population because that is what it was in the winter; in the summer, the population exploded to several times that number.

People often ask me what in the world ever prompted my father to move to the North Country, which in the 1920s was regarded as almost the end of creation. However, you must remember that in 1921 Fort McMurray was a boom town and was being heralded as the new city of the North. Fort McMurray had previously gone through a boom period in 1911, prior to the First World War. At that time, land prices skyrocketed and some of the residents sold their land for what in those days were fabulous prices, even though the town was 300 miles (500 km) from the nearest railroad point.

Prior to 1921, travel to Fort McMurray involved journeying by horse and wagon from Edmonton, the nearest rail point, to Athabasca Landing (the present town of Athabasca) and then continuing the trip by water via the Athabasca River. Scows, flat-bottomed boats used as barges, were formed up in a convoy and then, steered by "sweeps," were floated to Fort McMurray and points farther north as far as Fort Fitzgerald on the Alberta–Northwest Territories border. These craft had to "shoot" the rapids on the river, eleven in all, which made for some hair-raising rides, especially for newcomers. The largest of these rapids, Grand Rapids, is actually almost a waterfall and was usually bypassed by means of a railway track built around it. The scows were loaded onto wheeled trams on this track and manhandled to a point downstream where they were relaunched for the remainder of the trip downstream. One riverman by the name of Louis Fousseneuve was called "Captain Shott" because of his fame in shooting the rapids. I knew two of his sons, Joe and Emil Shott—they seem to have permanently adopted "Shott" as their surname.

When I was a child, Fort McMurray consisted of a few business establishments on Franklin Avenue, which incidentally was named after the explorer Sir John Franklin who went north via Fort McMurray on his voyage to the Arctic. At the east end of the avenue was the Franklin Hotel (later called the Oil Sands Hotel), which was owned by Frank O'Coffey. Sutherland's Drug Store was on the same site as the present drug store (adjacent to the Oil Sands Hotel), next to the Dominion Telegraph Station, which offered the only mode of communication to the outside world. Then came John Parry's General Store, Skelton's Butcher Shop, and the town water well, where the new Hudson's Bay Company (HBC) store was later built. My father's rooming house came next, followed by Charlie Mah's Union Cafe and the Board of Trade building.

The Board of Trade building was an old log structure where the Fort McMurray Board of Trade met during the early days. It then became George "Scotty" Morrison's residence. Morrison was a pioneer resident of Fort McMurray, having arrived there before 1911. He owned a barbershop and a bakery and was also the Dominion

Board of Trade members in Fort McMurray, ca. 1920. Seated left to right: "Scotty" Morrison, Kenneth Mackenzie, Zephyr Martin. Standing left to right: Annie Morrison, Mrs. Jeanie Morrison, Mrs. McTavish, Mrs. McVittle, Captain Williscroft, Reverend McTavish, Cecil Potts, Jack McDonald of Alberta Provincial Police.

Government's general representative for several different departments, acting as the sheriff, the registrar of births and deaths, and the land titles registrar. The old building was then used as a church by the Rev. Mr. C. D. McTavish, the pioneer Presbyterian minister. Later yet, it was used as a Sunday school by the United Church, which I attended. This building is now in Fort McMurray's Heritage Park. The present Morrison Centre in Fort McMurray is on the site where the old Board of Trade building originally stood.

Franklin Avenue ended at the HBC property, which was known as Hudson's Bay Flats (the original Hudson's Bay fort was near the Athabasca River, where the present bridge across the Athabasca River has its entrance). There were two buildings here. The largest was the residence of the superintendent for the Mackenzie District in 1921—Louis Romanet. The smaller was the residence of John Sutherland and his family.

Sutherland was the pioneer steam engineer on the original ss *Grahame*, the HBC steamboat built at Fort Chipewyan in 1883. When I was a boy, he was the engineer on the ss *Athabasca River*.

Bill Gordon owned all of the property on the north side of Franklin Avenue from Hudson's Bay Flats to somewhere opposite the Board of Trade building. Bill Gordon was a relative of the famous Major Charles George "Chinese" Gordon, who was famed for his military exploits in China in 1864 and his ill-fated defence of Khartoum against Sudanese rebels in 1884. Bill originally came to Fort McMurray during the Klondike Gold Rush and settled there to become a fur trader. On Bill Gordon's property were several houses, one owned by Sven Swanson, the Swedish carpenter and woodcutter who had constructed my father's building. Scotty Morrison built a house at the end of the Gordon property. Next to his property were several empty lots where Ronnie Morrison (Scotty's son), Real Martin, and some of the other boys and I played baseball. We hacked out a baseball diamond in the early 1930s, which was used for many years. At the east end of Franklin Avenue was the butcher Arnold Skelton's house, and beside it a building where the famous

FORT McMURRAY, July 1922   HILL PHOTO

Franklin Avenue, Fort McMurray, in 1922. Notice Sutherland's Drug Store and the Franklin Hotel.
(photography by Walter Hill, courtesy Ken Hill)

pilot Wop May lived when he first came to Fort McMurray.

In its early days, Fort McMurray's main source of income came from trapping. Most of the trappers were Native or Métis, but there were a number of white trappers as well. Almost all the trappers living within a 100-mile (160-km) radius of the village used it as a base to obtain supplies and sell furs. This meant that in winter there were always dog teams coming into town, mostly on the Athabasca River, which was essentially a winter highway for the dog teams once it had frozen over. Snowdrifts would fill in the toboggan trail on the river during snowstorms. This meant that the unfortunate musher traversing the trail by dog team after the storm would have to "break trail," which involved someone going ahead of the dogs on snowshoes to tramp down the snow. I have often wondered how anyone can consider snowshoeing a sport because breaking trail is such an arduous job.

When I was growing up, all heavy land transportation was conducted by horse-drawn vehicles—wagons in summer and sleighs in winter. The Ryan brothers operated the major share of the transportation business in Fort McMurray, with half a dozen teams of horses, their own livery barn, and a permanent crew of teamsters. They had one Model-T Ford truck, which was brought to Fort McMurray by Angus Sutherland in 1920. I don't see how it could have operated very successfully in the early 1920s because the roads between Waterways and Fort McMurray had not yet been gravelled and were a real quagmire.

The Ryans were an interesting pair. Pat, the eldest, was stone deaf and a blacksmith by trade. Mickey, his younger brother, had been a professional lightweight boxer in the United States. Pat ran the Fort McMurray branch of the business, and Mickey moved to Fort Fitzgerald and Fort Smith, where he obtained a monopoly on the haulage between the two towns. All the freight for the Northwest Territories came from Edmonton by rail to Waterways, then by boat to Fort Fitzgerald on the Alberta–Northwest Territories border. At this point, the freight had to be unloaded from the boats and portaged 16 miles (26 km) to Fort Smith because of the impassable rapids on the Slave River. From Fort Smith, boats could travel unimpeded all the way to the Arctic Ocean.

In the winter all transportation was by sleigh. Horse-drawn sleighs carried freight and people between Fort McMurray and Waterways. The Ryan brothers had a heated caboose on a sleigh for passengers. They also had a contract to carry the mail as far as Fort Smith. For this they used single horse-drawn flat sleighs, which were essentially extra-wide toboggans. A caravan of a dozen or more horses with their loads would make the round trip to Fort Smith several times a winter, following the frozen Athabasca River, Athabasca Lake, and the Slave River. To prepare food for the trip north, a huge pot of pork and beans was made and then ladled into pie plates, which were set outside to freeze. The frozen cakes of pork and beans were then stacked and sewn into used flour sacks, so that all anyone had to do was put a cake into a pot over a campfire to have a meal ready in no time.

In the summer the various waterways were the main channels of transportation. Of course, the canoe had been used for centuries, and it was still used by most of the Natives in the 1920s. By then, however, many of the canoes and skiffs (small boats) had outboard motors to make the trip upstream on the rivers, mainly the Athabasca River, which was the main artery running to the North. In the early days before

the railroad was built to Fort McMurray, scows were taken upstream by "trackers," who pulled them with long ropes attached to the bow, assisted by a man on board with a pole to keep the scow away from the shore. In this manner, scows were pulled all the way from Fort McMurray to Athabasca Landing, a trip of several hundred miles. After the trip the men would have to walk back to Fort McMurray. They would only be paid for the time they were tracking and had to find their own way back.

Sternwheel paddle-driven steamboats were the first mechanized craft on the Athabasca River. The first steamboat to ply the Athabasca was the ss *Grahame*, which was built in Fort Chipewyan in 1883. Stan Wylie, a grandson of William Wylie, told me that his grandfather,

Hudson's Bay Company steamer SS *Grahame* at Macdonald Island in "Snye" at Fort McMurray. The S.S. *Grahame* was the first steamboat on the Athabasca River at Fort Chipeweyan in 1883.

who had come out from Scotland as an indentured servant for the HBC, had become the company's blacksmith and had installed the boiler and engine on the *Grahame*. I remember as a boy playing on the hull of the *Grahame* in the 1920s, which after its useful life was over was left derelict on Macdonald Island in Fort McMurray. According to J. G. MacGregor, in his book *Paddle Wheels to Bucket-Wheels on the Athabasca*, the first hull of the *Grahame* was discarded at Fort Chipewyan in 1894, and the second *Grahame*, using the machinery of the first, plied the Athabasca River until 1914 when "her hull was broken up at Fort Chipewyan."[1] However, I remember very distinctly seeing the painted name "SS Grahame" on the remains of the boat when we used to go and rummage around the old hull on Macdonald Island. Recently, I have had this confirmed by Mr. Real Martin, an old-time resident of Fort McMurray and a boyhood friend, who also remembered seeing the *Grahame* on Macdonald Island. Gradually, over the years, the wreck disappeared as people tore it apart for firewood.

The two main steamboats on the river in my youth were the SS *Athabasca*, owned by the HBC, and the SS *Northland Echo*, owned by the Northern Traders. It was thrilling for us as children to hear the huffing and puffing of the steamboat engine as it came up the Athabasca. We would all run down to the riverbank to watch its progress as it neared town and hear the captain announce its arrival by sounding the whistle. The steamboats were quite luxurious for those days, with cabins and white-coated stewards and stewardesses serving sumptuous meals in the dining room.

Although the steamboats carried passengers, their primary function was to transport goods. Since the carrying capacity of the steamboat itself was limited, it usually pushed an accompanying barge, which could accommodate a heavy load of freight. At various spots along the river, the steamboats would stop to load cordwood, cutting wood being the main source of income for many people who lived along the river. They were paid three dollars a cord during the time I was growing up in Fort McMurray. This price included cutting, splitting, and piling the wood along the riverbank in a location where it could be loaded by the deckhands, who would carry one 4-foot (1.2-m) piece of wood at a time until several cords were loaded.

Unfortunately, none of the steamboats remain. The last steamboat on the Athabasca River, the ss *Athabasca*, had been beached at The Prairie in 1950, and when the municipality demanded that taxes be paid on the boat, the owner, the HBC, destroyed this priceless link to our past. The steamboats were superseded by the more economical internal-combustion-driven boats, especially the diesel-powered tugs. Thus a romantic era passed into history. I'm sure that all Northerners of my era mourned the demise of those behemoths of the water and their mournful whistle blasts as they huffed and puffed their way up and down the river. ■

Growing Up in
Fort McMurray

*L*ooking back it would appear that Fort McMurray was probably a very good place for me to grow up in. We were not subject to the many temptations that children are exposed to nowadays. The worst thing any of us ever did was try smoking, and even then I was lucky enough to have never picked up the habit. Another fortuitous result of living in Fort McMurray was that my brothers and I became thoroughly Canadianized in comparison with children of Japanese origin who grew up in the more or less ghettoized areas of British Columbia. My father insisted that we become good Canadians and was very strict about our conduct. We were taught to be absolutely honest, never to steal or cheat anyone, and to respect our elders. For example, we had to address a grown-up as Mr. so-and-so—even the town drunk, whom the other kids used to address by only his Christian name. We were also taught to be self-effacing, never to brag. In retrospect, this may have been a drawback, as I tended to stay in the background and sometimes let others take the credit when it would have been more advantageous for me to blow my own horn a bit.

All in all, Fort McMurray was a fascinating place, especially at Christmastime when all of the Natives would come in from their traplines to attend Midnight Mass. It was an exciting time for us when we were young to see all the dog teams with gaily coloured streamers flying from their harnesses and sleigh bells jingling. Some of the more affluent dog-team owners had their dogs' backs covered with beautiful blankets decorated with beadwork. The exciting thing for us children was to see the dogfights, when two teams would start fighting, tangling up all the harnesses, with everybody trying to pull them apart. I especially remember an English bulldog owned by John Richardson, a storekeeper. This bulldog always seemed to get loose when a dog team came to town and would immediately go for the throat of one of the dogs in a team. Mr. Richardson always kept a long iron poker (used for stirring up the wood fire in the stove) handy. He would come running out of his store with the poker to pry the bulldog's jaws apart. It was unbelievable, the death grip that that dog could get on another dog's throat.

Life in Fort McMurray revolved around the seasons, and the dominant season was winter. One lasting and abiding memory I have of Fort McMurray is the cold. Some days it felt like it was the coldest place in Canada, although it never did reach -70°F (-57°C) like Port Radium on Great Bear Lake did. On cold days the smoke from the stoves (everyone burned wood for heating) would rise straight up into the air, producing an eerie feeling with a sort of hazy fog pervading everything. You must remember, too, that this was in the days before insulated clothing and down-filled parkas. The hours of daylight were so short that we always seemed to be in darkness. We had to walk about a mile to school, and it was a cold walk home if there was a north wind off the Athabasca River—and there always seemed to be one.

Winters were usually so cold that none of us played outside very much. We did slide down the hills on our sleds or toboggans but did not skate, as there was usually no skating rink. One year, our teacher Mr. Bean and some of the older boys built a skating rink near the schoolhouse, but this was the only rink that was built, other than the ones we used to make on the river ice. Some years, the snow was cleared from the river for skating, but the lack of volunteers to keep the rink cleared doomed these efforts to failure and the ice was soon blown over again with snow. It wasn't until I finished school that I started playing hockey.

Summers were much better for sports in the community. Baseball games between Waterways and McMurray were held on Sundays at The Prairie, which was about halfway between the two villages. We boys played baseball on the diamond we had hacked out by clearing the bush from a vacant lot near Scotty Morrison's house. Well do I remember the pleas of my friends to hurry up and come and play ball when I was hoeing potatoes, but I had to finish my quota of so many rows before I could go and play. Our ballpark was across from the present Morrison Centre on Franklin Avenue and we played every Saturday. We were all obsessed with baseball. Herman Moldenaure and his brother loved baseball so much they would walk the 3 miles (5 km) from Waterways and return every

The baseball team I played with in Fort McMurray, the Cubs, ca. 1935.
I am kneeling on the far left. My brother, Harry, is holding the crossed bats.

Saturday just to play a game. The Native boys who came to town during the summer from their winter traplines loved to play as well. I remember them yelling *sooky* (hurry) to their teammates when they were running the bases. We were always short of equipment, so if one of the boys who owned a baseball glove did not show up, someone would have to play bare-handed. Eventually, we switched to softball, which was becoming popular in the early 1930s. That was when we formed a league with our teams—our team was originally called the Kids, later becoming the Cubs. The other teams in the league were the town teams from McMurray, Waterways, and Airways.

Boxing became another interest of mine when I was about twelve years old. Growing up, I got into a number of fights with kids who called me "Jap." Unfortunately, since I was smaller than most of them I usually lost the fight. I decided I would have to do something about learning how to fight. All the boys, and especially the Métis boys, loved to box. Even though money was scarce during the Depression, somehow we managed to rustle up some boxing gloves and we would have impromptu sparring matches. I saved up a dollar—a fortune to me in those days—and wrote away for a book called *How To Box*. With this book as my Bible, I practised every day for months but never seemed to improve and I became discouraged. However, after about six months, during one of our sparring sessions, all of a sudden I seemed to know exactly what to do. I could anticipate what my opponent was going to do, and I could land any punch where I wanted to. Soon I could outbox all the other boys in the group. As a result I never got into another fight because they were all afraid of me. This training and practising also stood me in good stead when I began to box in the army years later; I had learned the basics and therefore could really hit hard for someone my size.

Of all the days in summer, the first of July was always a memorable day. For one thing, it meant that school was out and our two-month vacation had begun. The town always put on a sports day with races, where fifty cents was awarded to the winner. There was also free ice cream and pop. Pop cost twenty-five cents a bottle back then, a prohibitive price for most of us. My friends and I would sometimes buy one bottle of cream soda to share amongst several of us, so getting free pop was a tremendous treat.

Fall meant a return to school. In my early years I did not enjoy school and, thinking back, I believe it was probably due to a variety of factors: the poor quality of the teaching, the crowding in the poorly heated shacks that were our classrooms, and the inherent difficulty of teaching young children with the limited time the teacher had with eight grades to control. I started school at the age of six in the old United Church building, which was then being used as a schoolhouse after the first schoolhouse, built by the pioneer Presbyterian minister Rev. Mr. McTavish, had burnt down. This original building was located on a site across the street from the present Peter Pond School. My first teacher, Mr. Perry, was only eighteen years old. He loved to play baseball, so during recess he and the bigger boys always played ball. He didn't last more than a few months.

The first schoolhouse at Fort McMurray (n.d.). (courtesy Heritage Park, Fort McMurray)

I don't think I learned very much during my first two years at school. However, I did learn to read after several months of reciting the few lines in the primer that I knew by heart from the illustrations with the text. Being able to read seemed to come suddenly one day. After that I read everything I could get my hands on, including the library of old books that were placed on the floor along the walls of the school, there being nowhere else to store them. These old books, probably brought by the McTavishes to Fort McMurray, were rescued from the original log school building when it burnt down. Among these piles of books were many volumes on old Greek mythology, and I avidly read these whenever the opportunity arose.

I did not enjoy my first years at school. I especially didn't enjoy the bitter cold days of winter when it was an ordeal to trudge through the snow to school, only to shiver in the poorly heated schoolhouse until the wood stove finally warmed up the building. Added to this was my fear of Donald Sharp, who was older and bigger than me and used to bully all the younger kids. He used to lie in wait for me and if Ronnie Morrison wasn't with me, he would beat me up. There was one other person I was afraid of—a girl! She was a feisty, black-haired girl named Ruby who would come at you like a wildcat if you did anything to incur her displeasure. The only time I ever got a strapping at school was when for some reason I had made her angry and she attacked me. Trying to defend myself, I stuck out my fist and made her nose bleed. She ran crying into the schoolroom, and I was hauled up before the teacher, who said, "Imagine. Hitting a girl. You should be ashamed of yourself!" Little did he know that she could have easily beaten me up, and it was only by a lucky punch that I had managed to hit her. I got three strokes of the strap on each hand—which I never told my father about, as I would have received a spanking from him for misbehaving in school. I felt it was a most unjust punishment. If anything I should have been rewarded for being fortunate enough to have survived without being beaten up by Ruby!

When I advanced to grade three, my desire to learn was awakened when a special teacher arrived. His vitality, vivacity, and interest in me changed my outlook entirely. He must have seen my potential and pushed me to achieve. He was a wonderful teacher and I grew to love him. Under Mr. Bean, I seemed to find myself and lapped up everything I could find. He had me skip two grades, from grade three to grade five. I was happy to be promoted but wasn't so sure it was a good thing for me in later years, when I found myself a couple of years younger than my classmates in high school.

Mr. Bean revolutionized the school system in Fort McMurray. He persuaded the school board to hire another teacher and to separate the lower grades from the higher grades. As a result another building was obtained for grades five to eight—Fred Parker's shack across the street from the United Church building. Parker was a trapper who was always out on his trapline during the winter. The shack was so small and the seats were jammed together so closely that there were no aisles and we had to climb over several seats to get to our own. The old stove also took a long time to heat up the inside of the building, which meant that in winter we usually had to keep our parkas on until it was warm enough to doff them.

Mr. Bean's powers of persuasion extended beyond the town's school board. He also persuaded the Burton brothers, Gene and Milton, to attend school even though they were in their twenties. When the Burtons started attending school, we got a skating rink. They brought their horses and a scoop shovel to level off the ground in front of the school and then they hauled water and flooded the ground for our rink. When I met the Burton brothers at a Fort McMurray school reunion several years ago, they laughingly spoke about the spelling bee the three of us had competed in—they were in their twenties and I was about nine or ten.

It was also Mr. Bean who brought the first movies that most of us had ever seen to Fort McMurray. Through the University of Alberta Department of Extension, he arranged for Mr. A. E. Ottewell, who headed the department as well as being the university's bursar, to come to town several times a year with his projector and cans of film. The expenses were covered by charging adults fifty cents and children twenty-five cents admission to McVittie's Dance Hall, where the movie nights were held. We would sit and watch the movies, enchanted by these views of an entirely new world. There was always a Charlie Chaplin comedy to finish off the show, making a wonderful climax to the evening.

Unfortunately, Mr. Bean was too forward-thinking for the old fogeys on the Fort McMurray school board. He lobbied them to build a decent schoolhouse, but they were too worried about the extra taxes they would have to charge to pay for a new school, so Mr. Bean ended up leaving. When I found out he had left, I was desolate and cried my heart out. In later years I often wondered where he had gone. I would have loved to see him again but never did manage to locate him.

Besides Mr. Bean, another contributing factor to my education was my love of reading. For some reason my father subscribed to the *Edmonton Journal*, the daily newspaper that arrived as a weekly batch every Wednesday when the meat arrived by train. Although my father could read English only with difficulty, he probably bought the newspaper so that my brothers and I could learn how to read. I would look forward to getting the paper, especially the sports pages. I was a Babe Ruth fan and followed baseball's 1927 World Series when the Yankees beat the Pittsburgh Pirates in four straight games. I must have been only eight years old. Looking back, I find it hard to believe that I could read the newspapers at that age, but I well remember reading about that World Series and the one after that in 1932 when the Yankees triumphed over the Chicago Cubs.

In 1931, I passed to grade ten and had to study at home since the school only taught to grade nine. The teacher, John Hammond, tutored me at night. Then in 1932 I attended Eastwood High School in East Edmonton, where I took grades eleven and twelve. Although I was only fourteen, I made some real friends there and enjoyed the opportunity to get my high school education. I think Eastwood had some of the best teachers anywhere, let alone in the city of Edmonton, and it was a privilege to be taught by them. I earned honours in both my years there and received an athletic crest for being on the champion city high school baseball team both years. Mac Colville, who became a prominent hockey player with the New York Rangers, was our catcher. He was also the star player on the school's football and hockey teams.

When I was growing up, life in Fort McMurray was very simple. The village was connected by the railway to Edmonton, but very few residents except for the well-heeled ever made the trip "outside." In the winter, one of our favourite diversions was to sit around the stove in the dark and listen to Ronnie Morrison's stories. Ronnie Morrison was an avid reader, especially of *The Shadow* pulp magazines. He would tell these tales of the Shadow catching criminals, weaving some of us boys into them. My friends and I were always clamouring to be included in the next Ronnie Morrison tale. Ronnie, who was my best friend, wasn't just a storyteller. He had many talents, including a talent for making model airplanes. He was also a skilled mechanic, but I've often thought that he would have made a great fiction writer, as he had such an inventive mind.

My memories also include listening to Scotty Morrison's radio in the evenings, which seemed like magic to us. This was in the days before the reliable superheterodyne sets were in use; the receiver on the radio was a regenerative type so there were terrific squeaks and howls before a station could be tuned in. The only station we could hear in the daytime was CJCA from Edmonton, and the favourite children's program on it was *The Farmer*, which always came on in the afternoon after school was out. A regular feature of the program was the announcement of children's birthdays—parents would write in beforehand so that the farmer could give the fortunate child greetings on his or her birthday. One of the stories going around at the time was about an incident that almost caused the farmer to lose his job. Thinking that the mike was switched off after ending a program one day, he was reputed to have said to one of the announcers, "Well, that should hold the little bastards for today." You can imagine the furor and indignation this must have aroused.

When fall came, we would listen to the World Series baseball games on the radio. Angus Sutherland, the owner of the drugstore, had the best and most reliable radio, and I used to go to his place to listen to the games. Well do I remember the St. Louis Cardinals, with Dizzy Dean and his brother Paul, and how Pepper Martin and the Gashouse Gang, which included Leo Durocher, ran wild and won the World

Series in 1934. In winter everyone listened to *Hockey Night in Canada* and Foster Hewitt was probably the best-known man in Canada with his trademark "He shoots. He scores!" Almost everyone across English-speaking Canada was a Toronto Maple Leafs fan and the great Maple Leafs hockey player Charlie Conacher was every boy's hero. I think hockey did more to achieve a united Canada than anything else in those days.

Fort McMurray was the "jumping off" place for the North Country as the only two routes to the North were via the Athabasca River or the Peace River. In the early days there was a steamboat on the Peace River, the ss *D.A. Thomas,* but it only went as far north as Fort Vermilion, and when it hit a rock and sank in the 1930s it was not replaced. Therefore, the only practical route was via the Athabasca and Slave rivers to the Mackenzie River and the Arctic Ocean. As a result, many famous people came through Fort McMurray. The Governor General of Canada, Lord Julian Byng, travelled north around 1926. Lord Tweedsmuir, who was the novelist John Buchan, visited the North Country in 1937 via the ss *Athabasca River* to Fort Fitzgerald and then the ss *Distributor* from Fort Smith to Aklavik. He was a very kind and warm person who walked unaccompanied down the street, speaking to everyone he met. He spoke to some of us children playing on the street, but I was too much in awe of him to say anything other than "hello."

One of the greatest thrills of my boyhood was in 1931 when I met the great Charlie Conacher and his older brother Lionel, who played for the Montreal Maroons. They were going north on a Mackenzie Air Services plane, wanting to do some duck hunting. I had hunted ducks at a place called Saline, near where the present Syncrude plant is located north of Fort McMurray. Charlie and Lionel came to our house to see the ducks I had shot, as they were considering whether or not to stop off to hunt ducks at Saline. What a thrill it was for me to shake hands with them and speak to them. I can well understand how Charlie Conacher could shoot the puck so hard, for he had the biggest and most powerful hands I'd ever seen. Lionel had a broken nose and looked every bit the tough guy he was reported to be as one of the most feared defencemen in the National Hockey League.

In the spring many well-known Northerners "laid over" in McMurray, waiting for "breakup" so that they could fly north. One whom I remember well was "Newt" Millen, the Mountie who was later killed by Albert Johnson, the Mad Trapper, near Aklavik in the Northwest Territories. Millen laid over in Fort McMurray in the spring before he continued on his way to Aklavik. He played softball with us, so we got to know him. He was well liked by everyone, and we felt a real sadness when he was killed. Newt became famous during the hunt for Albert Johnson, a story that headlined in newspapers worldwide and was later made into a movie.

Fort McMurray itself was comparatively crime free, with nothing much happening other than petty theft. The policeman in town was Corporal Jack McDonald. Jack had been in Fort McMurray for years, originally with the Alberta Provincial Police and then with the Royal Canadian Mounted Police (RCMP) once they took over the provincial force in the 1930s. Trouble only occurred in town when Jack was away on patrol. His territory extended some distance north, so he had to make regular patrols downriver on the Athabasca. I remember one famous "fight" during one of Jack's absences. Two men, both inebriated, were yelling and cursing at each other when practically the whole village arrived to watch the action. Hector Ducharme, a big French-Canadian carpenter, was yelling, with his fists up, "By gar, sacre bleu, I'll keel you!" Pete Baker, a little Palestinian trader, was shouting, "Come on, you SOB, I'll hit you so hard you'll never get up again!" One would take a step forward, and the other would take two steps back. Backward and forward they went, all the while yelling threats and cursing. Hec, although he was much bigger, was a pussycat and did most of the backing up. Finally, about 100 yards (90 m) or so from where they first started, they both tired from their efforts and the fight dissolved, each combatant walking away still threatening and swearing. By this time, there was a large crowd. All of us kids had as much fun watching the excitement as if it had been a real fight. Pete Baker later became well known as a member of the Northwest Territories Council in Yellowknife and wrote a book entitled *Memoirs of an Arctic Arab*.

Most of the children I grew up with were Native or Métis, and their parents would leave town to go to their cabins near their traplines each fall, not to return until after breakup in the spring. As a result, these children only went to school for perhaps a month in September and then a month or two before school ended in June, and many of them never learned to read or write. Some of the children whose parents remained in town went to school year-round and got more of an education.

Around the first of July each year was "treaty time" under the terms of Treaty No. 8, signed in 1899 by Paul Cree for the McMurray band. Paul Cree was the chief of the band for many years (I knew his son Rafael, who only died a few years ago at the age of 103). Under the terms of the treaty, each man, woman, and child in the band was to receive each year at treaty time the sum of five dollars, plus a supply of fishing nets and various other items. The chief was to receive twenty-five dollars, plus a blazer-type jacket and a peaked cap similar to a captain's regalia, which were to serve as his uniform. For some reason they were paid with two-dollar bills, and since most of the money was soon spent on candy and similar goodies, there were a lot of two-dollar bills circulating around town at this time. The treaty giving was performed with pomp and ceremony. The Indian agent, Mr. Gerald Card, sat at a table flanked by two Mounties in their scarlet dress uniforms. That evening there was always a tea dance, at least, that was what the white people called it. I think the Crees called it a *Moochigan*. There would be drinking by the younger fellows, but the older people, who were more steeped in the ancient traditions, did not drink.

Summer did not seem to last long and soon after what always felt like a short autumn season, winter would be upon us with a vengeance, bringing snow and bitter cold. However, our anticipation leading up to Christmas always brightened up the winter. As Christmas approached, Ronnie Morrison, his sister Annie, and I would spend the weekends tramping miles through the deep snow trying to find the perfect Christmas tree. Although the snow was usually 2 or 3 feet (0.5 to 1 m) deep by the time spring arrived and it was almost impossible to walk through the forests anywhere without snowshoes, in early December it hadn't reached these depths yet and we were still able to walk most places without snowshoes. It's surprising how difficult it was to find a tree that suited us amongst the thousands of trees that grew everywhere, but our tree had to be perfect before we would consider cutting it down.

As children we looked forward to Christmas for weeks and as the day approached we would get more and more excited. At school, lessons took second place to practising for the Christmas concert, which would usually take place a week or so before Christmas. At the concert, all the pupils went on stage to sing Christmas carols. Looking back I think it would have sounded a lot better if they had culled some of the nonmusical voices like mine and used only those who could sing. Everyone got a present from Santa Claus, who would arrive amidst ringing bells and ho-ho-ho's. The toys we received only seemed to last a few hours—they were of such poor quality—but that didn't seem to matter a great deal.

One of the most hilarious examples of miscasting in the Christmas concerts occurred when the bully Donald Sharp was cast to play the part of the Christ child. Donald was also a homely, bony, scrawny kid who always seemed to have a perpetual sneer on his face. When he came on stage with a sheet wrapped around him and one of the other players said, "Here comes the Christ child!" the place almost exploded there was so much laughter. What made the casting even more ludicrous was Donald's notoriety as a "firebug," or arsonist—he had set several fires around town, causing damage for which his long-suffering father had had to pay.

Although my friends the Morrison children and I were not Roman Catholic, we always loved to go to the local Catholic church for Midnight Mass on Christmas Eve to hear Father Letreste give his sermon in four languages—French, English, Cree, and Chipewyan. Chipewyan is such a guttural-sounding language that we used to marvel at how he could wrap his tongue around the words. I'm afraid we didn't receive much spiritual guidance from his sermons, as the English version always seemed to be so short. However, I found the solemn rites of the Roman Catholic Church very interesting. They were so much more expressive than our United Church liturgy.

My father was not a Christian, having been brought up to observe

Fort McMurray Sunday School at the United Church, 1925.
I am second from the right in the front row.

Shinto beliefs, but he insisted that all his children attend Sunday school at the United Church. This was fine with us, since my brothers and I always got prizes from the Sunday school for attendance! My first Sunday school teacher was Mrs. McDonald, Corporal Jack McDonald's wife. She had come to Canada from Scotland as a stewardess on the HBC steamboat SS *Athabasca River*. She told me years later that I was her favourite pupil because I could always remember the last Bible story she had told us during the previous class. Both Jack and she became lifelong friends of mine, and many years later when our son, Dana, was born, my wife, Kim, and I gave him the second name of Inglis, which was Mrs. McDonald's maiden name. ■

Fort McMurray's
Historic Roots

*T*he first white man to traverse Portage La Loche, also known as Methye Portage, was Peter Pond. This famous portage linked the water routes from Hudson Bay and eastern Canada to Canada's northern waterways all the way to the Arctic Ocean via the Athabasca, Slave, and Mackenzie rivers. In 1778 Peter Pond left Ile-à-la-Crosse, a fur-trading post in northern Saskatchewan, with a flotilla of four canoes laden with supplies. Guided by Natives, he paddled up the Churchill River and Churchill Lake, crossed what became known as Peter Pond Lake to the Methye River, and then crossed Methye Lake to the 12-mile (20-km) Portage La Loche.[1]

After carrying their canoes and supplies across this portage, which descended some 700 feet (210 m) into the Clearwater Valley, Pond and his party reached the Clearwater River, which flows into the Athabasca River some 70 miles (113 km) farther on. This junction, then known as "The Forks," became the site of the Hudson's Bay's Fort McMurray and the present-day city of Fort McMurray. From The Forks, Peter Pond had a leisurely voyage, with the strong Athabasca current carrying their canoes to the Athabasca River delta within four days. Here he built a new post. Although the exact site is unknown, it is probable that he built his fort at the Embarras Portage, where the Embarras River splits off from the Athabasca River to enter Lake Athabasca by another route. For the next one hundred years, the route via Portage La Loche that Peter Pond pioneered was the only route from Hudson Bay and eastern Canada to the Canadian North.

When the Hudson's Bay Company (HBC) amalgamated with its former rival the North West Company (NWC) in 1821, the company had a virtual monopoly on all transportation to the North. Portage La Loche thus became the meeting place for all the fur brigades: the men coming from the East with supplies and the voyageurs coming from the North with their bales of fur. They would meet at a central point on the portage and exchange loads. The Northerners would take over the supplies for their northern forts and those from the east would take over the precious bales of fur for their destinations, either via York Factory on Hudson Bay, Manitoba (the main HBC port until after the amalgamation with the NWC), for London, England, or the alternate route to Montreal in eastern Canada.

When canoes were first used, they had to be carried over the 12-mile (20-km) portage. This meant that canoes going east had to be carried up the back-breaking 700-foot (210-m) steep hill from the Clearwater River to the top of Portage La Loche. The trip down the hill while burdened was almost as arduous. When canoes were replaced by York boats in 1823, the latter were too heavy to be carried and had to be dragged. Eventually, in 1826, two sets of boats were provided, one on each side of the portage, so that only the cargoes and furs had to be toted. The voyageurs considered this mere child's play compared with the former back-breaking manhandling of the York boats. By 1862, as described by J. J. Hargrave in his book *Red River*, horses and oxen were employed to haul the furs and supplies across the portage, but as he pointed out, "should the supply of these animals not be sufficient to complete the work, the boatmen are always under contract to carry on their backs their respective cargoes to a point about the centre of the Portage."[2]

Crossing the Methye Portage on the crucial fur route to Athabaska Country by Hudson's Bay Company traders with their characteristic York boats. By Sidney Clark Ells. (www.canadianheritage.ca ID #10190, National Archives of Canada C-18665)

I remember as a boy hearing of the old Portage La Loche portages and of the men who could carry 450 pounds (204 kg) or more. The standard load was two 90-pound (40-kg) bales of fur. The men carried the loads on their backs using a broad leather band, called a portage strap, placed around the forehead and back over the shoulders. As a result they walked with a stoop when carrying their loads, their heads bent forward, their arms swinging at a forty-five-degree angle across their bodies. Years later, you could tell these old portagers by their characteristic walk, which they retained in their old age. I remember old Paul Fontaine, who had been a portager at Portage La Loche and who lived during the Riel Rebellion, walking in this manner.

Because Portage La Loche invoked such hardship and, more important, because the area around the forks of the Athabasca and Clearwater rivers was a prime source of furs, William McMurray, who had become chief factor at Fort Chipewyan in 1867, decided to establish a fort at this location. Accordingly, in 1870 he commissioned his friend Henry John Moberly to build a new fort at The Forks. Moberly had previously worked for the HBC but had left the company's service several years before. He had then engaged in trading and trapping and was, apparently, intending to go farther down the Athabasca to the Mackenzie River when he arrived at Fort Chipewyan in the fall of 1869. With the arrival of winter, McMurray gave Moberly temporary employment at the post. By the end of the winter McMurray had persuaded him to rejoin the HBC, and in the spring of 1870 he left Fort Chipewyan with two boats, their crews, and five men to help him construct the new post.

McMurray's plan to build the new post was the first step in a greater plan to develop an alternative route to Portage La Loche. In *Ribbons of Water and Steamboats North*, D. J. Comfort quotes McMurray from his personal papers:

> This post, situated at the confluence of the Athabasca and Clearwater Rivers, was established summer 1870. Mr Moberly, the person at present in charge, is a good and practicable man and appears to take an interest in his work. The complement of men for this place need not be large. If an overland route from Lac La Biche to some point on the Athabasca River below the Falls and Rapids [Grand Rapids] is practicable, the terminus must either be at the post or a mile above it. The site is a central one and is on the direct line of communication either to Lac La Biche or Portage La Loche.[3]

Moberly, not McMurray, has often been given credit for establishing the fort that bears the latter's name. Apparently one reason for this was that Moberly, in his later writings, took all the credit for establishing it. He did not even mention McMurray in his memoirs, saying only that "it was named after a Chief Factor, one of my oldest friends." This omission is curious given that it was McMurray's idea to have a post established at The Forks, and it was McMurray who acted as Moberly's benefactor,

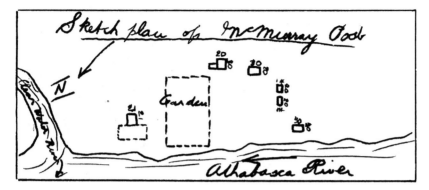

A sketch of the fort at McMurray twenty-two years after its construction by Henry John Moberly, showing the large garden, the Clearwater and Athabasca Rivers, and the six small buildings that made up the fort. The six buildings included a large dwelling with an attached kitchen, two smaller houses, a byre, and a river transport store. What is labelled the Clearwater River is actually the Snye, flowing in the opposite direction. (Hudson's Bay Company Archives, Archives of Manitoba)

hiring him to carry out the construction. Nowhere in his writings does Moberly even intimate that the chief factor in Chipewyan in 1870 and the friend after whom he named the fort were one and the same person. Moberly had initially been hired as a clerk by McMurray, and it seems unlikely that a lowly clerk would have been given the right by the company to name the new fort on his own. There is little doubt that McMurray considered himself the founder of the fort, as witnessed by James W. Taylor of the U.S. consulate in Winnipeg, who wrote that McMurray had informed him that he had established this post.[4]

William McMurray was transferred to Pembina in 1871, soon after he had commissioned Moberly to establish the fort at Fort McMurray. There, he was promoted to the rank of inspecting chief factor in 1875, a position second only to that of chief commissioner. He held this distinguished position for only two years before his death in Winnipeg at the age of fifty-three in 1877. McMurray was succeeded by Roderick MacFarlane, the chief factor at Fort Chipewyan, in 1875. MacFarlane was one of the most notable chief factors. He was instrumental in having steamboats built in the North and has been called the Father of Mackenzie River Transport. In addition to being an outstanding chief factor, he was a celebrated naturalist, contributing more than five thousand specimens of all sorts to the Smithsonian Institution in Washington, DC. Having arrived in the North as an apprentice fresh out from Stromness in the Orkney Islands of Scotland in 1852, he rapidly rose through the ranks and became a chief trader in 1868 and chief factor in 1875. He retired in 1895 and died in Winnipeg in 1920. Henry Moberly spent eight years in Fort McMurray, most of them under Roderick MacFarlane. MacFarlane instructed Moberly to improve the Portage La Loche trail. Accordingly, in 1874, a cart road was built down the hill so that loads could be moved by carts pulled by oxen or horses.

The first house in Fort McMurray was built sometime in the last half of the eighteenth century. According to J. G. MacGregor in his book *Paddle Wheels to Bucket-Wheels on the Athabasca*:

> [T]hree other outposts came into existence on the Athabasca River itself, all we know of them comes from the journals of Philip Turnor and Peter Fidler when in 1791 they descended that river to survey it and to locate Lake Athabasca on the map.[5]

What appears to have been the oldest house is what Philip Turnor noted as "an old Canadian House on the East Side of the Athabasca River which was left when they built one at the mouth of the Pillicon [Clearwater] River." This old house, which had been abandoned, was on the bank of the Athabasca directly east of the southern end of Mildred Lake.[6] Peter Fidler commented that the oldest house had been built by a man named St. Germain or Buffalo Head. The next outpost in order of age, the one at the mouth of the Clearwater River and the one Peter Fidler called "Mr. McLeod's House," had been "built about three or four years back [circa 1787], but now nobody lived in it."[7] It was stated to be on the right bank of the Clearwater near present-day Fort McMurray and, while unoccupied when Turnor's crew passed, nevertheless had a thriving garden planted with potatoes. ■

The Rivermen

*A*mong my strongest recollections of Fort McMurray are the wonderful people and extraordinary characters I encountered there. Many of the families I knew when I was growing up provided a direct link to the fort's origins as a fur-trading post and an important staging point for traffic via the North Country. People such as John Macdonald, who had been a very important riverman in the nineteenth century, and John Sutherland, who had helped build the first steamboat on the Athabasca River in 1883, connected me with those early days. Families such as the Loutits, Frasers, and Wylies had historic ties to the Hudson's Bay Company in its early days when it practically ruled the North Country. It was my privilege to grow up with these people, and so I wish to pass on what I remember of them.

When I was a boy in the early 1920s, the riverboat captains and pilots were elite figures. We admired them the same way we would look up to the airplane pilots a few years later. The rivermen provided a link to a past that was rapidly disappearing, so it was my privilege to have known some of these men. The steamboat pilots were the aristocrats of the rivermen. Although the captains had the papers to show that they were qualified to command the boats, it was the pilots who were at the helm and steered them through the tricky channels that abounded in the

43

river. They knew every landmark and snag throughout the whole system. To make matters more difficult for the pilots, the channel was constantly changing so they had to be able to "read" the water and know where all the sandbars and obstacles were located. This they had to do on pitch-black nights, as well as during the daytime.

When I knew him during the 1920s and 1930s, John Macdonald was quite old, but he was still a big, broad-shouldered, imposing figure and a grand old man. I remember seeing him row across the Snye in his skiff to go downtown to Franklin Avenue, where he would visit with his cronies. He had been a very important riverman for the HBC during the era when all the transportation to the North was via scow from Athabasca Landing to Fort McMurray and points north on the Athabasca River. According to author D. J. Comfort in *Ribbons of Water and Steamboats North*, John Macdonald was one of the earliest, if not the earliest, of Fort McMurray's pioneer settlers.[1]

Macdonald was mentioned by Ernest Thompson Seton, the eminent naturalist, who made a trip north from Athabasca Landing to the Arctic in 1907, in his book *The Arctic Prairies*.[2] Seton tells an amusing tale of how he cured John of his stomach trouble during their voyage down the river. Seton, who was known as quite a medicine man, had brought along some pills, which included "potent purgatives," and had been following his family physician's advice: "in case of doubt look wise and work on his bowels." John was in charge of the HBC brigade, which consisted of thirteen scows of freight with sixty men to man them. Seton wrote in *The Arctic Prairies*:

> One day, John Macdonald, the chief pilot and a mighty man on the river, came to my tent on Grand Island. John complained that he couldn't hold anything in his stomach; he was a total peristaltic wreck indeed (My words, his were more simple and more vivid, but less sonorous and professional.). He said he had been going downhill for two weeks and was so bad that he was "no better than a couple of ordinary men."

Seton gave him some pills and told him to come back the next morning, which he did, complaining that the pills had no effect. Seton then gave him a small amount of brandy in a tin cup and added an equal amount of painkiller. John gulped it down and "doubled up, rolled around, and danced for five minutes." An hour later he announced that he was about cured. The next day he came and said he was all right and would soon be as good as half a dozen men again!

In *The Arctic Prairies*, Seton also gave an illustration of the way in which John Macdonald managed the many men under his command in his flotilla:

> Sunday morning, 26th May, there was something like a strike among the sixty half-breeds and Indians that composed the crews. They were strict Sabbatarians (when it suited them); they believed that they should do no work, but give up the day to gambling and drinking. Old John, the chief pilot, wished to take advantage of the fine flood on the changing river, and drift down at least to the head of the Boiler Rapids, twenty miles away. The breeds maintained, with many white swear words, for lack of strong talk in Indian, that they never yet knew Sunday work to end in anything but disaster, and they sullenly scattered among the trees, produced their cards, and proceeded to game away their property, next year's pay, clothes, families, anything and otherwise show their respect for the Lord's Day and defiance of old John Macdonald. John made no reply to their arguments; he merely boarded the cook's boat, and pushed off into the swift stream with the cooks and all the grub. In five minutes the strikers were on the twelve big boats doing their best to live up to orders. John said nothing, and grinned at me only with his eyes.
>
> The breeds took their defeat in good part after the first minute, and their commander rose higher in their respect.

If Billy Loutit (William C. Loutit) had lived in the American West and had performed all his feats in the era of Wyatt Earp, Buffalo Bill Cody, and the other western heroes, he would have become a legend, just as they did.[3] I knew Billy and his wife, Jenny, in Fort McMurray and grew up with his children. Billy was born in Fort Chipewyan, the son of Peter Loutit who worked for the HBC. He was the nephew of William Cornwallis King, the Trader King of the book of the same name, and named after him. At the time I knew him, Billy was the pilot of Jim Cornwall's Northern Traders' steamboat, the *Northland Echo*.

William Cornwallis (Billy) Loutit, as drawn by Kathleen Shackleton in 1937. Billy was a Fort McMurray legend, nephew of William Cornwallis King, a trader with the Hudson's Bay Company. (Hudson's Bay Company Archives, Archives of Manitoba, HBCA P-262)

Before he became a river pilot, Billy had served as a guide for Ernest Thompson Seton on his trip to the Arctic in 1907. He is mentioned very favourably in Seton's account of the trip. Seton's first mention of Billy in *The Arctic Prairies* is as follows:

> I had made several unsuccessful attempts to get an experienced native boatman to go northward with me. All seemed to fear the intending plunge into the unknown; so was agreeably surprised when a young fellow of Scottish and Cree parentage came and volunteered for the trip. A few inquiries proved him to bear a good reputation as a river man and worker, so William C. Loutit was added to my expedition and served me faithfully throughout.
>
> In time I learned that Billy was a famous traveller. Some years ago, when the flood had severed all communication between Athabasca Landing and Edmonton, Billy volunteered to carry some important dispatches and covered the 96 miles on foot in one and a half days, although much of the road was under water. On another occasion he went alone and on foot from Horse River up the Athabasca to Calling River, and across to the Point to the Athabasca again, then up to the Landing—150 rough miles in four days. These exploits I had to find out for myself later on; but much more important to me at the time was the fact that he was a first-class cook, a steady, cheerful worker, and a capable guide as far as Great Slave Lake.

When Seton's party reached the "Barren Lands," where there were no trees and therefore no firewood, Billy showed his resourcefulness:

> Billy now did something that illustrates at once the preciousness of firewood, and the pluck, strength, and reliability of my cook. During his recent tramp he

found a low, rocky hollow full of large dead willows. It was eight miles back; nevertheless he set out, of his own free will; tramped the eight miles, that wet, blustery day, and returned in five and one-half hours, bearing on his back a heavy load, over 100 pounds of most acceptable firewood. Sixteen miles for a load of wood! But it seemed well worth it as we revelled in the blessed blaze.

Billy would show his true mettle, however, when he and Elzear Robillard were able to recover Seton's priceless bag of journals and sketches on their return trip up the Athabasca River from Fort McMurray. On October 20, 1907, Billy and Rob—the name by which Seton referred to Robillard—were hauling Seton's canoe through rapids on the Athabasca River when the strong waters whirled the canoe around suddenly and dashed it upon a rock. Seton, the sternsman in the canoe with him, their supplies, and Seton's precious journals were submerged. Seton and the sternsman were able to reach safety, but Seton was desolate over the loss of his journals. In his account, Seton wrote:

> I gathered all the things along the beach, made great racks for drying and a mighty blaze. I had no pots or pans, but an aluminum bottle which would serve as a kettle; and thus I prepared a meal of such things as were saved—a scrap of pork, some tea and a soggy mass that once was pilot bread. Then sat down by the fire to spend five hours of growing horror, 175 miles from a settlement, canoe smashed, guns gone, pots and pans gone, specimens all gone, half our bedding gone, our food gone; but all these things were nothing compared with the loss of my three precious journals; 600 pages of observation and discovery, geographical, botanical, and zoological, 500 drawings, valuable records made under all sorts of trying circumstances, discovery and compass

survey of the beautiful Nyarling River, compass survey
of the two great northern lakes, discovery of two great
northern rivers, many lakes, a thousand things of
interest to others and priceless to me—my summer's
work—gone; yes I could bear that, but the three
chapters of life and thought irrevocably gone; the
magnitude of this calamity was crushing. Oh God, this
is the most awful blow that could have fallen at the end
of the six months' trip.

Fortunately, Seton's worst fears were not realized. Thanks to the
grit, determination, and truly extraordinary physical efforts of Rob
and Billy, they were able to recover Seton's canvas bag containing his
journals, but only after they had scrambled on the rocks along the
shore of the river and risked drowning to retrieve it. Seton recorded his
gratitude as follows:

I never felt more thankful in my life! My heart
swelled with gratitude to the brave boys that had
leaped, scrambled, slidden, tumbled, fallen, swum or
climbed over those 14 perilous, horrible miles of icy
rocks and storm-piled timbers, to save the books that,
to them, seemed of so little value, but which they yet
knew were, to me, the most precious of all my things.
Guns, cameras, food, tents, bedding, dishes, were
trifling losses, and the horror of that day was turned
to joy by the crowning mercy of its close.

"I won't forget you when we reach the Landing,
Rob!" were the meagre words that rose to my lips, but
the tone of voice supplied what the words might lack.
And I did not forget him or the others; and Robillard
said afterward, "By Gar, dat de best day's work I ever
done, by Gar, de time I run down dat hell river after
dem dam books!"

In his book *Memoirs of an Arctic Arab*, Pete Baker also mentioned Billy and spoke warmly of him:

> Billy was an old timer. He worked on the boat "Bilot" and knew the river really well. He was employed by the Hudson's Bay Company and was now carrying cash to give to the company's post manager to purchase muskrat skins. I realized it was better for me to wait for him, as it was safer for two to travel together, particularly under such circumstances.
>
> Billy was one of Peter Loutit's family of Fort Chipewyan. Peter was originally a Scotsman. He worked for the Hudson's Bay Company as a blacksmith and did general repairs and construction work. He married a Flett girl, of a Metis family; they raised a family of six boys and two girls. George, Billy, John James, Alex, Tammy, Colin, Lora and Edith. These are the ones I am aware of, there may have been others. Most of the boys were employed by the Hudson's Bay Company as traders and post managers. Alex had a store of his own and Billie was a boatman and a river pilot. The whole Loutit family were, and still are, good people and desirable citizens. When I met Billie at Elmer Reid's place at the Embarras River, he was presumably in his middle forties, a man of long experience in the north's ventures, like canoeing, dog marching and steamship piloting. He also had a wonderful personality.[4]

My memories of Billy include an evening—it must have been in the mid-1930s—when I was visiting at the Loutit home and Scotty Morrison, who was in his cups, dropped in to see them. Billy loved to sing the hymns he had learned as a boy and he persuaded Scotty, who knew all the old hymns, to lead them in singing "Rock of Ages," "The Old Rugged Cross," and other songs. Jenny, Billy's wife, supplied the music with her accordion, stomping her foot to keep time. Billy was beaming with a smile that lit up the room and singing with great gusto. When they had finished one hymn, he would talk Scotty into starting another. Scotty knew the words to many hymns, and the singing went on for hours, with Scotty leading the singing, Jenny playing the accordion, and Billy joining in the singing. This was Fort McMurray's version of a riotous evening—hymn singing.

Another notable riverman was John Sutherland, who in 1883 had come from Thurso in northern Scotland to Fort Chipewyan at the age of nineteen to assist Captain J. W. Smith and William Wylie in the building of the first steamboat on the Athabasca River, the ss *Grahame*. He undoubtedly learned a lot from William Wylie and went on to help Captain Smith construct the *Wrigley*, which was a propeller-driven boat launched in 1886 and the first steamboat to go to the Arctic. Altogether, John Sutherland spent fifty-six years with the HBC on the riverboats as the chief engineer. He was a good friend of my father's and so I knew him quite well. When I was growing up in Fort McMurray, he was the chief engineer on the ss *Athabasca River*.

One of the famous rivermen was Colonel Jim Cornwall. Although he is perhaps more famous as being the foremost spokesman for the North, with the sobriquet of "Peace River Jim," he was a formidable pioneer in the business of steam boating. I remember him as a big man, with the heartiest laugh. It is easy to see how people fell under his spell; he had such tremendous charm. Andy Browning, an old friend of mine, had served under Cornwall in the army during the First World War and swore by him. Taking the *Northland Echo* through the Grand Rapids with Joe Bird[5] was a feat that should have been enough to put Cornwall in the history books, but he could claim many more accomplishments. Cornwall's Northern Traders had built and operated many of the sternwheeler steamboats in the North. Then in 1922, he obtained the contract to transport buffalo by steamboat to Wood Buffalo Park in northern Alberta. I remember seeing the scowloads of buffalo that would be unloaded from the Alberta and Great Waterways Railroad boxcars at Waterways and then loaded onto the barges for the *Northland Echo* to push down the Athabasca River to the park.

A transition from the pioneer rivermen was supplied by Julian "Hooley" Mills, with whom I used to play softball. He was the son of Captain J. W. Mills, who built many of the northern steamboats, including the ss *Fort McMurray* at Fort McMurray in 1915. Hooley was a true Northerner. He was born in 1897 at Fort Simpson in the Northwest Territories. After three years in the service during the First World War, he worked for the HBC for the next twenty years, first as an engineer on the *Nechimus* and then as captain of the *Canadusa*, both gasoline-engine-powered tugs on the Athabasca River. In 1940 he joined the Northern Transportation Company and was captain of several of its tugboats.

An eminent riverman who was of a different brand than most of

The Grand Rapids of the Athabasca River were not easy to navigate. (courtesy Ken Hill)

the others was Captain Owen Forrester Browne, whom some ignorant Northerners referred to as "Nigger Brown." He was actually of Polynesian descent—his grandfather was a Tahitian by the name of Kanahana, who had settled in Hawaii and was called David Browne. One of Kanahana's sons, Owen Wamsley Browne, married a Hawaiian woman named Teresa Oponi and the couple came to British Columbia, first residing near Fort Langley and then near New Westminster. One of their sons, Owen Forrester Browne, became a steamship captain on several sternwheelers on the Fraser River. He then became a skipper on various sternwheelers on the Athabasca River for the HBC. Remembered as a proud, reserved man of the utmost integrity, he retired to New Westminster where he died in 1948. According to his

descendants, in all his years on the Fraser and Athabasca rivers, he never mentioned his Polynesian background.

One of the well-known riverboat captains who had retired from river boating was Captain Williscroft. I remember him riding his bicycle downtown from The Prairie, where he lived with his sister, Mrs. McVittie, who owned the town dance hall. He was a stern man who was probably used to being obeyed. There was a story about him ordering a deckhand to throw the boat's anchor overboard, and on being told that there was no chain on the anchor, he roared, "I told you to throw the anchor out." Whereupon the deckhand did so, and he was promptly chewed out for being an idiot.

Pilots and captains aside, the steamboats could not have operated without the services of the woodcutters. All of the wood was cut into 4-foot (1.2-m) lengths and measured in cords, thus called "cordwood." The wood would be cut and split, then piled along the riverbank at spots where the water was deep enough to tie up the boat and throw a gangplank ashore. When the boat had been moored, the gang of deckhands would run ashore and hoist as many sticks of cordwood as they could carry on their shoulders, then rush back to pile the fuel on board. Several cords would be loaded in this way, and woe betide the deckhand who was slow in doing his share for he would be sure to receive a chewing out by the captain.

One of the well-known woodcutters was Bill Burns, who had previously been a noted boxer but had worked as a woodcutter for several years. However, the record for the most wood cut in one woodcutting season—that is, from fall through spring breakup—was set by Sven Swanson, the Swedish carpenter and woodcutter who built my father's rooming house and barbershop. I believe it was around 1933 or 1934, at the height of the Depression, when Sven came back to Fort McMurray from his downriver cabin somewhere north of Fort McKay. He had cut, split, and piled on the riverbank 333 cords of wood, and at the rate of $3 per cord, received $999 for his winter's work. In those days, a thousand dollars was a huge sum, so everyone congratulated him on his achievement. He told everyone he was going back to visit his home in Sweden with his newly won wealth and left for Edmonton on the weekly train. However, in a couple of weeks he was back in McMurray, having gotten no farther than Edmonton, where he drank up all his money.

The era of the rivermen reached a climax during the Second World War when the U.S. Army transported a huge assortment of material north for the Canol Pipeline. Some of the descendants of the pioneer captains and pilots came into their own as they piloted a myriad of craft down the Athabasca River. Although perhaps not as glamorous a calling as we deemed it to be in our youth, it remains an important vocation for Northerners who still depend on the river to transport their supplies. ■

Early Residents
and Characters

Early Fort McMurray had its share of characters. Some were fugitives of one sort or another. One man, for example, had run away from his wife in Kitchener, Ontario, and had a common-law Native wife and a family by her. During the boom of 1911, he and several others walked out to Edmonton via Athabasca Landing to finalize the sales of their property in Fort McMurray. Unfortunately for him, he was recognized by a woman in Athabasca who promptly wrote back to his wife in Ontario. As a result the wife came north and lived in comfort from the sale of his land, while the unfortunate common-law wife and her children had to live in poverty.

Although most residents of Fort McMurray were ordinary folk, two German counts contributed a bit of glamour to the scene. Count Alfred Von Hammerstein and Count Von Auberg, known simply as "Von," were residents of Fort McMurray at various times. Count Von Hammerstein had acquired a large number of tar sands' leases and lived off the options on these that he sold to various companies. Count Von Auberg was a civil engineer who came to Canada in 1880 and was the city parks engineer in Edmonton when the First World War broke out in 1914. Because of growing anti-German sentiment during the war, he quit his job and travelled all over the North Country as far north as Great Slave Lake until the war ended. He was quite a lady's man and had several of the local matrons enamoured with him. He wrote children's stories in German and managed to live off the proceeds of his writing for many years.

Fort McMurray also had its fair share of remittance men and, of these, the most famous was probably George Bennett, the brother of former Prime Minister R. B. Bennett. George was an alcoholic and R. B. kept him in isolation in Fort McMurray. He was paid three hundred dollars a month as the agent for one of the trust companies that R. B. controlled, with the stipulation that he was to stay in Fort McMurray. This was a tremendous sum of money in those days, but before the end of the month George was always broke and came to borrow money from my father. Since my father was not very affluent, I think the reason George borrowed from him was that he knew my father would be discreet and not mention it to anyone.

Despite his money problems, George pretended to be quite wealthy and always acted very pompously. He always wore a bowler hat and walked down the street carrying a cane held in his elbow. He was a delight to listen to, as he spouted his fractured French phrases. For example, instead of "thank you," he would say, "mercy caboo," and for "fine," he would say, "trays beans." A favourite form of entertainment was watching George feud with his next-door neighbour, who happened to be Jack McDonald, the Mountie. George's grudge against Jack stemmed from the time Jack had taken George's revolver away from him when he was shooting it during one of his drunken sprees. When R. B. became prime minister in 1930, George became even more cocky. Whenever Jack McDonald was standing talking to someone on the main street, George would strut by in his bowler hat and black suit, with his gold chain dangling from his vest pocket and his cane hanging from his elbow. As he strutted by, he would bump into Jack. Jack would then follow him down the street until George turned around and headed back home. When they were away from the centre of town, where they thought no one was watching, they would begin to grapple and wrestle on the ground. Of course, all of us kids would be following at a discreet distance to watch the fun.

George was interdicted, which meant he couldn't enter a beer parlour. He still found a way to satisfy his habit, though. At that time there was a tonic called "Beef Iron and Wine," which was sold in drugstores, even though it had a high alcohol content. When I went with my father to help him do some work in George's yard, I always used to see a huge mound of empty "Beef Iron and Wine" bottles behind his house. Incidentally, with respect to alcohol, my father told me that during the Prohibition period, when he was in Edmonton pre-1920, people obtained liquor by getting prescriptions from doctors and then purchasing the liquor from a drugstore. There were long lineups at doctors' offices for prescriptions and at drugstores to buy this "medicine."

Next door to George Bennett's house was a one-bed hospital, which although sponsored by the Presbyterian Church was believed to have been funded by R. B. Bennett so that the nurse in charge could take care of George during his binges. The nurse was Miss Olive (Dolly) Ross. She was the daughter of Donald Ross, a pioneer hotel man in Edmonton, who had arrived in the city in 1872 and four years later opened Edmonton House, the first hotel west of Portage La Prairie, Manitoba. Dolly Ross was also one of my Sunday school teachers and was always very good to my family, although she was very stern. She remembered the early days in Fort Edmonton, and I've since regretted that I didn't find out more from her about the early days in Alberta. When Dolly died in Edmonton, I think she must have reached the century mark.

Another famous Fort McMurray character was Cassie Owens. She was the daughter of Billy Biggs, one of the village's early settlers. Cassie was famous as the owner of a team of dogs that were supposed to be part wolf. These dogs attacked Ronnie and Annie Morrison, when they were about nine and six years old, respectively, and almost killed them. However, the dogs—or wolves—were never destroyed, although that would be almost routine practice in this modern age. Cassie later became one of the two local taxi drivers when the motor car finally made its appearance in Fort McMurray in the late 1920s.

Some of the old-timers were living history books, like Paul Fontaine, who was born in 1843 and had lived through the Riel Rebellions. He had worked for the Hudson's Bay Company, portaging over Portage La Loche on the historic water route from Manitoba to the Athabasca River. He stood and walked with a permanent stoop, which was said to have resulted from the huge loads, up to 400 pounds (180 kg), that he toted over the 12-mile (20-km) portage. He had a long beard, always wore a bowler hat, and used a cane. During the winter he lived in a log house near Bill Gordon's property at the west end of Franklin Avenue, but as soon as spring came he and his family moved into a teepee. He hated airplanes, as he didn't think God had intended man to fly, and would curse them every time he saw one in the air. It was frustrating trying to squeeze information out of Paul about the Riel Rebellions. All he would say was, "Bad times. Those, bad times." My favourite memory of Paul is when my father had him to lunch one day. The main course was steak with potatoes and vegetables, and there was apple pie for dessert. I watched fascinated as Paul ate the apple pie first, then the steak, then the potatoes, and then the vegetables. I guess he ate the things he liked the most first.

Two of the prominent early residents of Fort McMurray were Bill and Christine Gordon. As I mentioned previously, Bill and his sister Christine were related to the famous "Chinese Gordon," who had taken part in the Boxer Rebellion and the relief of Khartoum. In his book *Paddle Wheels to Bucket-Wheels on the Athabasca*, J. G. MacGregor stated that Bill Gordon arrived in Fort McMurray in 1905 and that he and his sister had opened a restaurant in Athabasca Landing around 1900.[1] (However, Scotty Morrison told me that Bill had arrived in the area in 1898, en route to the Klondike on the "Trail of '98.") Bill owned the land on the north side of Franklin Avenue from Hudson's Bay Flats to a point approximately opposite to where the present-day Morrison Centre stands.

I remember Bill as a big man who had become quite obese by the time

I knew him. He was a fur trader, and it was on one of his winter trips by dog team from the Athabasca delta that my father had accompanied him from Embarras Portage to Fort McMurray. He had the highest regard for my father, who had probably saved his life by building a fire to warm him up after their axe had been found and brought to them by Jim Darwish. Bill was also the first postmaster in Fort McMurray, and his sister Christine ran the post office. Christine was the first white woman to permanently reside in the village. The Christina River in northern Alberta near Fort McMurray was named after her, although her name is misspelled. Gordon Lake was named after her and her brother. The Gordons had a large garden and demonstrated that wonderful crops of vegetables could be grown in the area.

During my early days in Fort McMurray in the 1920s, the only means of communication with the outside world was through the telegraph line operated by the Dominion Government telegrapher. This line ran from Athabasca to Fort McMurray and was serviced by a lineman, Frank Goodwin, as far as House River. Charlie Somers, who had been a telegrapher in the Signal Corps during the First World War, arrived in Fort McMurray in 1922 and was the operator until the line closed in 1954. His son, also named Charlie, became my brother Harry's business partner in the 1950s in Uranium City, where they owned and operated the Uranium City bus line and a general store. In the days before anyone had radios, some of the men would chip in to have the heavyweight championship fights come in by wire on the telegraph line. Charlie Somers would receive the description of each round and then post them outside for everyone to read. My hero was, of course, Jack Dempsey, and I cried when he lost to that "tooney" (Gene Tunney)—we knew he must have been robbed by the now-famous long count.

Charlie Eymondson, one of Fort McMurray's pioneer residents, was an Icelander who built the first telephone system in the village in 1924. The telephone line zigzagged through the village, with wires being supported by insulators nailed to the most convenient tree. Most of the business establishments had a battery-operated telephone that was housed in a large wooden box about 24 inches (60 cm) high, 12 inches (30 cm) wide, and 12 inches (30 cm) deep. This box would be fastened to a wall in a convenient place, with a handle on the side of the phone so the caller could ring the other party. The system was a party line and each site was assigned a certain ring (for example, one short and two longs). This system operated until 1958. Although Eymondson lived in Waterways, the system didn't extend there and was confined to McMurray.

One of the most prominent citizens of Fort McMurray was George "Scotty" Morrison, whom I have described earlier. His son Ronnie and daughter Annie were my boyhood chums. Scotty came from Aberdeen in Scotland. After working on the Grand Trunk Railway, he must have arrived in McMurray prior to 1911, as I remember him telling me about the land boom of that year. His wife-to-be, Jeanie Polson, arrived in 1911. She told me about her arduous trip from Athabasca Landing. She had been brought over from Scotland by Christine Gordon in 1912. She and Christine had been booked to cross the Atlantic on the *Titanic*, but for some reason they were—fortunately— unable to get passage on it. After this narrow escape, they obtained passage on another ship to Halifax. Then, they took the long train trip from Halifax to Edmonton and then rode on top of a wagonload of freight pulled by horse team from Edmonton to Athabasca. Despite these hardships, she said the worst part of her journey was the scow trip down the Athabasca River.

Jeanie would never go into much detail about her scow trip down the river but with much shaking of her head and clicking of her teeth would only say that it was a terrible experience. I'm not sure if she was on the scow that foundered in the Grand Rapids channel and sank with the complete loss of thirty-five hundred dollars worth of goods in 1912. According to J. G. MacGregor in *Paddle Wheels to Bucket-Wheels on the Athabasca*, Bill Gordon had three scows in a flotilla on that trip. Two of them managed to navigate the channel safely, but the scow that Bill and Christine were on sank.[2] I am sure that Jeanie would have been on the same scow as Bill and Christine, not wanting to be too far away from her friend on such a perilous journey. Christine was an athletic tomboy, so she managed to get a canoe afloat and get to shore. This would have been typical of Christine Gordon. Scotty Morrison used to say that when she was young, she was a fine figure of a woman and that she would gallop by on horseback with her hair flying behind her with not a care in the world.

The year 1913 marked the arrival of several notable people in Fort McMurray. The redoubtable Mountie Sergeant Denny Lanauze, who became famous for his exploits, arrived from Athabasca Landing. Sydney C. Ells also arrived to map the tar sands, thus beginning his long and illustrious career in oil sands research. The village's first lawyer, the kindly gentleman Cecil Potts, also settled in Fort McMurray in 1913 and was promptly made a justice of the peace, an office he retained until the end of his life. Mr. Potts's home was located right in the middle of a road allowance, as he had settled there before the land was surveyed. His beautiful garden was famous throughout the whole of the North Country. Even though his property was in the middle of the avenue running just south of Franklin Avenue, it was left untouched during his lifetime. Mr. Potts was well loved by everyone and was so well respected that I don't think anyone ever called him by his first name—he was always "Mister" Potts.

One of the town's most lovable characters was Mrs. Mackenzie, the wife of Kenneth Mackenzie, one of the first white settlers in Fort McMurray. When I was growing up, she and her family lived at Willow Lake (now known as Gregoire Lake), about 25 miles (40 km) south of McMurray, where they had started a homestead. I remember her coming in regularly on the Wednesday train for her weekly visit to town. A small, squat woman with a perpetual smile on her face, she punctuated her speech with "Wha Wha!" and "Chee Wheeze!" Scotty Morrison described her as being a beautiful Indian princess when she was young. She would always visit Scotty's wife, Jeanie, when she came to town, and it was fascinating to listen to her talk and tell of her week's activities. She seemed to be the happiest and sunniest person I'd ever known, but one day she was in high dudgeon and told in great detail of her quarrel with Maggie Cheecham, who also lived at Willow Lake. She said, "Chee Wheeze! I'm so mad, I'm trow im down and choke it, dot

Maggie! Wha Wha!" I couldn't ever imagine Mrs. Mackenzie getting angry enough to throw anyone down, let alone choking them. The Mackenzies had two sons who grew up in the Willow Lake area, and I believe their descendants are living there still.

The most important resident in Fort McMurray was Louis Romanet, who was the HBC's district manager for the Athabasca and Mackenzie districts. I had always thought Romanet was French Canadian, but he was born in Saint-Nazaire in the south of France. He had come to Canada in 1903 with Revillon Frères, the French fur-trading company, and managed its first trading post in Canada, located near Fort Chimo in northern Quebec. He joined the HBC in 1916 as an inspector. However, when word of the war in Europe finally reached him, he left his family and returned to France to rejoin the regiment in which he had been commissioned as a lieutenant prior to leaving for Canada. In 1919 he returned to his position with the HBC and in 1923 was promoted to district manager of the Athabasca and Mackenzie districts, as well as of the company's river transportation throughout the North.

Romanet was initially stationed at Fort McMurray but after only a few years moved his headquarters to Edmonton where he was based and where, in 1933, the HBC unceremoniously fired him, presumably because revenues had fallen off during the Depression. He was very bitter at what he considered to be his unjust treatment after his many years of loyal service during which he had contributed a great deal to the company. Romanet learned English in his early days in Canada through his contact with English-speaking traders and Natives. He attained such facility in the language that in 1920 he won an essay competition put on by the company to mark its 250th anniversary. He also collaborated with the writer Lowell Thomas, who turned Romanet's autobiography into a book entitled *Kabluk of the Eskimo*, which was published in 1932. Romanet spent the last years of his life in the veterans' home at Government House in Edmonton and died in January 1964. He is buried in the Field of Honour at the Edmonton Cemetery.

Many Americans came to Canada, and especially to southern Alberta, to settle. However, the more adventurous filtered north and amongst these was Fred Murray, who had fought with the American army in the Spanish-American War. In 1914 Otto Bushner, a German trapper who lived across the Clearwater River, killed two men and became the object of a manhunt. The Mountie "Nitchie" Thorne had organized what the Americans would call a "posse," and Mickey Ryan and Fred Murray were amongst this group. One party located Bushner and, according to them, Bushner had shot himself through the head. When I was a boy, people still discussed the Bushner killings and the manhunt, which had remained etched in the memory of the locals since it had been the only violent occurrence of the sort in the community's history. Even at that time there were rumours that Fred Murray had actually shot Bushner, and these rumours gained more resonance after Fred stabbed another local resident, Ed McQueen, during a quarrel sometime in the 1920s.

Of all the characters in McMurray, Gilly Sigurder used the most colourful language, having a way with words that I doubt anyone could have duplicated. Gilly was of Icelandic origin and had grown up in Winnipeg, where he became an expert fisherman. As a boy I was impressed with how he could fillet dozens of whitefish in just a few minutes. Gilly had a vocabulary all his own, and I wish I had written down or recorded some of his turns of phrase, but the originality of some of them is etched in my memory:

> Well, I was haulin' a load of popple [poplar] on the opposide the river!
> One time when I was a-fishin' on Lake Winnipeg I fell through the ice and bloody near froze to death until I got home and put my dry goods on.
> When I was in Edmonton I got on the street car and went across the High Liver Bridge.

Of course everyone understood what he meant, and as young as I was, it didn't seem strange—I thought that was the way everyone spoke!

In addition to the old-timers and historic figures, my brothers Bob, Bill, Harry, Jack, and George Morimoto also played a role in the development of the North. Bob went to Port Radium in 1934 to work

65

for Vic Ingraham, who owned the only hotel there. Bob later went to Yellowknife with Willie Wylie and helped Willie and Smoky Stout build the first restaurant in Yellowknife in 1937, the famous Wildcat Café, where I worked as a dishwasher when I first arrived there in 1938. Bill went to work for Discovery Mines in the Northwest Territories in 1948. He was only twenty-three when he was made mill superintendent by the Byrnes brothers, the main owners and operators of the mine. He then worked for Iron Ore Company of Canada in their pelletizing plant. With the experience he gained on these projects, he became a foremost consultant on iron-ore pelletizing and worked throughout the world. My brother Harry, who died several years ago, operated general stores in Fort Chipewyan and Uranium City. Along with Alex McIver and Charlie Somers, he also owned the Uranium City Bus Line in Uranium City. Jack and George were younger and did not go north until after the Second World War, when they went to Yellowknife and Uranium City to work in various mines. ■

The Fort Chipewyan Families

*A*lthough Fort Chipewyan is some 150 miles (240 km) north, it has always had close ties to the then village and now city of Fort McMurray. One reason for this, of course, is that the only way out of Chipewyan to the "outside" was via the Athabasca River to Fort McMurray—even in the days of travel via Portage La Loche. Another is that practically all the Fort Chipewyan families had one or more members residing in Fort McMurray at one time or another. As a result we felt that Fort Chipewyan was really an extension of Fort McMurray.

Fort Chipewyan was the oldest trading post in the North. A post had originally been built in 1778 by Peter Pond of the North West Company, 30 miles (50 km) south of Lake Athabasca on the delta of the Athabasca River; it was the first fort on the Mackenzie watershed and the first white man's house in Alberta. It was probably at Embarras Portage, where the Athabasca River splits and the Embarras River flows to Lake Athabasca. In 1788, Alexander Mackenzie had his cousin Roderick Mackenzie build a new post on the lake at Fort

Chipewyan, which he then made his headquarters for eight years. In 1789 he started his journey to the Arctic Ocean from here, down the river that is named after him, and then in 1792 he left Fort Chipewyan on his historic trip to the Pacific. Sir John Franklin obtained his supplies at Fort Chipewyan for two trips to the Arctic, first in 1820 and then in 1825. According to entries in HBC journals cited by Agnes Dean Cameron in her book *The New North*, Franklin conducted two weddings while in Chipewyan.[1]

When I lived in Fort McMurray there was an aristocracy in Fort Chipewyan. Practically all the Natives and Métis were Roman Catholics but the families within the patrician group were Anglicans. I remember their distinctive accent, which was quite unlike any I have ever heard elsewhere in Canada, as it neither sounded Scottish, English, nor French. The members of these families were all very intelligent and many were well educated, and from these families came such men as George and Billy Loutit. Other families that made up the aristocracy included the Wylies and Frasers. They were of mixed blood, their progenitors having come from Scotland to Canada where they married Native girls. Within a generation or two, there was so much intermarriage between the members of these families that everyone seemed to be related to each other.

When Agnes Dean Cameron, the author of *The New North*, went north in 1908 she stopped off in Fort Chipewyan, where she met the well-known members of these elite families. Of the Loutits, she said, "There are Loutits in Chipewyan as far back as the old journals reach. The Scottish blood has intermingled with that of Cree and Chipewyan and the result in this day's generation is a family of striking young people." She went on to say: "George Loutit without help brought a scow worth four thousand pounds from Athabasca landing to Chipewyan through the ninety miles of rapids. Rivermen tell of George Loutit quarrelling with a man one afternoon in a saloon at Edmonton and throwing his adversary out of the window. When he heard him slump, George immediately thought of the North as a most desirable place and started hot foot for Athabasca Landing, a hundred miles away. He arrived there in time for noon luncheon next day."[2]

Another notable member of the Loutit family, a brother of Billy and George, was John James Loutit, who was the first factor in the newly reactivated post of Fort McMurray in 1907. He served the HBC faithfully for many years as a factor at various posts, mainly at Fort Chipewyan and Fort McMurray. He was the factor at McMurray when I was growing up there, and I attended school with most of his children. As a mark of "appreciation" for his many valuable years of service, John James was discarded during the Depression years when he was the factor at Fort Chipewyan—presumably because he didn't turn in enough profit for the year. Another example of the "magnanimity" of the Bay toward its loyal employees was the manner in which it treated Billy Loutit's widow, Jenny, after he died in a hospital in Edmonton in July 1947. Jenny stayed at the Corona Hotel during his last days, and on arriving back home she was puzzled as to why her next pension cheque was so small. On inquiring she discovered that the grateful company had deducted her hotel expenses from the cheque. Their son Paul, who was attempting to follow in his father's footsteps and was apprenticing with the Bay, became so disgusted he promptly left the company.

I don't have much love for the HBC, or should I say the original company before it divested itself of its northern trading business (to be distinguished from the modern department store complex). This is mainly based on personal experience, namely, how the company treated some of my friends, and because of other dealings of which I have knowledge. During my time in the North and especially in the early days, the Bay held sway over the North, although its grip was slightly loosened by the competition from fur traders. From the way in which loyal and faithful servants of the company were treated dating from the days of Roderick MacFarlane, it seems evident that after HBC governor Sir George Simpson retired, it was run by men in London who never set foot in Canada and were only interested in the profits that accrued.

I knew several of the Bay apprentices who had come out from

Scotland to work. As indentured servants they received a salary of one hundred dollars per year, which was increased by one hundred dollars each subsequent year so that at the end of their five-year contract they would receive a salary of five hundred dollars per year. They also received free accommodation and meals. According to these lads I knew, they were filled with tales by the company of how they could trap for furs in their spare time and make much more money than their actual wages. To young lads in Scotland, the glamour of the Canadian North and the lure of the wealth they were told they could amass was a magnet that drew them irresistibly to this country. Little did they comprehend the isolation and loneliness of some of the northern posts. Neither did they have time to trap once they got here, as they worked all hours of the day, performing menial tasks around the trading post at the whim of the factor. Everything, of course, depended on whether or not they had a reasonable factor, because at the post he was king.

In 1870 the HBC sold the bulk of the land that had previously been its domain to the Government of Canada for three hundred thousand pounds. Until 1871, the officers were partners and received forty percent of the net profit. This was divided into eighty-five shares, with chief factors holding two shares and chief traders one share. Thus the factors and traders expected to receive a share of the three hundred thousand pounds received for the land. However, they did not receive a penny. In 1871 the company revised its "Deed Poll" and refused to give the officers a share of either the money or the land that it had retained. The company had retained choice grants of land throughout the country, including the mineral rights to that land. An example of how the HBC acted in ways that were detrimental to Canada is the way in which it handled these mineral rights when oil and gas were found in abundance in certain parts of the country. Some of the most valuable of these rights were on HBC land, and these the Bay practically gave away in 1926 to the American company Continental Oil, which called its Canadian subsidiary Hudson's Bay Oil and Gas.

Notwithstanding the shortcomings of the HBC, it must be admitted that many of the people who opened up northern Canada were "Bay" men or their descendants. For example, the members of another

Chipewyan family, the Frasers, were descended from Colin Fraser, who had been brought over from the highlands of Scotland in 1826 to be the eminent HBC governor Sir George Simpson's piper. Sir George added a touch of pomp by having Colin, clad in a kilt, pipe in his arrival at any of the forts he visited. The piping impressed the Natives, who thought Simpson was a great chief. Colin's grandson, also named Colin Fraser, settled in Fort Chipewyan, where he became the foremost fur trader and the head of the Fraser clan in the area. Horace Wylie, a grandson of both Colin Fraser and William Wylie, still owned Colin Fraser's original bagpipes in the 1980s, but then donated them to the Government of Alberta museum in Edmonton.

Probably the most distinguished citizen of Fort Chipewyan was William Wylie, the ancestor of the Wylie clan, who arrived in 1863 from the Orkney Islands as an indentured servant of the HBC and became the company's blacksmith. He had come to Canada via the company ship to Hudson Bay, then went with the brigade up the rivers and across the various lakes on the original route from Hudson Bay to Portage La Loche and down the Clearwater and Athabasca rivers to Fort Chipewyan. He was still in his teens when he came to Chipewyan and never saw a city until he was an old man, when he went as far as Winnipeg in 1907, intending to make his way back to Scotland for a visit. However, he couldn't stand being in the city, so he abandoned his trip and went back to Fort Chipewyan, where he lived until his death.

William Wylie made all the nails and ironwork used in the rebuilding of the fort at Chipewyan. He also manufactured the ironwork for the building of the ss *Grahame* in 1883. In *The New North*, Agnes Dean Cameron said of him: "Talking with the old gentleman, you are conscious of the innate moral strength rather than the mechanical skill of the craftsman. Instinctively you feel the splendid power of his presence and come out from his forge murmuring 'thank God I have seen a man this day.'" She said that throughout the HBC journals in Fort Chipewyan, there are entries such as "Wylie making nails"; "Wylie straightening the fowling pieces"; and "Wylie making sled runners." She was clearly impressed by the man, for she wrote:

No one feels like smiling a smile of superiority in talking with old Mr. Wylie. He has taught himself the gentle arts of gunsmithing and blacksmithing. The tools that we see all around us are marvels of a modern arts and crafts exhibition. His sledges and augers, planes and chisels have been made by the old man out of pig iron which came as ballast in the holds of those old sailing ships which beat their way into Fort Churchill through Hudson Strait. The hand made tools are set into convenient handles of moose-horn and bone. Clean indeed is the workmanship that Wylie has done with them. The last triumph from this unique forge was the welding of the little tug *Primrose*. The steamer *Grahame* was built at Chipewyan of whip-sawn lumber, and much of her steel and ironwork was wrought on Wylie's forge.[3] ∎

The Coming of
the Airplane

ero worship changed for the boys of Fort McMurray with the arrival of the airplane. Whereas the objects of our adulation had previously been riverboat captains and pilots—just as in Mark Twain's day—abruptly our heroes became airplane pilots and mechanics. We wanted to be like them, and some of my friends, including Rex Terpening and Ron Morrison, would go and help the mechanics service the planes, working full time without pay in order to learn the trade and earn their licence.

Since Fort McMurray was such a small community, we got to know all the pilots and mechanics, as well as their families. They became our friends, as well as our heroes. Although I had not thought of it before, I now realize that when it came to the airplane pilots and mechanics, we kids didn't follow my father's instruction that we should address all adult men using the title "Mr." That rule of etiquette didn't seem to apply to the airmen as we called all of them by their first name—it was Wop, Con, Archie, and even Punch. As for the airmen's wives, I always called them "Mrs." except for Vi May, Wop's wife, who played ball with us and was just "Vi."

Wop May and John Michaels with a lake trout from Great Bear Lake.
(courtesy Denny May)

All of the fliers and aeromechanics were based in Fort McMurray, and in the summer they played softball with us. Our league included the Airways team, the town team from Fort McMurray, the Waterways team, and our team of kids, called the "Cubs." Wop May was the pitcher for the Airways team and Vi May, who was a very good athlete, played first base. Lou Parmenter, Punch Dickins's air engineer, was English and had played a lot of cricket. He could really wallop a low ball and hated it when pitchers threw balls above his knees.

Although the airplane people were the upper crust of society in Fort McMurray, none of them tended to act "uppity" and all of them were respected and accepted by everyone. As the years went on, some, because of their acts of kindness, became almost household gods to the people whom they had helped. The airplane transformed the life of Northerners. Before the coming of the airplane, during the winter people north of Fort McMurray were almost completely isolated from the outside world. The only previous means of long-distance transportation was by dog team, which meant days or even weeks of arduous travel with temperatures ranging as low as -65°F (-54°C). If someone contracted a life-threatening illness or suffered an accident, it was practically impossible to get medical help unless the community was fortunate enough to have a doctor. With the coming of the airplane, "mercy flights" were conducted, which helped save many lives. The airplane also erased the winter's long isolation by bringing in news from the outside world. It seemed almost like magic to the northern settlements to receive mail within weeks, rather than six or eight months.

The first airplanes I remember seeing were Royal Canadian Air Force (RCAF) aircraft in 1924. These were Vickers Vidette flying boats that had been brought over from England. All the kids in town, including myself, would run down to the "Snye" (a backwater of the Athabasca River) with great excitement to watch them taxiing to shore. These planes were so underpowered, however, that we never saw them take off—the Snye did not provide enough length for them to get airborne, and they were forced to use the Athabasca River, which afforded them a long enough runway.

The RCAF used these Vickers flying boats to perform aerial mapping of the country, as many of the existing maps were inaccurate and vast areas of the North were unmapped. The air force eventually switched to Fairchild 71s, and these and the Fokkers were probably the most popular planes in the late 1920s and the early 1930s. In 1928 the mining magnate Jack Hammell started Northern Aerial Mineral Explorers (NAME), using Fairchild 71s. Some of the most famous bush pilots, such as Doc Oakes, Bill Spence, and Bill McDonough, flew for NAME. These pilots flew prospectors all over the North Country looking for gold and other minerals. Following the RCAF flying boats, the next airplane I saw was Doc Oakes's Fairchild in the summer of 1927 or 1928. After that, airplanes became commonplace and we quit running down to the Snye to see them land.

In 1928 Punch Dickins became the first commercial pilot in the North, flying for James Richardson's Western Canada Airways.[1] In the summer of 1928 Punch and his mechanic, Lou Parmenter, had flown Colonel C. D. H. MacAlpine of Dominion Explorers on a trip from Winnipeg to Hudson Bay and across the Barren Lands, finally arriving back in Fort Smith and then travelling on to Fort McMurray. They had also flown in the dead of winter to Fort Smith and various other northern ports that had previously only been accessible by dog team at that time of year.

In the winter of 1929 there was great excitement as Wop May and his band of flyers and mechanics descended upon Fort McMurray to start their assault on the North Country. The coming of May's Commercial Airways was a great boon to McMurray, as the community's economy had previously depended primarily on the fur trade. The additional revenue from the airline and its personnel provided a welcome fillip for local businesses. I especially remember fellows like Casey Vandelinden, an airplane mechanic just out from Belgium, either still in his teens or barely twenty, getting outfitted with winter clothing in bitterly cold -50°F (-46°C) weather. He must have had second thoughts about coming to such a God-forsaken country, where servicing airplanes involved warming up the engines with gasoline-burning blow-pots, on which the engine oil was heated before it was poured into the engine. Commercial Airways' financial backers Solloway and Mills went bankrupt in the crash of 1929, and after that the airline was taken over by James Richardson's group, which by that time had changed its name from Western Canada Airways to Canadian Airways. However, the personnel of the old Commercial Airways were all retained, with Wop May becoming the superintendent of this new branch of Canadian Airways.

As uranium ore, gold, and other minerals were discovered in the North, the activities of the airlines expanded. This began with the discovery of pitchblende, an ore from which uranium oxide is extracted, at Great Bear Lake by Gilbert Labine and his partners in 1932. A lot of freight went north by boat in the summertime, but a lot was flown from Fort Norman to Port Radium on Great Bear Lake because of the rapids in the Bear River. A lot of material that was required on a rush basis was also flown in from Fort McMurray. Then gold was discovered at Goldfields on the north shore of Lake Athabasca in northern Saskatchewan in about 1932. This resulted in the development of the Box Mine by Consolidated Mining and Smelting and a flurry of activity in that area. The property was later abandoned when it was discovered that, due to sampling errors, the grade of the ore had been overestimated and was actually too low to be profitable. However, uranium ore was discovered nearby some years later, and this resulted in more flying activity out of Fort McMurray.

The discovery of gold in northern Saskatchewan and at Yellowknife in the Northwest Territories during the early 1930s caused a boom in the previously Depression-ridden North. During these years, practically the only place to find a decent-paying job was in the North Country, either in the mines or with companies supplying services to them. The only access was through Fort McMurray—all of the traffic funnelled through it to the North. Prior to the Goldfields discovery, Major Lauchie Burwash (who had become famous for determining the location of the North Magnetic Pole in the Arctic) had been working on a gold discovery on what is now the Giant Mine property. Although it seemed to be a promising prospect, the main Giant ore body had not yet been discovered. I remember Johnny Baker, who was prospecting on the property, telling us in 1932 of the riches that would come from this mining claim.

In 1935 Consolidated Mining and Smelting discovered the property that became a rich gold-producing mine—the Con in Yellowknife. Following this, two more gold-producing mines were discovered nearby: the Ryan and the Negus. With these discoveries Yellowknife became a boom town, and the gold rush was on. In 1935 Leigh Brintnell's newly formed Mackenzie Air Services obtained a large Bellanca Airbus, with which they began flying pitchblende concentrate from the Eldorado Mine at Port Radium on Great Bear Lake to Fort McMurray. This ore was sent to the Eldorado refinery in Ontario, where uranium was extracted from it, which was utilized in the first atomic bombs from Oak Ridge in the United States. Brintnell had been a pilot for James Richardson's Western Canada Airways (later Canadian Airways) before he formed Mackenzie Air Services. He was built like a tank and was reputed to have been a sparring partner for Jack Dempsey. He looked like a tough customer, and I don't think anyone would have liked to tangle with him.

One other airline in addition to Canadian Airways and Mackenzie Air Services was started in the North in the early 1930s. Spence-McDonough was inaugurated by two well-known northern pilots, Bill Spence and Bill McDonough, but their company was absorbed by Canadian Airways in 1933. By 1932 Fort McMurray had become the busiest airport in Canada. All the planes used the Snye as their landing field, landing on floats in summer and skis in winter. The Snye was an ideal landing site in winter because the quietness of the backwater allowed the ice to freeze as smooth as a billiard table; the main channel of the Athabasca usually had hummocks and bumps that made it unsuitable.

Other than the outmoded RCAF Vickers flying boats, the airplanes most commonly in northern service in the early days were Fokkers and Fairchilds. Of course, there was a whole variety of other airplanes in use, as well. Canadian Airways had several German-built, low-winged Junkers. The Junkers had been developed in post-First World War Germany and were actually disguised military airplanes—disguised since Germany was not allowed to build military aircraft after the war. In Canada the Junkers were fitted with American air-cooled Wasp radial engines, rather than the original German water-cooled engines. With this set-up, they proved to be dependable, rugged workhorses. One of the original airplanes in commercial use in Canada was a Curtiss Lark that was purchased by James Richardson for Doc Oakes to begin a service from Winnipeg to Red Lake, Ontario, in 1926. Sammy Tomlinson was the air engineer for this original member of the Western Canada Airways fleet. Sammy maintained that it was the first commercial air service in Canada.

Wop May's Commercial Airways used Bellanca Pacemakers. These were smaller than the Bellanca Airbus that was later used by Mackenzie Air Services to haul pitchblende ore from Port Radium to Fort McMurray. Canadian Airways had sold its Universal Fokkers, which were powered by smaller engines than the newer Super Universal Fokkers it had acquired, to Grant McConachie's fledgling airline Universal Air Services in 1930. McConachie used them to fly frozen whitefish from lakes in northern Saskatchewan to Fort McMurray for the McInnes Fish Company until he formed Yukon Southern Air Transport in 1937 and obtained a mail contract from Edmonton to Whitehorse in the Yukon.

Bill Jewett of Consolidated Mining and Smelting (CM&S) started flying in the North during the early 1930s in a DeHavilland Gypsy Moth, which was an open-cockpit, two-seater plane. CM&S then switched to twin-engine De Havilland Dragons, but these were so underpowered that they usually had to taxi miles before they were able to take off. When CM&S started developing the Box Mine at Goldfields in northern Saskatchewan, it began utilizing Fairchild 71s for transporting equipment. Ken Dewar and Paige Macphee of CM&S spent hours each day ferrying material to Goldfields from McMurray.

Many of the pilots, including Con Farrell, had flown Fokker aircraft on the first scheduled western Canadian airmail flights between the prairie cities. However, these planes were not the Universal or Super Universals that were used in the North from 1928 onward. In the Fokkers that were used for the Prairie Airmail run, the pilot was seated in an open cockpit toward the rear of the fuselage rather than in the front. Con told me that airmen hated these flights. One can understand why, since the pilot's location at the rear impeded their sight and they had to land on grass airfields with no lights other than those used to mark out the edges of the landing strips. There was, of course, no radio communication and all flying had to be done by dead-reckoning. This must have been a nightmare during snowstorms and blizzards. The Prairie Airmail only lasted from 1929 to 1931 to the obvious relief of the pilots, to whom flying in the North Country seemed like a piece of cake after their night-flying ordeals. The first plane specifically designed for northern bush flying was the Norseman, which made its debut in the latter part of the 1930s. It was a dependable, sturdy plane that could carry a good payload and was the forerunner of the acclaimed Beaver and Otter, which were developed by DeHavilland for bush flying after the Second World War.

The decade before the Second World War was the heyday of bush pilots like Punch Dickins, Wop May, Con Farrell, and the many others who were flying to still-unmapped areas in northern Canada. Since I worked for Canadian Airways in 1935 and 1936, when I was seventeen, I got to know the company's pilots quite well, especially Wop May and Con Farrell, with whom I had considerable contact when delivering radio messages that required a reply.

Wop May was an ace pilot in the First World War and became famous because he was involved in the shooting down of the great German "Red Baron" Manfred von Richtofen.[2] In 1927 Wop was a flying instructor for the Edmonton Flying Club when an urgent call came in for serum to combat a diphtheria outbreak in the northern Alberta village of Fort Vermilion. In an open-cockpit Avro Avian, he and Vic Horner flew the serum in -33°F (-36°C) weather from Edmonton to Fort Vermilion. In 1930 he again made headlines with his flights to assist the posse chasing the "Mad Trapper," Albert Johnson, in the Richardson Mountains west of Aklavik in the Northwest Territories.

Wop was a hero to all the western Canadian boys of my generation. However, to me, he was also a warm-hearted friend who was very kind when I needed help. In 1938 when I was languishing in Fort

McMurray without enough money to purchase a ticket to Yellowknife, where I wanted to go to find a job, somehow Wop found out about my predicament and let me earn my fare by painting the front of the McMurray Canadian Airways hangar. I am sure he performed many such acts of kindness throughout the North that were never publicized.

Con Farrell, who had also been a First World War flier, was the assistant superintendent for the Northern District of Canadian Airways under Wop. He was a very good manager and administrator, as well as being a great pilot. Once, Con and his mechanic were forced down by engine trouble in the Arctic in 1935 and were sitting it out on a small lake. They had been down several days, with several Canadian Airways planes out searching for them, when fellow pilot Matt Berry spotted them and flew over, pretending not to see them. (You would not have expected Matt to play such a practical joke as he always seemed to be such a serious fellow.) Knowing that Con would be ranting and cursing at him for not sighting them, he landed some miles away before taking off and coming back. All of us who knew Con could imagine the blast that Matt received when he landed to pick them up.

Although I didn't know Punch Dickins as well as the other pilots, I knew him well enough to call him "Punch." Of course, this probably doesn't count for much as everyone called him that. In the North Country no one seemed to call anyone "Mister." Punch was the dean of the bush pilots. He had served as a bomber pilot during the First World War with the Royal Flying Corps and incredibly had shot down seven enemy aircraft while flying a bomber. He flew a total of seventy-three missions. He was one of the first pilots hired by James Richardson's Western Canada Airways in 1926, and he piloted the first aircraft on the newly inaugurated Prairie Airmail in 1929. He was responsible for a number of landmark flights, such as the first aerial survey of Canada in 1928 and the first airmail run to the Northwest Territories in 1929. He was the first to fly the full length of the Mackenzie River and to fly over the Barren Lands in the Northwest Territories. He also flew the first prospectors, including Gilbert Labine, into Great Bear Lake where they discovered uranium.

Prior to the Second World War, Punch was general superintendent for Canadian Pacific Airlines. When war broke out, he headed the Atlantic Ferry Command, which flew desperately needed combat aircraft to Britain. He then played a major part in developing the Commonwealth Air Training Program, which trained thousands of combat fliers in Canada. After the war he played a major part in the design of the famous Beaver bush plane with DeHavilland Canada Aircraft. He received numerous honours and awards and didn't stop flying until he was seventy-eight years old. He died in 1995 and his ashes were scattered from an aircraft along the Mackenzie River by his son John.

Another outstanding airman I want to mention here is Cy Becker. A friend of Wop May's, he had been a flyer in the Royal Flying Corps during the First World War and helped found Commercial Airways. He was a practising lawyer in Edmonton but still retained his commercial pilot's licence and was one of the pilots who flew with Wop on the historic first airmail flight by Commercial Airways in 1929. Whenever anyone needed any legal help, they went to Cy, who never let them down. When I returned from overseas after the Second World War, I had difficulty buying a house because a bigoted contractor and the North American Life Insurance Mortgage lender felt that my being of Japanese origin would be detrimental to their selling other houses in the area. Cy soon put them straight, but I had trouble getting a bill from him. He eventually charged me twenty dollars. Needless to say, Cy was tops in my books.

The unsung heroes of the early days of bush flying were the air mechanics. Instead of a co-pilot, each airplane carried an aero-engineer (they are now called aircraft maintenance engineers). In order to obtain an aero-engineer's licence, they had to undergo a long period of training, so all of them were skilled mechanics. Some of the aero-engineers I remember are Don Goodwin, Lou Parmenter, Sammy Tomlinson, and Rex Terpening.

Don Goodwin had been on the ill-fated MacAlpine expedition that was lost in the Arctic for weeks in 1929 and for which the most extensive air search to date was made. Don lost several toes to frostbite from that ordeal. He later became the chief mechanic for Canadian

Airways in Fort McMurray. The MacAlpine expedition had been launched by Colonel MacAlpine, the president of the Dominion Explorers mining company, who was intent on scouring the North Country for minerals. They set out in two airplanes piloted by G. A. Thompson, who headed up James Richardson's Western Canada Airways and whom we always referred to as "Gat," and Stan McMillan, who later became chief pilot for Mackenzie Air Services. Due to several unfortunate incidents, they were forced off course and after landing did not have enough fuel to proceed. They were unable to travel because of open water and had to wait until the water froze to make the trek on foot to Cambridge Bay. It was during this trip that Don Goodwin's toes froze. Remarkably, Don's toes seem to have been the only casualties suffered during their ordeal.

Lou Parmenter was a Cockney who had served in the Royal Air Force (RAF). He was Punch Dickins's mechanic when Punch was making some of the first commercial flights from Fort McMurray to the North Country in 1928. On one landing at Fort Smith in 1928, Punch hit a hummock on the ice and the Fokker airplane nosed over, bending the propeller. As it was the only aircraft flying in the North at that time in the dead of winter, there was no way of getting a spare propeller flown in. Lou straightened the bent propeller out as much as possible, then sawed off the end, which was bent too much to straighten. He then had to saw a piece off the other end to match. By the dint of much filing, he balanced the prop so they could try it out on the plane. It's hard to believe that he could have adequately balanced the prop by manually filing it so that it didn't tear the engine apart when running at flying speed, but they managed to fly back to Fort McMurray with the sawed-off prop, and both Lou and Punch just treated it like it had been a routine flight.

Sammy Tomlinson served with the RAF in the First World War and then came to Canada as an aero-engineer with the first Vickers flying boats purchased by the RCAF in the early 1920s. When Doc Oakes began an air service from Winnipeg to Red Lake in 1926, Sammy served as his aero-engineer and stayed with Western Canada Airways, which became Canadian Airways. He then joined the RCAF and went

83

overseas at the outbreak of the Second World War. I became quite good friends with Sammy years later, when we both lived in Calgary, Alberta, and he had been retired for some years. He once asked me, "What do you think was the item that contributed most significantly to bush flying in the North?" When I replied that I didn't know, he said, "It was the Nelson heaters, which allowed the aircraft to fly no matter how cold it got in the winter." During the winter, whenever an airplane stopped at its landing spot, the mechanic would drain the lubricating oil from the engine. Then, in the morning, with a large canvas tarp enclosing the engine, the mechanic would light the Nelson heater, place it under the engine, and put the can of oil on top of it to heat it up. The heater thus performed two functions: it heated the oil so it would flow freely when put into the engine, and it warmed up the engine so it would start easily. The Nelson heaters allowed aircraft to start in -60°F (-51°C) weather with no trouble.

Another of the aero-engineers was Rex Terpening. We were in the same grade at school in Fort McMurray and became very good friends. However, after we left school our paths never crossed again until many years later, when Rex was inducted into the Canadian Aviation Hall of Fame in 1998. Rex very kindly sent me an invitation to attend the induction ceremony, which was held at the Calgary Petroleum Club. Rex had gone to work for Canadian Airways after leaving school and worked for a year at no salary until he obtained his aero-engineer's licence. After that, he flew throughout the North with all of the well-known bush pilots. When Canadian Pacific Airlines took over Canadian Airways in 1942, he was put in charge of the company's maintenance in Vancouver. His book *Bent Props and Blowpots*, which chronicles his experiences flying in the North, was published in 2003. ■

Striking Out
on My Own

I was sixteen, I had just finished high school during the height of the Depression, and there weren't any jobs around. Hundreds of men had come to Fort McMurray via rail on the boxcars, looking for work. I had a job working in my father's market garden, hoeing potatoes and weeding vegetables, then harvesting the crop in the fall. Finally, I did get a job in the spring of 1935 with Alex McIver, who took a scow loaded with merchandise down the Athabasca River delta each spring to trade for muskrat pelts.

In the 1920s and early 1930s, before the discovery of gold in the North Country, the primary industry, especially during the winter and spring months, was the fur trade. During that period, aside from cutting wood for the steamboats, it was practically the only source of income in the Fort McMurray area. Other than muskrat and beaver, the fur trade relied on the abundance of snowshoe rabbits, upon which other fur-bearing animals, such as foxes and lynx, depended for food. The population of rabbits was cyclical, starting with lean years in which there were practically none, then increasing each year until finally there were so many that the only sustenance available to them was the bark off young trees, which they denuded. The rabbits would then die off, either from a disease called myxomatosis or from lack of food. The cycle would then repeat itself, occurring every seven to ten years. Dr. William Rowan, a prominent naturalist at the University of Alberta, believed this phenomenon was due to the sunspot cycle, which seemed to correspond with the rabbit cycle. It is interesting to note that in a paper entitled "The Ten Year Cycle,"[1] Rowan's graph plotting of records for the Hudson's Bay Company's fur sales going back hundreds of years produced an almost-perfect sine curve demonstrating the seven- to ten-year cycle.

With the decline in the number of fur-bearing animals due to extensive trapping, the main source of income during the 1930s was the spring muskrat crop. The mecca for muskrat trapping was the Athabasca delta, where the Athabasca River flows into Lake Athabasca. Here, there were thousands of muskrats, so there was invariably a bountiful harvest for the cash-starved people who had been waiting impatiently for the season to start.

Alex McIver was a trader in partnership with Sam Kushner, a local merchant in Fort McMurray. McIver had a scow, some 50 feet (15 m) in length, covered with a roof, which he would cram full with merchandise and foodstuffs to sell in trade for muskrats. It was, in effect, a travelling general store. The scow was propelled by two ten-horsepower Johnson outboard motors mounted at the rear. Since the end of the scow was too high to permit the propellers to reach the water, wells were cut in the sloping back end so the propellers could operate below the water's surface. Normally with outboard motors, steering is accomplished by turning the motor but since there were two motors and only one steersman, the motors were lashed into place and steering was accomplished by means of a long sweep mounted on a swivel at the rear of the scow. The sweep was a long spruce pole with a board fastened to the end. It was manned by our pilot, "Curly" Jewett, an experienced riverman.

As soon as the ice broke on the river in April we embarked, but we were soon stopped by the ice jamming a few miles down the river.

The winter had been quite cold and the ice in the river had frozen to a thickness of 3 to 5 feet (1 to 1.5 m). As a result, when the ice broke in the spring the floes were huge. Anyone who has not seen the spring breakup in the North would be amazed at the raw power unleashed when the huge ice masses—they can be several feet thick and some 20 to 50 feet (6 to 15 m) in breadth and length—grind together and roll over as they rush onward. The roar they make is deafening and frightening when first heard. When the ice on the river is thick, like it was in the spring of 1935, ice jams often occur wherever there is some obstruction in the river, such as an island in midstream. Behind the jams, water backs up and floods the countryside. In 1935 the ice jams caused a huge flood in the Athabasca River valley.

As our scow moved down the river, the water level was so high that we found ourselves riding along at treetop height, some 40 feet (12 m) or more above the normal level. The ice jam would eventually break and then jam again a few miles farther downstream so that we were continually tying up and starting again. We had several passengers on board who had paid to be taken north, men who were heading north to look for work. During the Depression, men were always on the move, and since there was little hope of getting work on the Prairies, there were always some who thought that the North Country would offer something.

When we finally reached the delta of the Athabasca River we tied up our scow in a more or less permanent location. The delta is a large, marshy area where the land is practically floating on top of the water. It is the natural habitat of muskrats and waterfowl, and the trappers in the area would shoot or trap hundreds of muskrats during the spring season. Some often obtained as many as a thousand skins a season. At a dollar each, this was a lot of money during the Depression years, especially when it was earned in just a few months during the spring.

Once we had tied up in the delta, I stayed on the scow and acted as the local storekeeper, while McIver went around in his canoe, powered by a kicker (an outboard motor), and visited the cabins of the various trappers to buy muskrat pelts for cash. The Native women would paddle up to our scow in their canoes and buy things from me, using muskrats as currency. All the Natives knew who I was because my father had trapped in the delta years before, and they recognized my resemblance to him. Although my knowledge of Cree was limited, I managed fairly well. I soon also discovered why the women would point to the summer sausage and then giggle—in the limited Cree vocabulary, the same word was used for both sausage and penis.

I learned how to grade muskrat pelts from a man I knew only as Ned, a fur buyer from Winnipeg who accompanied us. From him I also discovered what a risky business fur buying was. In those days, when it was impossible to communicate with the outside markets, no one knew the current price of muskrats or other fur. Therefore, if a buyer paid a dollar for each muskrat, it was quite possible that, when he finally got them to the fur sales, he might only get fifty cents for each pelt and take a terrific loss.

When the spring trapping season was over, we began the long journey upstream back to Fort McMurray. It was boring sitting in the scow, watching the shoreline creep past. Anyone who has ridden upstream in an underpowered boat will understand how slowly you seem to travel. However, it was interesting and almost unbelievable to see where the water level had been on our downstream voyage—we could see the waterline on the tree trunks some 40 feet (12 m) above us as we inched our way upstream. After we got back to Fort McMurray, I was paid for my labours, a dollar a day for thirty-some days. Then it was back to hoeing potatoes for my father.

After I finished high school in 1934, I helped my father with his potato farm and vegetable garden. Going to the garden each day I would pass by the Canadian Airways radio station, located at the end of Franklin Avenue, just on the edge of Hudson's Bay Flats. One day as I was passing by, Bill Hartree, the operator, came out and asked me if I was interested in learning how to become a radio operator. I said, "Anything's better than hoeing spuds." So it was arranged that I would work around the radio station for free and in return I'd learn Morse code and radio theory with a view to becoming a radio operator. I had to start the fire in the radio shack at 6:00 AM so it would be warm enough for the first schedule, or "sked," at 8:00 AM. Part of my duties included delivering radio messages, which were mostly for Fred Lundy, the local station agent.

Fred was a big, broad-shouldered man and a great guy—but an alcoholic. When he went on a tear, it was my job to find him and try to get an intelligible answer out of him. This was sometimes a real chore. I often had to keep prodding him awake until I finally got a reply to the wire I had brought him. The messages for Fred were usually from Wop May, the district superintendent for Canadian Airways, who would send them during one of his flights. He demanded answers immediately, so Fred would have been in trouble if I didn't get the information from him. Amazingly, Fred seemed to be able to reason even while totally inebriated, although I usually had to read him the message as he would be too drunk to read it himself. I'm sure I saved Fred's job for him several times.

The radio transmitter we used at Canadian Airways would be considered archaic by today's standards and was even becoming out of date by the late 1930s, as it did not have quartz crystals to ensure that the frequency did not waver. It had two large vacuum tubes about 24 inches (60 cm) in length, arranged in what was known as a push-pull arrangement. The frequency was set by copper coils and large condensers. To change frequency, the coils had to be changed and the dial setting on the condensers altered. The coils were made of quarter-inch (half-centimetre) copper tubing. The plates on the vacuum tubes had a voltage of 1,500 volts, which was supplied by a 1,500-volt direct-current generator, driven by a gasoline engine.

At that time in 1935, Canadian Airways had radio stations at Fort Rae in the Northwest Territories and at Goldfields on Lake Athabasca in northern Saskatchewan. The Fort Rae station was later moved to the Burwash Camp, which was later to become the Giant Mine in Yellowknife. Since there were no Royal Canadian Corps of Signals stations in these locations, the Canadian Airways stations were also allowed to handle commercial radio messages. The Signals Corps established a station at Yellowknife in 1937, and Canadian Airways' handling of commercial traffic ended.

The Signals Corps had been given the task of providing radio communication for the North Country in the early days of radio in the 1920s. This network extended all the way from Edmonton to Aklavik in the Northwest Territories and was a godsend to the people in the North who previously did not receive news or could not get in touch with anyone from "outside" for months. The corps was able to use long-wave radio, which gave them reliable channels at all times. This type of radio wave powered along the ground and unlike short-wave was not dependent on being bounced into the stratosphere to be reflected back by the Kennelly-Heavyside Layer. Short-wave radio signals could travel long distances with small power input because they were reflected back to Earth by this medium. However, short-wave communication, at least in those days, was unreliable at times of high sunspot activity such as occurred in 1936. There were periods when no signals could be received for weeks on end by the short-wave stations utilized by Canadian Airways, whereas the Signals Corps was able to get through at all times on long-wave, since all this medium required was a lot of power.

My days at the radio station consisted of learning Morse code when I had free time and learning radio theory and practical radio from Bill Hartree, who was always building radio sets. Bill had been a wireless operator in the Royal Navy in England before immigrating to Canada. Working for Canadian Airways, I also came to know all the pilots and air engineers. Punch Dickins was by then general superintendent for western Canada but was not often in Fort McMurray. Wop May was superintendent of northern Alberta and the Northwest Territories and was based in Fort McMurray, while Con Farrell was assistant superintendent. I got to know Wop and Con quite well, as I was always delivering messages for them. I would often be with Con when he was making up a message to reply to one of Wop's wires. By the end of a year I was put on the payroll as assistant operator, at a salary of thirty dollars a month.

In 1936 Canadian Airways moved its northern headquarters from Fort McMurray to Edmonton, and I was out of a job as the company had decided that an assistant radio operator at Fort McMurray was no longer required. Fortunately for me, Bill Hartree, my boss and mentor at Canadian Airways, had negotiated a deal with Bob Fitzsimmons, the owner and president of the International Bitumen Company at Bitumount, to build a radio station for the company. The station would operate on the Canadian Airways network when all Canadian Airways traffic was completed for the day. Bill recommended me for the job as radio operator at Bitumount, which was 55 miles (88 km) north of Fort McMurray. This station was not licensed, and I was not a licensed commercial operator, only having my amateur radio operating licence. However, the only Canadian Airways operator working in the North Country at that time who had a commercial licence was Bill Hartree. All the other operators had only an amateur licence, even though they were very qualified operators. In those days no one bothered much about details like obtaining a licence. I accepted the offer from Bob at a salary of sixty dollars a month plus board, and it was arranged that I would go to Bitumount to visit the site. I was to go with Bob Harrop, who was taking care of the plant during the winter season and had come to Fort McMurray by driving up the frozen Athabasca River in the Model-T Ford that Fitzsimmons kept at Bitumount.

The weather in March of that year (1937) had been very mild. The snow cover on the river ice melted during the warm days and refroze at night to form an almost continuous sheet of ice. It was like a giant skating rink all the way from Fort McMurray to Bitumount. Bob and I set out in the Model-T on a beautiful spring day, driving down the Athabasca River at the tremendous speed of 15 to 20 miles (24 to 32 km) per hour. We really felt like lords of all we surveyed as we clattered along with the old Model-T put-putting along with nary a hiccup. We went downriver in the morning and came back upriver in the afternoon.

Bob Fitzsimmons had a tar sands' lease at Bitumount, on the east bank of the Athabasca River. It was a very rich deposit, quite easy to mine, and Bob had been trying to build a plant to separate oil from the tar sands for several years. He obtained financing by travelling all over Canada and the United States selling shares in his International Bitumen Company. He was a real pioneer in the development of the tar sands and, unfortunately, was years ahead of his time. He was

Bob Fitzsimmons and the Model-T Ford at Bitumount in the 1930s. This was the car that I rode in to and from Bitumount in 1937. (Provincial Archives of Alberta, image no. 71.356/604)

unfortunate in that although the hot-water process he employed was on the right track, the equipment that had been installed was not adequate to remove enough of the very abrasive sand, so that the plant couldn't be kept operating for any length of time. I feel that he has not been given due credit for his early work in this field.

Bob was an innovator in many ways. For example, he obtained a speedboat powered by a Curtiss-Wright airplane engine and air propeller that could travel 50 miles (80 km) per hour. This boat was similar to those now in operation in the swamps of the southern United States but was unique at the time and was the only such craft on the Athabasca River. It had the advantage of drawing only a few inches of water and was not bothered by the many sandbars in the river that often impeded the progress of other boats with a larger draft. It could make the journey from Bitumount to Fort McMurray in an hour or so, versus the many hours that normal boats took to make the same upstream voyage. Bob also had a farm near Bitumount, complete with horses and cattle, which was located at his residence, a few miles from the plant site. The farm was taken care of by a man and his wife who lived there year-round and grew vegetables and feed for the animals. When the summer plant crew arrived to start work, there were always fresh vegetables for the kitchen from Bob's garden.

The same spring that I went to work at Bitumount, I was offered a job as a radio operator on the sternwheeler the ss *Athabasca River*, owned and operated by the HBC. In the early days in the North, the Bay had almost a monopoly on transportation by water. The company had decided to modernize and install radios on its steamboats so it could communicate with them during their voyages north. The radios operated on continuous wave (CW); they were not radiotelephones and so required an operator to send and receive messages in Morse code. The job I was offered included acting as purser in my spare time, all at a salary of forty dollars a month plus meals and accommodation when I was on the boat. (This salary was to last only during the actual working season from mid-May until September. After the boats stopped running in the fall, you had to fend for yourself.) This was typical of the wages the Bay paid their employees. Without hesitation I turned down its offer in favour of the one from Fitzsimmons.

When Bill Hartree finally completed building the radio transmitter, I went to Bitumount. I was booked to travel on the ss *Athabasca River* and had gone on board at Waterways the night before we were due to embark. I got to sleep in a stateroom on the boat and was waited on by a steward in a white uniform. I thought this was the height of luxury and especially relished the experience of eating in the ship's dining room.

The next morning the steamboat headed downstream for Fort Fitzgerald, 300 miles (483 km) to the north, and soon reached Bitumount, which was only 54 miles (87 km) from Fort McMurray. While the steamboat was standing in midstream waiting for a motorboat to come out and pick me up, the wind caught it and blew it off course, so that the barge it was pushing became stuck on a sandbar. Steamboats like the *Athabasca River* had a very high profile because of the upper decks and this, combined with their shallow draft and flat bottoms, made them very difficult to control in a high wind. The steamboat had to be unhooked from the barge and manoeuvred in several directions until eventually, after pulling backward, forward, and sideways, the barge was loosened from the sandbar. This was accompanied by much cursing and arm-waving by the captain, Harvey Alexander. Captain Alexander—known behind his back as Sandbar Harvey—was just a little guy, but he had a voice like a foghorn.

He paced the upper deck outside the wheelhouse in his battered captain's hat, vest, and armbands that held up the shirtsleeves on his short arms, roaring at the deckhands scurrying about trying to carry out his orders. "Throw them goddamned lines over to port!" and "What the hell are you bastards doing with them lines?" It was a hilarious scene to watch from shore, but he must have cursed me for causing so much trouble. The cost to the HBC must have been much more than my fare.

Soon after I arrived at Bitumount, I set up my radio station and started communicating with Bill Hartree at Fort McMurray. I would go on the air several times a day and cut in when Bill had signed off with all his northern stations. I had some problems with the steam engineer on night shift, who was trying to sleep and was bothered by the noise of my gasoline-engine-driven generator whenever I went on the air. Eventually he accepted it as one of the drawbacks of the job

Hudson's Bay Company sternwheeler steamboat SS *Athabasca River* at Bitumount in 1937. (Provincial Archives of Alberta, image no. 71.356/614)

and became a friend. However, he may have had an ulterior motive, because when he couldn't sleep he would come and talk with me. He was a dedicated Communist, the first one I had ever met, and did his best to convert me. I suppose a lot of men who went through the terrible times of the Depression became Communists. However, he didn't stay too long at the plant and didn't succeed in converting me.

The plant at Bitumount was a marvel of design. It looked like it had been built by Rube Goldberg, who was famous for his cartoons of complex arrangements of machinery that performed simple tasks. The motive power at the plant was the steam supplied by two wood-

The International Bitumen Company plant at Bitumount in 1937.
(Provincial Archives of Alberta, image no. 71.356/615)

fueled, fifty-horsepower Scotch Marine boilers situated outdoors. There was a plentiful supply of fuel, as there was an abundance of fire-killed spruce nearby. The only problem was the amount of work necessary to get it. It required a gang of men to cut wood in the bush, another gang to load it onto wagons, and teamsters to drive the horse-drawn vehicles to the plant site. There, another gang had to saw it into cordwood lengths, using a gasoline-engine-driven power saw. Then, of course, the firemen had to feed the wood into the boiler furnaces. The boilers supplied steam, which powered a large steam engine that drove most of the separation machinery. Steam also supplied power to reciprocating pumps for pumping the separated bitumen. Steam and hot water from the boilers were used in the separation process. Electrical power for lighting was obtained from a steam-driven electrical generator. The main steam engine drove a huge flywheel, about 10 to 12 feet (3 to 3.7 m) in diameter. To this flywheel were attached belts, which drove the machinery. There were belts going in all directions to drive various machines.

The process used by Bob Fitzsimmons to separate oil from the tar sand was a hot-water process similar to that developed by Dr. Karl Clark at the University of Alberta and to a later process used by Great Canadian Oil Sands and Syncrude. However, Fitzsimmons's process was much "cruder." The raw tar sand feed was conveyed by a scoop operated by a dragline, which was powered by a "donkey engine," a wood-fired combination steam boiler and engine. The tar sand was dropped into a "grizzly," which was essentially a coarse screen composed of iron bars to get rid of any rocks. The tar sand was then mixed with hot water and steam and sent to a mixer—a vessel with paddles—to mix the tar sand and water into a pulp. This pulp was then fed by gravity into a separation tank, a steel tank approximately 25 feet (8 m) in length, with a rotating spiral screw about 12 inches (30 cm) in diameter at its bottom. Hot water and steam were injected into the separation tank to supply heat and to separate the bitumen from the sand—the bitumen floating to the top and the cleaned sand sinking to the bottom to be removed by the rotating spiral screw. The bitumen was removed by paddles that continually scraped the surface of the tank, depositing the bitumen in a surge tank from which it was pumped to the refinery. All the moving parts in this system were powered by the belts and pulleys driven by the main flywheel.

The refinery consisted of a wood-fired furnace, a small, six-tray distillation tower, and an overhead condenser. The bitumen from the separation plant was pumped through the 3-inch (8-cm) furnace tubes and then sent to the distillation tower. This tower separated the lighter compounds, which came out from the top of the tower. These compounds were sent to a condenser, which consisted of coils of 1-inch (2.5-cm) pipe over which river water was sprayed to condense the diesel oil product. The material from the bottom of the tower was the asphalt product.

The process worked—albeit with many interruptions—and produced some beautiful asphalt from the bottom of the tower and a few barrels of very sour distillate from the overhead condenser. However, the problems and shortcomings soon became evident after

A scoop digging bitumen is hauled by a dragline to be processed at the plant. (Provincial Archives of Alberta, image no. 71.356/604k)

the operation began. First, the process as installed did not entirely remove the sand. As a result, when the steam pumps started to pump the liquid bitumen to the refinery, the abrasive sand wore out the valves in the pumps within a couple of hours. What had not been accounted for was how abrasive the sand was. It was beautiful white sand, and with all of the oil removed from it I believe it would have made good glass sand. When Sun Oil started its Great Canadian Oil Sands plant many years later in 1967, I thought they had solved all the problems that Fitzsimmons had encountered. However, they, too, soon discovered just how abrasive the sand was when they found that the cutting teeth on their rotating mining wheels only lasted a few hours before they were abraded to the point of having to be replaced.

Getting back to the problems with Fitzsimmons's plant, as I've stated the sand was so abrasive that the small amount left in the bitumen kept wearing out the valves in the steam-driven reciprocating pumps within a few hours. If the pumps could be kept going long enough, the sand in the bitumen would wear a hole in the piping wherever there was an elbow. You can imagine what a gooey, messy job it was taking these pumps apart, when everything was covered with the tarry bitumen. Another problem was that, because the specific gravity of bitumen was very close to that of water, some water would be present in the feed to the furnace, and when a shot of water hit the furnace tubes, the temperature of the distillation-tower bottom would drop and interfere with the quality of the asphalt produced.

The Bitumount plant kept going long enough to produce some eleven hundred barrels of asphalt and fifty barrels of distillate. Based on this level of production, I believe R. C. (Bob) Fitzsimmons should be given credit as the first producer of commercially processed bitumen from the Athabasca tar sands. This was in the summer of 1937, before any oil was produced at Abasand or any of the other tar sands plants.

I acted as radio operator at Bitumount for several months. Because I had nothing else to do when not on the air, I also worked in the plant, helping the pipefitters. One day, one of the radio transmitter's tubes burned out, and I didn't have a replacement. Although I asked for replacement parts for my radio they never arrived—probably because Fitzsimmons didn't have time to order them or didn't want to spend the money to get them (Fitzsimmons was obviously having trouble raising financing as none of us was getting paid). With no replacement parts, I had to abandon the radio station, so I went to work full time in the plant. Since they weren't receiving any pay, men were deserting the place whenever they could, but most of us didn't have the money to pay the fare on the steamboat or any other means of getting upstream to Fort McMurray. If Fort McMurray had been downstream, we could easily have paddled or even drifted there. Quite a few of us had to wait for the river to freeze in December to make the journey on foot.

During my time at Bitumount after my radio transmitter went kaput, I gained some good working experience. I learned how to handle logs with a peavey, which is a lumberjack's cant hook with a projecting spike near the end. A log retaining wall was being constructed along the bank of the river, and I worked on this project for a while. The foreman was a crusty old bird by the name of George Anderson, who owned a farm near Olds, Alberta. He had been a bridge and building foreman on the CPR and knew all about timber construction. Since farmers were hit by the Depression just like the rest of us, he had taken the job at Bitumount to try and earn some cash. However, just like the rest of us, he never got paid. He resented me at first, probably because he thought I was a softie and of no use to him, but because I worked hard and became very adept at handling the big logs, he grew to like me and we became good friends.

I also worked in the plant. I swore I would never work with bitumen again after changing the valves in the steam pumps several times a day. Our clothes were so saturated with the tar they became stiff, so stiff that we could barely move. Another of my jobs was working in the refinery, firing the wood furnace, and one day I was elated to see that I had got the temperature in the still bottom up to over 300°F (149°C). It was a reason to celebrate, since the higher the still-bottom temperature, the better the quality of the asphalt at the bottom. (That was the only instrument in the refinery—a big temperature gauge showing the still-bottom temperature!) After a couple of weeks of operation, the tower became clogged with sand, and I, being the only one who was small enough to get inside (I think the column was 14 inches [36 cm] in diameter), volunteered to go into the tower and remove the trays. It was plugged with sand from top to bottom. Luckily or unluckily, depending on your point of view, I only had to climb into the tower once, since we were never able to operate the rest of the plant long enough to clog it again.

There were approximately seventy men in Bitumount at the peak period that summer. With the exception of a few married men, we all lived in the bunkhouse. This building had been constructed using single one-by-eight boards with no tarpaper lining or insulation. The lumber had been green at the time it was built, so there were cracks over an inch (2.5 cm) wide between the boards. We all slept on steel cots with cotton mattresses; each man supplied his own bedroll. There were hordes of mosquitoes and these, of course, came through the cracks in the walls and filled the bunkhouse each night.

One of the men in the bunkhouse was a big Hungarian miner who was supposed to be an expert on blasting with dynamite. He hated the mosquitoes and built a smudge in the bunkhouse to try and fend them off—this lasted until the others complained about the smoke. He would go to bed with socks over his hands and arms and a towel around his neck. He would snuggle down into his bedroll so all you could see were the towel and the socks on his arms that were flailing away at the mosquitoes. This flailing was accompanied by a continuous stream of curses in his thick Hungarian accent: "G– D– F– mosquitoes." He stayed at the plant for only a few weeks before grabbing the first boat out. I think he went north to the mines at either Goldfields or Yellowknife.

Even though we weren't getting paid, we were fortunate. Although we never received any money for our labours, we did not go hungry and ate well with two Chinese cooks to feed us. The cookhouse and dining facilities, as well as the kitchen, were excellent. I believe that if more care had been taken to provide bunkhouse facilities comparable to the dining facilities, morale would have been much higher. (Of course, when men are not getting paid, I suppose it's hard to improve morale.)

We always looked forward to hearing the dinner bell. One thing that really interested me was watching Andy Anderson, the blacksmith, at mealtime—especially when he ate beans with his knife. It was fascinating to watch the skill with which he took a knife full of beans and slid it right across his mouth without dropping a single bean. I had never seen anyone do this before, although it was probably routine in some of the lumber camps. The only man I ever saw who matched his skill was a Canadian Army forestry lumberjack who was eating pork and beans in a tea shop in Aberdeen, Scotland, one evening during the war. Another skill that Andy had was drinking tea or coffee out of his saucer. His expertise at this—he didn't spill a drop—testified to years of practice.

There were some good men at the plant that year. The chief engineer was an American, Harry Everard, who had brought his wife and sixteen-year-old daughter with him. He became discouraged with the failings of the plant and left after a few months. The first chemical engineer I had ever met, Elmer Adkins, came to Bitumount right out of university. He later became president of Dominion Tar and Chemical. He got me interested in chemical engineering, and I believe his talks with me had quite an influence on my choosing chemical engineering as a career later on.

Finally, in December the ice on the Athabasca River was strong enough that we could walk to Fort McMurray. Alex McDonald looked after the horses at the plant and he hitched them to a sleigh and loaded our baggage onto it and away we all went—we being everyone who was still working at the plant, with the exception of two married men who had their wives with them. However, after travelling a short distance, we discovered that there was a thin crust of ice and snow on top of the frozen river, which the horses broke through. Underneath this crust was water, several inches deep on top of the main sheet of ice. It was soon evident that we couldn't use the horses, so we abandoned this plan and had to carry our belongings on our backs. We walked the first day to Fort McKay, a distance of about 20 miles (32 km). There was a Hudson's Bay post there that, fortunately, was being run by an old friend of my father's, Mr. Bob McDermott, who had been the factor at Fort McMurray some years earlier. He and his wife, "Granny" McDermott, let us sleep on the floor of the store that night. The next morning we took off again for Fort McMurray, which was now about 35 miles (56 km) away. I have never been so tired in my whole life and still remember the relief at arriving back home. Thus ended my sojourn in Bitumount. I met Bob Fitzsimmons some months later, and he gave me fifty dollars and some shares of International Bitumen stock. The fifty dollars was all that I was ever paid for the summer's work, but it was probably more than any of the others received. Unfortunately, I don't know what became of the shares. They would have made a good souvenir. ■

A copy of 50,000 shares in the International Bitumen Company. This copy is courtesy the Provincial Archives of Alberta—mine has been lost to time.
(Provincial Archives of Alberta, image no. 71.356/516)

PART TWO

YELLOWKNIFE

The Lure
of Gold

I first heard of Yellowknife in connection with gold in 1935 from Johnny Baker, who had discovered gold there in 1934. Johnny was an English civil engineer who was prospecting in the Yellowknife area but had been laid over in Fort McMurray during the spring breakup, when planes could not fly because they could not land on the melting ice. In those days, Northerners going to the Northwest Territories had to go through Fort McMurray, the only gateway to the North. As a result I got to know most of them when they would have to lay over during the spring breakup or the winter freeze-up period. During his sojourn in Fort McMurray, Johnny used to visit the Morrison family and tell them about the fabulous gold deposits that existed in the Yellowknife area. I was often there during these times and would be fascinated by his tales. Most of the mining activity at that time was concentrated on Goldfields in northern Saskatchewan, where Consolidated Mining and Smelting had a large, low-grade gold property known as the Box Mine. However, Johnny said that Goldfields was nothing compared with

Yellowknife and he was absolutely right. The "Box" never got into production, while the mines in Yellowknife proved to be very rich and are still producing.

In 1934 Johnny Baker and Hugh Muir, who later became the manager of the Discovery Mines in the Yellowknife area, had been working as prospectors for a subsidiary of Bear Exploration and Radium under Major Lauchie Burwash, the Arctic explorer who had become famous for locating the Magnetic North Pole in 1930. Baker and Muir discovered a quartz vein with very good gold showings and traced it for several hundred feet before it disappeared under the muskeg. After their discovery, others began staking claims in Yellowknife. Murdoch Mosher, an experienced prospector from Ontario, arrived in late 1934 and staked claims that later became the Ryan Gold Mines property. In 1935 Bill Jewett, who was in charge of the area for Consolidated Mining and Smelting, told pilot Mike Finland to get to Yellowknife and begin staking immediately. Mike and his mechanic flew to Yellowknife in his open-cockpit DeHavilland Gypsy Moth airplane and began staking the property that ultimately became the Con mine. Ollie Hagen, with whom I later worked at the Negus operations, staked the adjoining claims, which became the Negus mines. In 1935 Johnny Baker, still working for Burwash, staked the claims that later became the very rich Giant mine, which still operates today.

The Mining Act then in force in the Northwest Territories required that one hundred dollars worth of assessment work (such as trenching and diamond drilling) per claim be performed on the property each year. If this was not done, the claims would lapse. This is what happened to Murdock Mosher, who had returned to eastern Canada and allowed the claims he had staked in 1934 to lapse. His claims were then re-staked by Tom Payne and Gordie Latham in the dead of night—immediately after midnight when the claims became "open"— just ahead of twenty or thirty others who had the same idea. Tom was an Englishman who had done various jobs for the Ryan brothers, and I knew him when he stayed for a few months in Fort McMurray, sleeping in the loft of the Ryans' livery barn. He had gone to

Yellowknife, after having been grubstaked by the Ryan brothers. Gordie Latham, who became a good friend of mine, was an ex-school-teacher who was also part owner, along with Pete Racine, of the Corona Inn in Yellowknife. He later became a well-known flyer and the chief pilot for Eldorado mines. The claims he and Tom re-staked became the Rycon mine, and a sixty percent interest in this property was sold to Consolidated Mining and Smelting by the Ryan brothers for half a million dollars, a huge sum in those days.

Once the Mosher property had been re-staked, Tom Payne, Mickey and Pat Ryan, and Billy Wilson, the Ryan brothers' accountant, formed Ryan Gold Mines and sold shares to raise one hundred thousand dollars. I persuaded my father to part with two hundred dollars to buy two hundred shares and he eventually received about fifty times this amount for his investment. Although I didn't know Tom Payne well, I knew the Ryans and Billy Wilson as they had been Fort McMurray residents for years. They all became rich men as a result of that middle-of-the-night staking venture.

Following on the heels of the discoveries that led to the Con, Rycon, and Negus mines, Yellowknife became a hive of activity in 1937—and even more so in 1938, the year I arrived there. My brother Bob had preceded me. He had been working for hotelier Vic Ingraham at Great Bear Lake, but when business there began to get slack, Willie Wylie, Smoky Stout, and Bob travelled by dog team, first to Hottah Lake and then to Yellowknife, in the winter of 1936–37. After arriving in Yellowknife, they helped to build the famous Wildcat Café. Unfortunately, none of the historical material relating to this Yellowknife landmark mentions my brother's contribution. In 1984 I spoke with Smoky Stout's sister Margaret, who confirmed Bob's involvement and was quite indignant about this oversight.

By 1938 my brother Bob had a job at the new Negus mines camp on Yellowknife Bay. That year, as soon as the ice had melted off Great Slave Lake and the planes started flying, I flew into Yellowknife to look for a job. At that time there was a regulation that you had to have an eiderdown bedroll before you could enter the Northwest Territories. So I bought my eiderdown, and away I went. I arrived in Yellowknife and pitched my tent on the rock just above the Royal Canadian Corps of Signals station, overlooking what became known as "Glamour Alley" and later, Peace River Flats. Yellowknife would play an important part in moulding my young life, as it was there that my transition from boyhood to manhood occurred. It was there that I matured socially and became economically independent. I immediately got a job with Pete Racine as the night cook at his Corona Inn, although I knew nothing about cooking. That didn't really matter, however, as my only duties were making coffee and toast and frying bacon and eggs.

Yellowknife was a real boom town in the summer of 1938. People were arriving in droves, as it was relatively easy to get there by boat from Peace River or Fort McMurray. All you needed was something that floated—the rivers ran north and you could go downstream all the way. Because of this, some of the strangest craft ever built would come into Yellowknife. The place was a hive of activity, with buildings going up everywhere and airplanes landing and taking off continually. There were two main airlines in operation at the time: James Richardson's Canadian Airways and Leigh Brintnell's Mackenzie Air Services. Both companies had radio stations, although commercial telegrams were handled by the Signals Corps station.

Several general stores were in operation by early 1938. Weaver and Devore had a log building near the Signals station, and Eddie Jones had a store on Latham Island. The biggest store was Yellowknife Supplies, owned by John Michaels[1] of Edmonton and operated by his adopted son Otto Thibert. Another store was started by Sam Kushner of Fort McMurray and run by his son Les, a boyhood friend of mine. In 1938 Les managed to get the jump on his rivals by bringing the first boat into Yellowknife after the spring breakup. He had a scow loaded with provisions, including the fresh produce that everyone was hungering for. Items such as oranges and real eggs were snapped up, even though he put a steep price on them.

Yellowknife was a magnet that drew characters from all over Canada. It was probably similar to every gold rush town that ever mushroomed in the United States or Canada. Along with the honest, hard-working, Depression-driven farmers who streamed into town from the Prairie Provinces, shysters and hucksters arrived daily, trying to milk the public at any opportunity. One of the interesting things I discovered when I first arrived in Yellowknife was that many of the characters who had previously frequented the Fort McMurray/Waterways area, and whom we had not heard of for years, had gravitated to Yellowknife. One of these notable characters was Doc Griffin. Doc had become addicted to lemon extract during his many years as a cook. (A great many cooks became addicted to drinking extract in those days because it contained so much alcohol and was readily available.) In Yellowknife, Doc's modus operandi was to approach you and say that he had a big deal for some mining claims just coming up and had wires coming in from all over the country about them but was just a little short of cash at the moment—so could you lend him fifty cents? This just happened to be the price of a bottle of lemon extract. The only way to counter Doc was to ask him to lend you fifty cents first. I did this once and he promptly dug in his pocket and offered me the money, which I, of course, refused.

My favourite Yellowknife character was Joe Veitch, who was described in Ray Price's book *Yellowknife*.[2] While Price was writing about Joe from stories told to him by others, I knew Joe personally. What Price says is generally true: Joe was a kleptomaniac, not particularly sanitary, and loved his dogs, and they did live with him in his house—although I don't think the dogs slept with him, as Price stated.

I first met Joe in the Fort McMurray area, when he lived there in the early 1930s, and I had a great affection for him despite his being light-fingered. He had a heart as big as a house. When he lived at Waterways, he housed and fed dozens of men who had arrived there via boxcars on the train from Edmonton. This was during the Depression, when hundreds of men would come north to Fort McMurray every summer looking for work. During that time, Joe was a big, raw-boned man in his early seventies, with three visible black teeth, each separated by huge gaps. Between these teeth he smoked a corncob pipe. His accent was true Northern English—he came from Durham County and was not a Scot, as Ray Price described him. He had been a coal miner in Durham and, more especially, a poacher.

He told me how he had come to leave England, never to return.

One night Joe and his pal were poaching on the local lord's estate when the gamekeeper caught them red-handed and shot and killed his mate. Joe said, "So, I up and shot gamekeeper." He then ran home and announced, "Mother, I've shot gamekeeper," and described to his mother how the gamekeeper had shot his friend. His mother replied, "Good for you, son. Someone should have done it a long time ago." Joe had to hide out and finally escaped by sea on his Uncle Tom's sailing vessel. From then on, he led a varied career, including a spell in the British Navy. Eventually, he came to Canada and ended up following the different mining booms that occurred across the country.

While he lived at Waterways, Joe procured a Buick automobile engine from an old abandoned taxi and installed it in a boat he had built and christened the *Old 97*. He used to keep his boat engine supplied with gasoline stolen from the Canadian Airways base at Fort McMurray. As a result, he was well known to Wop May, the company's district superintendent. In 1936 Joe took his *Old 97* down the Athabasca River and ended up at Yellowknife. There he built himself a log shack just below the Canadian Airways radio station on the "Rock," where the original town of Yellowknife was situated. He survived by doing odd ferrying jobs and, of course, always managed to find something of value somewhere, especially from the Yellowknife Supplies store operated by Otto Thibert.

In the spring the airlines hired Joe to use his boat to clear ice out of the narrow channel between Latham Island and the town. One day, Wop May was in Yellowknife on an inspection trip when he happened to kick the side of a gasoline barrel in the fuel dump near the radio station, and also near Joe's home. When he discovered the drum was empty, Wop said, "What the hell's going on? Somebody is stealing gas from this dump." Then he noticed Joe standing nearby, trying to look innocent. Wop swore and said, "Joe, you SOB. You're at it again." Joe replied, "What do you mean? I ain't done nothing." Since Wop knew that Joe would steal the gasoline anyway, he let him have anything that was left in the drums after they had been pumped out. They could never completely pump all the fuel out of the barrel with the hand pumps they used, so there was always a bit left in the bottom. In return for this concession, Joe promised not to touch any of the full barrels and to keep an eye out for other would-be gas thieves.

Joe was a kleptomaniac, but one that you couldn't help liking—unless you were one of his victims. When winter came, Canadian Airways had several loads of wooden logs brought near the radio station and sawn up for firewood. After this had been accomplished, Joe came barging into the radio station and said to Harry Hardham, the radio operator, "Harry, you bastard, you've cut all your wood too long for my stove." Ken Razzell, the ticket agent, was present and after Joe left he spluttered, "Did you hear what he said? The nerve of the guy," and went away muttering to himself. Two days later Joe came by again and said, "It's okay, Harry. I've made a new stove out of a gas barrel, and you can cut the wood any length you want."

Another time the Mounted Police, whose barracks were just down the road from Joe's place, came and asked him to drag the lake near their pier for their outboard motor, which had dropped off the back of their skiff into the water just opposite the pier. Joe took his *Old 97* and dragged for the motor, found where it was, and announced to the Mounties that he hadn't been able to locate it. Later, Joe said to me, "I went back last night and pulled it up in the middle of the night. I've taken it all apart and have all kinds of kicker parts now. Do you need any?" I said, no, I didn't need any, and beat a hasty retreat.

Ray Price's story in his book *Yellowknife* about Joe cutting wood in jail in Fort Smith differs from what Joe told me. In Joe's version, the events took place in Fort Norman—not Fort Smith—where Joe had been during freeze-up several years before. A Métis woman had a sick child, and there was no milk available in the stores in the community. Joe went to the village's Signals Corps station and asked the sergeant in charge if he could borrow some powdered milk, which he knew they had. The sergeant refused him, so Joe went to their storehouse and broke down the door and took the milk. He was hauled before the local justice of the peace and sentenced to thirty days in jail. Joe was put to work sawing wood. However, Joe, being Joe, carefully measured the stove length and cut every stick several inches too long.

The Mounties didn't discover this until after he had left jail.

Being in jail in Fort Norman could not have been very confining for Joe, especially since the Mountie in charge often had to go out on patrol and would leave him to look after the remaining sled dogs. While in jail, Joe also had the job of cooking up the dog feed in a nearby shed. In those days, it was customary to use "crackling" for dog feed. Crackling was a mixture of pork rind, fat, and odd bits of pork meat that the packing plants compressed into large, round cylinders. This was cooked up, mixed with whatever else was available, and fed to the dogs. Once when the Mountie was away on patrol, Joe started a mash for moonshine. On his return, the Mountie went into the shed and was led to the mash by the strange smell. Joe tried to say it was only dog feed, but the Mountie insisted on having a look at the concoction and when he saw what it was he swore and said, "Get out of here, you scoundrel. And don't show your face around here again." Joe later bragged, "I'm the only man who was ever kicked out of jail in the Territories, and maybe anywhere!"

Another incident Joe used to recall with many a chuckle involved the wife of the stipendiary magistrate J. E. Gibben, who had been appointed and sent to Yellowknife in 1938. Joe disliked Otto Thibert, the operator of Yellowknife Supplies, the main store in town, and I suppose the feeling was mutual, as Joe took every opportunity to steal from the store. The store warehouse had a small track on which a small hand-pulled trolley was run whenever supplies had to be unloaded from a boat. One day, a quantity of frozen meat was unloaded and left sitting unattended on the trolley when Joe wandered by. He helped himself to a couple of beautiful roasts and took them home. A short time later, Mrs. Gibben came by and said, "Joe, would it be possible for you to get me some caribou meat from the Indian village sometime when you go that way?" Joe said sure he would, and the next day he presented Mrs. Gibben with one of the thawed beef roasts he had purloined from Otto Thibert, but telling her he had gone over to the Native village and got some caribou meat from them. He saw Mrs. Gibben the next week and she said, "Joe, that was the nicest caribou meat I've ever eaten."

We used to say that Joe would give you the shirt off his back, even though he may have had to steal it. My friendship with him probably seemed strange to some people given the disparity in our ages, and later I heard that some suspected that we had a homosexual relationship—which was not true. I know that Joe thought a lot of me. During the war he went around Yellowknife telling everyone that he'd received a letter from me and that I'd been promoted to the rank of colonel (I was only a lowly signalman at the time). I lost track of Joe after the war but know he ended up in Aklavik, Northwest Territories, probably arriving there in his *Old 97*. I heard that he died at Aklavik at the age of eighty-nine in 1957.

Yellowknife was fast becoming a town, with a bank, restaurants, a bakery, a laundry, and a barbershop among the new establishments. However, liquor was still obtained by the time-honoured custom of getting a permit for a case of twelve bottles of hard liquor per year.[3] This system led to bootlegging, as most of the men didn't want to buy a whole case at one time—they would have just drunk it all immediately and then have had nothing left for the rest of the year. So everyone would give their permit to a bootlegger in return for a free bottle, and then purchases could be made at anytime from the bootlegger for ten dollars a bottle.

The government in far-off Ottawa still treated the Northwest Territories as a sort of feudal fiefdom, so the old permit system stayed in place all the time that I was there. The government thus seemed to condone bootlegging. The chief bootlegger was Vic Ingraham, who owned and operated the Yellowknife Hotel. He had been crippled in an accident several years before and had become world famous for his heroic behaviour during the ordeal.

Vic and his partner, Gerry Murphy, had a boat transportation service and a general store at Cameron Bay, near the Eldorado uranium mine, which had been discovered a few years earlier, in September 1934. Vic and his crew were making a last run before freeze-up across Great Bear Lake in his schooner *Speed*. The schooner was towing a scow with five men and five dogs on board and laden with their winter supplies. A terrific storm arose and Vic had to cut the scow loose. The wind finally blew the scow ashore and the men scrambled for shelter. One of those men was Stan Hooker, a high school classmate of mine.

Not long after the scow was abandoned, the schooner caught fire when gasoline was spilled on the exhaust while the crew tried to refuel in the storm. Two of the crew, Harry Jebs and Tommy Potts, were engulfed in flames in the engine room. Vic tried to save them, but was driven back by the fire and was badly burned. Vic and the other crew member, Stu Curry, managed to escape in a rubber life raft just as the schooner exploded and sank with the two men. After much hardship, Vic and Stu were finally located eleven days later by Harry Hayter in his Curtiss Robin airplane and flown to Cameron Bay. Vic was eventually sent to an Edmonton hospital where he had both his legs amputated above the knee and lost most of his fingers. Perhaps the authorities felt he deserved to be able to earn a living from bootlegging because of his physical disability. At any rate, he ran his bootlegging operation with minimal interference from the Mounties.

The system of limiting the legal amount of liquor coming into the Territories to twelve bottles per person per year inevitably resulted in a shortage. This shortfall was alleviated by cheap fibre suitcases filled with liquor flown in from Edmonton. These suitcases made up a considerable amount of the freight carried in by the airlines in 1938, and there was soon a glut of fibre suitcases in Yellowknife. The policy of the Territories' administration seemed to be like that of an indulgent father—as long as nothing got out of hand, things were allowed to proceed as before.

Yellowknife was a contradiction. It was a wide-open town but usually quite orderly. There was a twenty-four-hour gambling den operated by Oscar Landry and a whorehouse run by "Red," a red-haired prostitute. The whorehouse wasn't a "house" per se, but two tents, complete with wooden floors and walls, set up in Peace River Flats. Red resided with her maid in one tent, while the other served as her work tent. You could tell how many clients she had had the day before by the number of towels the maid hung out on the wash line. In spite of these nefarious activities, things seldom got out of hand. Although there were only two Mounties in Yellowknife at the time, they didn't have too much trouble maintaining order. However, I do remember a huge drunken brawl that broke out one evening and lasted for over an hour. The two constables were unable to control the combatants, but there weren't any resultant injuries or ill effects, so everyone soon forgot the incident. In fact, I don't think anyone remembered how it had started in the first place.

I had only been in Yellowknife for a couple of months in 1938 when my mother died. I will always be grateful to Wop May for flying my brother Bob and me back to Fort McMurray, even though we didn't have the money to pay the fare. I stayed in Fort McMurray long enough to earn my return fare back to Yellowknife. Again, I was able to do this because of Wop's kindness, when he gave me work painting the hangar at McMurray.

My mother's death was very traumatic for me. As well as being my first experience with the death of anyone close, I had just lost someone I could always run to when I needed help. When I was young, my mother would even sympathize with me when she felt my father had gone too far in punishing me. I've always regretted that she died before I was successful enough to give her some of the things she had yearned for, such as a trip back to Japan to visit her relatives. I remember being quite surprised at the size of her funeral—practically the whole town came out to pay their last respects to her.

I returned to Yellowknife early in September 1938 and immediately got a job washing dishes at the Wildcat Café for two dollars a day and my meals. I still had my tent near the Royal Canadian Corps of Signals station so had a place to sleep. The Wildcat, which was operated by Carl Jensen and his wife, was the only eating establishment in Yellowknife and did a roaring business. (One of the waitresses at the Wildcat, Lil Bretzlaff, later opened her own restaurant.) Since it was the only restaurant in this gold rush boom town, if you wanted to know which big mining men had arrived in Yellowknife, all you had to do was dine at the Wildcat. Of course, as a lowly dishwasher, I was too busy to do anything but keep my head down and work.

Although I had a job and was getting my meals, I still lived in my tent and was worried about finding a place to stay for the winter.

I am standing in front of the Wild Cat Café in 1984. This was where I washed dishes in 1938.

My problem was solved when in October 1938 Pete Schwerdt, a prospector, and Pete Oleinek, who worked for Canadian Airways as a helper around the office, came to me and offered to let me in on staking some very promising claims. They knew I didn't have any money, but they wanted to use my licence to stake the claims and wanted someone they felt they could trust. At that time anyone in the Territories could get a licence to stake six claims. You were also allowed to stake twelve other claims by proxy, that is, you could stake six claims each for two other people who didn't have to be present or even reside in the Northwest Territories when the claims were staked.

Territories Exploration, a subsidiary of the Mining Corporation of Canada, a large mining company, had discovered a fabulously rich gold showing at Wray Lake, about 150 miles (240 km) northwest of Yellowknife. (Wray Lake was later renamed and is now known as Indin Lake.) Pete Oleinek had found out about the strike because Canadian Airways was flying supplies into the site, which Territories Exploration had kept secret. Although Territories Exploration had six men at its camp at the site, it had not staked a large number of claims as it wanted to keep the strike secret until more work had been done to ascertain how rich it was. The company was also limited to the number of claims it could stake by the licences held by the men on the property. Pete Oleinek made a deal with some of the pilots who knew the location of the site that he would stake claims and share them with the pilots. He formed a partnership with Pete Schwerdt, who had worked as a prospector for a mining company all summer and was the only one of the three of us who had any money. So Pete Schwerdt supplied the financing for the trip to Wray Lake and for purchasing the canoe, tent, and supplies, as well as paying for the airplane flight. There were, as yet, no maps of the area, but there were RCAF aerial photographs available, and Pete Oleinek had obtained a pencil tracing of one of these photographs. Copies of this tracing served as our map.

Yellowknife was fascinating in 1938 because of the intrigue and secrecy that abounded. There were always rumours of new finds, and everyone watched everyone else to see if they were flying off to some new strike. When airplanes took off, the pilots would often fly in the opposite direction from their intended destination to confuse any watching prospectors. Our venture was no different. All our meetings were held in secret. Looking back, I can't help but think we acted overly suspicious, with all the furtive looks we threw over our shoulders before anyone spoke. We would usually wait until after dark to meet on the end of a pier so no one would overhear us, and even then we spoke in whispers. It was exciting for me, a young greenhorn, to be involved in this quest for gold, and I was elated at the prospect of going on the adventure of a lifetime to make a fortune.

Finally, the day of our departure arrived. It was mid-October 1938.

I was up at 6:00 AM. Pete Oleinek had asked me to wake him and told me he would be sleeping in the Canadian Airways oil shed, which had a cot in it. I went into the shed and whispered, "Pete." When he didn't wake up I shone my flashlight and scared the daylights out of one of the airline mechanics and a magazine sales girl who were sleeping on the cot. This young lady had just come to Yellowknife and had obviously sold a lot of subscriptions. I beat a hasty retreat and finally found Pete.

We took off at daylight in a Norseman airplane, piloted by Jack Crosby. In an attempt to mislead any overly curious observers, we flew south before finally turning northwest toward Wray Lake. We had a canoe lashed onto the floats of the Norseman, which would violate safety regulations now but in those days was common practice. In the early days of the Great Bear Lake pitchblende rush, lumber was often lashed onto the floats of planes and freighted in this manner. We landed some miles from the Territories Exploration site and set up our camp. Immediately after we had landed, a quarrel broke out between the two Petes. The quarrelling would continue for the two months that we spent there and would make things difficult for me, the youngest and the man in the middle.

Shortly after we had set up camp, we were surrounded by caribou on their annual southern fall migration. Thousands of them poured through a draw beside our camp, paying no attention to us. However, apart from shooting one for food, we were too busy to watch them. The caribou meat was welcome because we only had the food we had flown in with and had to supplement this in order to survive. In fact, food was one of the first contentious subjects that caused arguments between my two partners. Pete Oleinek had been filling up on bread and jam, saying he needed it for "quick energy," and Pete Schwerdt began to berate him for using up all our supplies at once.

Another bone of contention was farting in the tent. We were living on caribou and beans, which meant a lot of gas was being passed between the three of us. Pete Oleinek objected to everyone farting, so whenever I felt one coming on, I went and stuck my backside outside the tent flap. Pete Schwerdt refused to do this, and it would lead to a tremendous argument between the two Petes. Another squabble broke out when Pete Oleinek forgot to tie up the canoe after we had landed at a spot on the edge of the lake. The canoe drifted out from shore, and we watched helplessly as it drifted away. Luckily, we were saved by the grace of God when a wind came up and blew it back to shore.

As soon as we had established our camp, we immediately began staking claims. Territories Exploration had made two finds—one was known as the South Showing and the other as the North Showing. These were several miles apart and each consisted of some eighteen claims. Presumably these were on a line of strike, as there seemed to be a main fault line that ran north and south through the properties. The South Showing looked to be the most promising. When the Territories Exploration crew had hand-steeled and blasted a pit on a quartz outcropping in the South Showing, they had uncovered spectacular free gold in the quartz rock. Even the rusty loose rock on top of the outcropping panned about an ounce of gold from a shovelful of rock. When they had first blasted and looked at the pieces of rock, one of the workmen, a young farm lad from Alberta, had picked up a piece of rock and asked Slim Gamey, the geologist in charge, "Is this gold?" He had never seen gold ore before. Slim looked at it and said, "Is it ever gold!" The piece of rock was entirely studded through with gold. They excavated a small pit and bagged 1,500 pounds (680 kg) of ore, which they flew out to the Negus mines mill in Yellowknife. From it they obtained 235 ounces (6,660 g) of gold.

Since the property between the North and South Showings was open, we began staking there. Pete Schwerdt staked claims nearest the south end of the North Showing; Pete Oleinek began staking immediately south of the South Showing. Luckily, winter was late arriving that year and there was still open water, even though it was mid-October. The weather held, and we were going from dawn to dusk running claim lines. We would cut corner posts, squaring the top portion of each post, and write the claim description with a crayon pencil on the surface. We only ran the claim lines that ran north and south, intending to run the east-west lines later. This method, of course, caused our claims to be irregular in shape, as we measured with paces. We used a Brunton compass to take a bearing on some landmark, such as a tall tree, and then walked off one thousand paces, blazing trees with a small axe as we went. We stopped to set up our claim posts and then repeated the process. The inside claims required four posts—one for the northeast corner and one each for the southeast, southwest, and northwest corners of the adjoining claims. Wherever there was water, a small lake for instance, we would have to set up posts on shore and state that they were for locations so many yards out in the water. It was tiring work, and I remember once having to go around a lake that lay in the path of my claim line. On my pencil-traced map, it looked as though I would have to walk only about a mile (1.6 km) east and then back west another mile to pick up the claim line. However, when I came to the end of the lake, there was a small creek that did not show on the tracing. I couldn't cross it, so I had to walk another 3 miles (5 km) around another lake and then back several miles before I could reach where I wanted to go. I almost cried with frustration.

Within two days of landing, however, we heard the sound of airplanes. I was with Pete Schwerdt at the time, and he almost went berserk, saying, "They've double-crossed me—they weren't supposed to come for a week." Apparently, he had double-crossed Pete Oleinek and, unknown to Pete, had made a deal with a couple of other prospectors— Ed Medvedt and a fellow named Walter Despard—as well as with his own brother Chuck Schwerdt. He had given the three of them details of where to fly, with the understanding that they would allow us a week before coming in to stake. Soon we heard the sound of other planes, and we knew the rush was on. A couple of days later, Chuck Schwerdt and Ed Medvedt came to our camp and told us that Walter Despard had gone crazy and was wandering around the lake armed with a rifle. Apparently, the prospect of sudden riches from gold had driven him mad. After that, we were afraid to light a campfire because we weren't sure when a bullet might come winging out from the bush.

We later learned that during his meandering, Despard had entered the Territories Exploration camp and walked in on Charlie Skelding, the radio operator, who was on the air with Yellowknife. He told Charlie he could read Morse code, so Charlie had better not try anything funny. Charlie was frightened but took a chance and told Yellowknife about the crazy man on the loose. As a result of Skelding's message, the Mounties flew in and took Despard back to Yellowknife. As soon as Despard arrived in Yellowknife, though, he seemed to recover and began to act normally again. After freeze-up, he flew back to our camp at Wray Lake, but he hadn't been there a day when he went off his rocker again. Archie Vanhie flew in to take him back to Yellowknife. I heard later that Walter Despard had joined the Canadian army, received a commission, and ended up a captain in Italy. Being only an NCO (non-commissioned officer) myself during the war, this helped to reinforce my opinion concerning the behaviour of some of the officers.

When freeze-up arrived, the rivers and lakes froze over so we didn't have to circumvent them but could walk straight across to run our claim lines. One disadvantage was the snow on the spruce trees, which would cascade down on us when we blazed a tree. I had a caribou parka that kept me warm and with the hood up the snow didn't bother me too much. Incidentally, no one has been able to come up with clothing that has better insulating properties than caribou skin. The only problem is it sheds. For this reason, the best caribou hides are those from caribou killed during the summer months. These can only be obtained in the regions of the far North.

By midwinter of 1938 the several groups of stakers had gathered together with their tents near each other into a small community, and we all used to get together to tell stories in the evening. Among those present were Sleepy Jim McDonald, a well-known old-timer in Yellowknife, and Pete Davidson, probably the senior and most famous prospector in Canada at that time. I remember being fascinated by the tales this tough old prospector told us, although I regret to say that I've forgotten most of them. One story I do remember was that he had been responsible for the federal department of mines changing the way in which claim lines were run. According to him, claim lines had originally been run toward magnetic north, but the federal government had changed this so that the lines ran true north and south. In some areas of the North this made a considerable difference—for example, at Wray Lake the declination of magnetic north from true north was approximately thirty-seven degrees.

I have already mentioned how claims could be very irregular in shape because of the crude methods of measuring used while staking. This often gave rise to the creation of fractions, which were small areas between some of the claims that could be staked. Pete Davidson claimed to have staked one of these fractions at the Eldorado property at Great Bear Lake before the Eldorado people got around to it. This fraction ran right across the main ore body of pitchblende, and so Pete stood to make a lot of money because he could prevent Eldorado from mining ore from his property. However, by this time, Gilbert Labine, the original discoverer and by then president of Eldorado, had enough influence with the federal government to have the law changed retroactively so that claim lines ran true north and south, rather than magnetic north and south. This eliminated Pete's fraction and deprived him of his share of the ore body.

By December, the weather had turned very cold, dropping to -50°F (-46°C) or so. We had built a pole floor and sides for our tent and could keep reasonably comfortable if we kept a fire going in our little sheet-iron stove. This meant a lot of work chopping and sawing firewood, however, and led to further dissension between the two Petes—Pete Schwerdt claiming that Pete Oleinek didn't cut his fair share of the wood. During those cold days, it took a lot of willpower to get out of bed in the morning. We would cut kindling the night before and have birchbark ready to light the fire in the morning. I did more than my share of being first up to start the fire.

Living in the wilderness in the winter could be hazardous. One day one of the fellows, Wilbur McDonald, went out hunting caribou. He was part Native and had been hired by Vic Ingraham to come out with Pete Davidson and Sleepy Jim to help them stake. We assumed that, being Native, he knew his way around the bush. However, he never returned from his hunting trip, and although we searched for him for several days, we finally gave him up for lost. After about a week, one of the fellows, while staking, came across Wilbur wandering in the bush. He had been lost all this time but was none the worse for wear. It was a miracle he didn't freeze to death.

Soon after freeze-up I was crossing an arm of the main lake following my compass course when Pete Schwerdt yelled out to me to check the ice. I stopped and dropped the blade of my axe onto the ice and it went through. I very gingerly retraced my steps over the rubbery ice to shore, thanking my lucky stars I hadn't broken through. Even if

I had managed to get out of the water, which was unlikely because of the thinness of the ice at that point, I would have been lucky to have survived in my wet clothes as we were a long distance from our campsite. Another evening I was returning to camp from staking and was walking across a lake at dusk when I heard a rumbling noise far down the lake. The noise became louder and louder, and I could see a huge shadow coming toward me. It turned out to be a herd of about twenty caribou. I had only a small staking axe in my hand, and they came right at me. They were only 30 feet (9 m) or so from me when they must have seen me, and they circled right around me before running off. Wolves must have been chasing them and they were probably as surprised to see me as I was to see them.

Another day Pete Schwerdt decided that he and I would go off to another area about 20 miles (32 km) away and do some staking. This was known as "blanketing"—we didn't have licences to do it and it was illegal. The idea was to get a jump on the staking and then obtain the necessary licences later on. We started out, taking our eiderdowns and some food with us. The weather turned bitterly cold—it must have been at least -50°F (-46°C). That night we built a big fire under a large spruce tree, spread spruce boughs on the ground, placed one eiderdown on the bottom with the other on top, and crawled in between them. The eiderdowns were supposed to be good for -60°F (-51°C) weather, but I can testify that even at that night's temperature they didn't provide much comfort. We didn't stake any claims and the next day made our way back to camp. It was now a matter of waiting for the ice to freeze to a thickness great enough to sustain the weight of a plane to land and take us back to Yellowknife. We flew back to Yellowknife on December 15, 1938.

Looking back on my time at Wray Lake, I think I was lucky to have survived. I have never had a very good sense of direction and could easily have gotten lost. However, at the time I never worried about it, or even thought about it, as I had my Brunton compass and my little map. I suppose at times ignorance is bliss. In the end, despite the risks and gruelling work involved, I received nothing for the claims. According to the law, in order to retain the claims, the claim holder had to do one hundred dollars worth of assessment work per year on each claim—alternatively, the claim holder could do all of the required assessment work on one claim. For my eighteen claims, I would have had to do eighteen hundred dollars worth of work on some part of the property. When war broke out in September 1939, the market for gold properties collapsed and no one was interested in buying claims. Nor did I have the money to do the assessment work, so I had to allow the claims to lapse. I later learned that an act had been passed to allow a moratorium on assessment work for anyone who had joined the forces. I joined the army in June 1940 but was unaware of this new law. In 1942, when I was overseas, there was a gold rush to Wray Lake, and I believe a lot of claims were sold. However, I didn't benefit: all I got out of my Wray Lake adventure was experience. However, Pete Schwerdt did become a millionaire by his staking claims.

Before his death, I had a chance to talk to Pete Schwerdt about how he made his fortune after Territories Exploration allowed the claims it had staked to lapse. In 1941 several groups in Yellowknife were aware that these claims were coming open and were poised to fly to Wray Lake to re-stake them. However, they were delayed due to nasty weather that made it impossible to fly for some days. Meanwhile, Pete had gone to Wray Lake by dog team with Fred Camsell. Fred was a brother of the then federal deputy minister of mines, Dr. Charles Camsell. Pete beat the others by a day or two and re-staked the South Showing, which he renamed the "Vidie" claims after his wife.

Pete's account of his dog team trip from Fort Rae up the Snare River to Wray Lake included an interesting story about encountering Natives hunting caribou. Pete said that he and Fred were camped one night when they heard the sleigh bells of dog teams coming north on the river. The travellers were Natives who somehow—possibly through what we called the "moccasin telegraph" because of the mysterious way in which news travelled in the North Country—knew that the caribou were coming through farther north. Natives didn't normally travel by dog team after dark, but their hunger for caribou urged them irresistibly onward and so they drove through the night. Pete told of how the Natives, after they had killed their first day's caribou, would feast through the night. In those days the caribou meant life or death. If for some reason the caribou changed their migration pattern and the Natives missed them, the Natives would starve to death. So it is understandable how, after being on a near-starvation diet, they would gorge themselves when they finally got all the meat they could eat. They would put the meat into large pots, and when the meat was all eaten they cracked the bones to get the marrow, which they considered a delicacy.

The summer after re-staking the claim, Pete and his brother Chuck went to Wray Lake and were digging in the pit where Territories Exploration had first found the fabulously rich ore. All of a sudden, Pete discovered a piece of rock that bent. Pete and Chuck took out enough ore to be refined into thirty-nine thousand dollars worth of gold. With this money, Pete bid for and obtained leases for oil and gas in northern British Columbia. From these leases, he made millions of dollars, which he unfortunately later lost, a lot of it because he was hounded by the federal income tax department for taxes. Pete eventually died broke in Calgary, sometime in the late 1980s.

Pete Schwerdt was the one who came to the rescue when he, Pete Oleinek, and I arrived back in Yellowknife in time for Christmas 1938. At the time my prospects seemed bleak: no place to stay, no money, no job, and the temperature was -30 to -40°F (-34 to -40°C). However, Pete Schwerdt found a shack near the Signals station that was owned by Fred Furlough and managed to rent the shack from Fred, who was not in Yellowknife at the time. Inside, against the walls of the shack, were half a dozen double bunks constructed from spruce poles. It was here that Pete started bootlegging and so kept his brother Chuck, Ed Medvedt, and several others—including me—from starving and freezing that winter.

The way that Pete got into the bootlegging business was quite simple. He contacted various fellows and obtained their liquor licences, which they were happy to let him have as they thought Vic Ingraham had too much of a monopoly and needed some competition. By offering either ten dollars or a free bottle, Pete managed to get some seventy licences and was soon in business. In later years, my wife could never understand how I put up with Pete and all his dodgy schemes. It was just that I had not forgotten how he had helped me and the others for those two frigid months at the beginning of 1939, when I was living off the avails of his bootlegging.

Pete had been in business for a while when he went to see the new Mountie, a constable who had recently been transferred to Yellowknife. Pete introduced himself and said, "You know what I am doing for a living?" The Mountie answered, "Yes, you're a prospector." Pete replied, "Well, I'm bootlegging just now, because it's winter and I can't get a job prospecting and I have to make a living. There's talk around town that you are going to close down us small bootleggers and only allow Vic Ingraham to stay in business." The Mountie asked, "Who says so?" Pete replied, "Well, a lot of the businessmen around town, people like Jock McMeekan and others." At that, the Mountie brought his fist crashing down on the table and roared, "I say who bootlegs in this town, not those bastards." And then he said, "I'll tell you what I'll do Pete. You can bootleg until spring, but as soon as open water comes, you had better be out prospecting or else." Pete said, "Fine. And do I still leave the forty-ounce bottle of rum under the doorstep every Friday like I did for the other Mountie?" The constable mumbled, "I don't know anything about that." However, there were no objections when Pete continued the practice.

By 1939 Yellowknife had quite a thriving business centre in Peace River Flats, which became known as "Glamour Alley." All three whorehouses were there. The original was run by "Red," who had supplemented her tents with a real frame house and employed several girls, so that she now acted as a madam and rarely worked herself. A number of other girls worked in the other two houses, which added up to about twelve prostitutes operating in the little community. Under local police orders, all the girls had to go to see Dr. Stanton at the Con mine each week for a checkup. One day, one of the girls was put on the shelf by Dr. Stanton's holiday replacement, and since there was nothing else for her to do, she got drunk. Late one evening, when a lot of men were in from the mines, she went downtown, threw up her skirt, and yelled, "A million dollars worth, and I can't get a nickel for it because of that GD doctor."

Right next to the whorehouses was a drinking establishment, which made things very convenient for any miner who wanted to enjoy himself. This was operated by a small-time racketeer from New Jersey named Corona. He had built a shack near Red's place and was living there with Red's erstwhile maid. Corona made moonshine and sold it for three dollars a bottle. He did such a landslide business that the hooch didn't have time to age, and there were a lot of complaints that it was too "green."

Early in the summer of 1938, I had been in Kushner's store when Corona ordered six hundred cases of dried fruit. He called himself "The Corona Diamond Drilling Company" and ordered the dried fruit in that name. Les Kushner asked, "What do you need all those raisins and dried peaches and apricots for?" and Corona replied, "To make moonshine." Les said, "You'll never get away with doing that in the Northwest Territories. This isn't like the United States." Les then asked, "Are you sure you'll take delivery of the stuff and pay for it when it arrives?" Corona replied, "Don't worry, I'll take it and you'll get paid. Let me worry about any problems with the police. I'll operate okay." Corona then told me about his problems trying to run a speakeasy in New Jersey and how he had had to pay off the police on the beat, in the precinct, and at headquarters, as well as the politicians, until there was no money left for him. I guess that was when he decided to look for greener pastures and came to Yellowknife. Corona operated until the spring of 1940, when he was raided by the police who seized his supply of dried fruit and hooch. As it turned out, he was only fined one hundred dollars and his material was returned, but he continued to operate for just a short time afterward, before leaving Yellowknife.

After living in Pete Schwerdt's shack for a couple of months, I finally got a job working in the kitchen at the Negus mines in February 1939. Bill Stewart, the mine manager, had been reluctant to hire me, even though my brother Bob was working there and had proven to be a good worker. Bill is supposed to have said he was worried about people protesting that he was hiring too many "Japs." However, he must have overcome this worry, which soon disappeared in any event when Bob left Negus some months later, and I was the only "Jap" left.

Anyone who thinks a kitchen worker's job in a mining camp is a snap is mistaken, as I soon discovered. There were five men working in the kitchen to feed some eighty men. Our crew consisted of the chief cook, a baker, and three kitchen helpers, or "flunkies," as we were called. The head flunky was a little Irishman by the name of Jimmy Mulholland, who taught the rest of us what to do. He was a professional and had been doing this job his entire working career—he must have been in his forties then. I've never seen anyone who was faster at the job than he was.

The flunkies had to set the tables for each meal and then wait on the tables during mealtimes. Everything was placed in large bowls on each table so everyone could help themselves. Desserts were on a separate table, and each man helped himself to those as well. Our job at mealtimes was to keep all the containers full and pour coffee. After the meals were over, we had to clean the tables and, of course, wash the dishes, cutlery, and pots and pans. We had a unique method of drying cutlery. After the cutlery was washed, it was rinsed and boiling water was poured over it. The cutlery was then placed in a pillow slip and shaken for a couple of minutes and, presto, it emerged bone dry! Each week the two junior helpers—the other assistant flunky and me—alternated as the dishwasher. The dishwasher was referred to as the "pearl diver." Jimmy, being the senior flunky, didn't have to pearl dive. The efficiency of the whole kitchen operation depended on the pearl diver. If he was slow, the others couldn't get finished on time and as a result would not get a rest break before it was time to prepare for the next meal. I soon became expert at it and finished in rapid quick time. However, my partner was so slow that when his week came to pearl dive, we barely had time to get ready for the next meal, let alone squeeze in a rest period. In spite of our berating him and cursing him and urging him to speed up, nothing could make him get a move on.

The meals were terrific, and to men brought up in the penurious 1930s it seemed like paradise at first. However, once they had been there about six months and their bellies were full, some would find fault with the meals. It was too much the same, there wasn't enough variety, they would complain. Caribou meat is delicious when you first eat it, but it doesn't have the body of beef and soon palls. Similarly, the potatoes and eggs we had were dehydrated. It got so that the men ate less and less. In June when the first boats arrived, it was like a feast being able to dine on fresh eggs, fresh vegetables, and fresh beef and pork. Finally, in late 1939 the meat packers Burns & Co., under Bill McGruther, erected a cold-storage plant, so that frozen meat was available year-round and the days of caribou meat were gone forever.

Working in the kitchen at Negus was sort of an apprenticeship. The policy at that time seemed to be that any young fellow who was hired had to undergo this kitchen apprenticeship: if you did well there it was possible to move on to the much higher-paying jobs in the mine or the mill. I suppose it was a good way of assessing a fellow's worth. For example, I would never have hired my pearl-diving partner for any other job whatsoever. ■

Into the Negus Mine

*A*fter having worked in the kitchen at Negus for about three months, I was given a job in the mine as the "sampler." It was a tremendous boost in pay—from seventy-five dollars a month to five dollars a day. I thought, "I'm going to be rich." As the sampler I had to go underground and take samples wherever the mining engineer wanted them taken. Usually when the miners were drifting along a vein—drilling a tunnel horizontally along the vein is called "drifting"—I would have to go to the face with a hammer and chisel and cut a sample of rock across the vein, noting at the same time the width of the vein and whether any mineralization was visible. This had to be done before each round was blasted out. A round usually consisted of 5 or 6 feet (1.5 to 1.8 m), which was blasted out at the end of each shift.

The tunnel created by drifting along a vein is called a "drift" and drilling upward in the vein from a drift creates a space called a "stope." After ore is blasted down from the stope, timbers are set in place to hold the ore. Chutes are set in these timbers so that this ore can be drawn out into tram cars. As stoping is done upward on the vein and the ore is blasted down onto the timbers, enough ore is drawn out to drill another upward round. My job was to cut samples at set intervals across the vein before each round was blasted out.

When I first went into a drift where a miner and his helper were drilling, I was shocked at the terrific noise. It was so deafening it was difficult for me to make my body move, and it took me quite a while to get used to this nerve-shattering din that seemed to numb all my faculties and rob me of the power to do anything. Unfortunately, this was in the days before men wore ear protection, which is compulsory now. I'm sure most miners suffered considerable loss of hearing if they worked at the trade very long.

I used to help the miners set up their equipment in the stopes. This wasn't part of my job, but I suppose it was egotism on my part: I wanted to show them I could do the work despite my small size. I would carry 120-pound (55-kg) stopers with one arm up a 20- to 40-foot (6- to 12-m) ladder. The miners were impressed that someone my size could do this. I know I couldn't do it now! Our lamps were not the electric battery-operated type in use today—ours were carbide lamps mounted on our hats. These lamps consisted of a small container into which water was added to carbide to generate acetylene gas, and I soon learned how to adjust the lamp to get a beautiful bright flame. If your lamp ever went out, you would find yourself in pitch blackness. Until you have been down a mine, you do not know what total darkness is.

In most mines, gold is not visible in the ore since it is usually finely disseminated throughout the quartz. However, Negus was a high-grade mine and there were some veins that had spectacular showings of free gold. Once you see it, you can always recognize it and distinguish it from "fool's gold" (pyrite).

At that time the miners on the Negus crew were the elite of the mining world. Since Negus paid higher wages than the Con mine, which was only a few hundred yards away, it attracted the best miners available. Everyone who worked there was proud to be a Negus man, and the Negus miners looked down their noses at the Con men because they felt they were the best. This was probably true when you consider that they would "pull" a 6-foot (1.8-m) round when they tunnelled, while the normal maximum elsewhere was 5 feet (1.5 m). Even the whores in "Glamour Alley" would jibe at the Con men when they walked past, jeering at them that they were too cheap and "jerked off" instead of acting like real men and coming to use their services like the Negus guys did.

The men I worked with were hard as nails, with muscles built up and toughened by the hard labour they performed. Mining in those days was all hard work—there were no soft jobs. After the rounds were blasted out, the rock had to be "mucked out" by shovel. Steel sheets were set down so the rock could be blasted onto them, making the mucking easier. However, the portion of ore nearest the face did not have sheets under it, and the men had to shovel this part out by brute force over a base of jagged rock. This was called "mucking over the boot" and was very hard work. Nowadays, mucking is done by machines, which has eliminated a lot of the back-breaking work.

The veteran miners were mainly Norwegian. They were the toughest, strongest men you could meet, the epitome of the "hard rock" in which they toiled, yet many like Carl Nicklund, the mine captain, Carl Anderson, the shift boss, and Ole Gullickson were also the kindest, gentlest men you could meet. Many of the less-experienced miners were young farm boys from the Peace River country and the Prairies. Initially, the old-timers derided these stubble-jumpers, but eventually the farm boys became expert miners. Fellows like "Pud" McAusland, Jack Perkins, Bill Day, and Charlie Bothwell were among the best anywhere. Charlie Bothwell and his helper "Gentleman Jock" Mackinnon would put in a shift, go to town, get drunk, and come back in the morning the worse for wear, put in another shift, and repeat the process for several days. Gentleman Jock was a Cape Bretoner who had been an amateur boxer in the Maritimes. He was built like a brick house and was strong as an ox, but he never raised his voice or used his strength to intimidate anyone. He was a true gentleman and lived up to his nickname.

Probably because of the Depression, the miners I knew came from all walks of life and ranged from the deeply religious to those who were masters of obscenity. One miner's favourite saying was, "If I'm wrong, I'll wash your ass and drink the water." Some were real artists at manufacturing sometimes comical blasphemies. Some of the more blasphemous expressions were "By the hind quarter of the Lamb of God" and "By the balls of the Seven Ragged Apostles." As well as these linguistic artistes, we had characters like Jim Kelly.

Jim was a master diamond driller and one of the few men in the country who could set the diamonds in the bits. He was employed to punch diamond drill holes from underground rather than from the surface in an attempt to find further ore veins. We became good friends from playing table tennis together. After the Second World War, Jim made a lot of money as the owner of several diamond-drilling rigs that kept busy during the mining boom that took place during that period. When he got drunk, he would light a cigar with a ten-dollar bill. When I was going to university after the war, he came to visit me in Edmonton and took my wife, Kim, and me out to dinner. He came in a taxi and when we went into the restaurant, he brought the taxi driver along to eat dinner with us, with the taxi's meter running the whole time.

In 1938 Bill Stewart, the mine manager, and Tommy Macnab, the chief engineer, left Negus for British Guiana in South America to develop some placer deposits there for Negus's main shareholder Joe Errington, one of the foremost mining men in Canada at the time. Tommy died there from some tropical disease, but Bill later returned to Canada and worked on building the Snare River dam for the federal government. When Bill left, Jock McNiven, who had come to Negus previously to be manager of the mill, became the new mine manager. McNiven was a good mine manager who was affectionately referred to as McFoo. (He became a legend and eventually the mayor of Yellowknife.) McNiven was given the name "McFoo"—behind his back—because of a song some wit made up about Negus miners who missed their shifts. At times, some of them would go to town, get drunk, and not make it back in time for their shift. McNiven didn't want to fire anyone, though, especially since he had such a good crew, so he devised a system whereby a man would receive a warning for his first offence but would be suspended for seven days for his second offence. Part of the song, as I remember it, went:

Too late, too late to go to Negus,
Too late, too late to see McFoo.
So, my boy, it's seven days for you.

McNiven's name didn't rhyme with "you," so the songwriter changed it to "McFoo."

An incident occurred during the winter of 1939 that caused an uproar in the Negus camp. Two Negus men, Scotty Alexander and Slim Munroe, had gone into town and, of course, had been drinking, as all miners did when they went to town, but they were both good-natured fellows who wouldn't harm anyone. Scotty, a little Scot, had trapped in the North but eventually ended up working as a miner on a stoper at Negus. Slim was a big, happy-go-lucky farm boy with one crossed eye, which gave him a slightly peculiar look. They were in one of the cafés in town and were singing when Constable McManus, an unpopular Mountie, came in and tried to arrest them for disturbing the peace. When they protested, McManus threw them into jail, charging them with disturbing the peace, resisting arrest, and assaulting a police officer.

The injustice of the charges aroused the ire of the whole Negus camp, since there were several witnesses who swore that Scotty and Slim had done no wrong. However, each of them stood to receive several years in jail if the maximum sentence was imposed, so a collection was taken up and enough money was raised to bring in a lawyer from Edmonton to fight their case. The lawyer was Cy Becker, whom I've mentioned before as a man known and honoured throughout the North. When the trial came up in Yellowknife, Cy made a monkey out of McManus on the witness stand and, with the help of the testimony of the many witnesses, demolished the Crown's case. There was great cheering when Scotty and Slim were acquitted.

The Negus was a very rich mine. The veins varied in thickness from 6 inches (15 cm) to 20 feet (6 m) and sloped downward at an angle of approximately seventy degrees. In later years, a huge body of ore was found at a much greater depth, but when I was there, all the ore was obtained from the various veins.

135

Preliminary work had been performed at the Negus to determine whether it was worth developing into a mine. To this end an inclined shaft was sunk from the surface on a vein down to the 100-foot (30-m) level. When it became apparent how rich the ore was, a decision was made to immediately construct a fifty-ton-per-day mill to process the ore. At the same time a vertical shaft was sunk to the 100-foot level and mining began there. Thus, the mill was constructed before the mine was fully developed. Normally, ore is blasted for at least a year before a mill is installed to leave enough ore in a stope so that miners can use this buildup as a floor while they drill. However, because of the shortage of mill feed at the Negus, all the ore had to be drawn out of the chutes on the first level (100 feet). As a result, miners had to drill from staging set as much as 70 or 80 feet (21 to 24 m) above the floor of the drift.

The staging was constructed by driving "sprags"—pieces of timber—into both the footwall and hanging wall. To do this, notches were cut into the rock, so that the sprags would support the planks laid across them. Drilling was then done off these planks. The staging had to be sturdy enough to support the men working on it and withstand the pounding from the stopers being drilled from it. If the sprags were not securely fastened into both walls, men and machines would go plummeting down the seventy-degree slope and end up in the timbers below.

One of the "muckers"—he wasn't a miner because you had to start out as a miner's helper to become a miner and none of the miners would have him—was a powerfully built young fellow by the name of George Shanks, who was unpopular because of his bullying tactics. He fancied himself a heavyweight boxer and eventually left Negus and went to Edmonton to pursue his boxing career. He won several fights by knockouts and was heralded as an up-and-coming champion. Whenever any of the Negus men were in Edmonton, if George happened to be fighting, they would attend the match with the hope of seeing him get beaten. One night, Shanks had a bout with a young light heavyweight who was a member of the fighting Lust family from Medicine Hat and had the ring name of "Young Tunney Lust." At one point, George had Lust on the verge of a knockout and, throwing caution to the winds, was about to finish him off. But Lust was an experienced boxer and even though he was tottering on his feet, he caught Shanks flush on the chin with a desperation right as he came charging in. Shanks went down and he was out for the count. The Negus fellows who were present that night cheered so loudly they almost brought the roof down. I would meet Lust later, when he fought in the Canadian Army Championships in Europe in 1945.

I enjoyed working in the mine at Negus, my only worry being that I'd get silicosis from the rock dust in the air following blasting.[1] However, it turned out there was something else I should have been worried about. One day, I had just taken samples from the face about 80 feet (24 m) up and was going down the ladder carrying my samples in a box, which was attached to a strap over my shoulder. Because the roof of the stope was so high, two 40-foot (12-m) ladders were required to reach it, but I had forgotten the two ladders were staggered—the bottom ladder was not directly below the top one but to the side of it. When I came to the bottom ladder, I stepped into thin air and tried to grab the rung of the top ladder with my left hand. I had torn a tendon on the little finger of my left hand playing softball a few days earlier though, and it was encased in a huge aluminum splint. The splint interfered with my grip and I couldn't grab the rung and I went plummeting 40 feet down the stope. My hard hat and lamp went flying off into the darkness below, and I thought, "God, this is it!" However, I ended up in the bottom of the ore chute without injury, except that my ankle hurt. I yelled up at Frank Winters and Donnie Sheck, the two miners above me, not to throw down any old steel as I was in the chute, and they laughed uproariously when I told them I had walked off the ladder.

Several days after my ladder mishap, I was standing on a ladder some 80 feet (24 m) up in the same stope while the same two miners, Frank Winters and Donnie Sheck, were installing new staging. Donnie was walking toward me, saying, "Tommy, don't stand on those planks. They are only nailed to—," when he stepped on the plank himself and went hurtling down the seventy-degree slope. There was a rumbling noise as he fell and his partner, Frank, went white and called out,

"Donnie, are you all right?" There was no sound for some time, so Frank ran down the ladder to see how serious the situation was. Then there was a loud moan and Donnie said, "Oh, the cheeks of my arse." We were certainly relieved that he was okay, and they didn't rib me about falling off the ladder after that.

As well as being the mine sampler, I worked at several other jobs in the mine. As the "machine doctor" I repaired the drilling machines, such as the liners and stoppers. Although the title sounded impressive, the job was relatively simple—it mainly consisted of replacing worn-out items with spare parts. As the "powder man" I had to make sure that each miner got his required supply of dynamite (which was called powder), fuses, and caps. The powder was kept in a steam-heated shed, as dynamite cannot be allowed to freeze. Fuses had to be cut to the proper lengths and detonator caps attached to the fuses. The fuses were cut to specific lengths so that different holes would detonate at different times. When drilling in a tunnel, holes would first be drilled so that there was a "cut" near the bottom or floor. These "cut" holes were drilled inward at an angle to form a pyramid and were blasted first so that there would be a cut, or opening, 5 or 6 feet (1.5 to 1.8 m) into the rock. The other holes would then be blasted toward the cut, thus extending the tunnel 5 or 6 feet further into the face.

Drilled at an angle, the "cut" holes were the most difficult to drill and sometimes the drill steel would get stuck. I've seen miners practically crying in frustration, desperately trying to loosen the stuck drill rod with wrenches. When this proved impossible, a new hole would have to be drilled before the round could be blasted. Today, specially hardened, factory-made bits are used, but in 1939–40 all the bits were formed and hardened by a blacksmith, called the "steel-sharpener," who heated the steel bits on the end of the drill steel in a charcoal-heated forge, placed them in a machine to form the drilling bits, and once they had reached the proper temperature, plunged them into cold water to harden them. Because the steel-sharpener's decision on when to harden the bits depended on his estimation of the correct redness of the heated steel, it was important that he be in possession of all his faculties. If the steel-sharpener's judgment was impaired, perhaps by a hangover, the resultant used steel would come back up from underground with a round blob on the end of it and the steel-sharpener would be on the receiving end of every blasphemous name under the sun. Good steel-sharpeners were jewels beyond price; the success of the mine's operation depended on them.

When winter came it was hockey season. Yellowknife went hockey mad during the winter of 1939–40. There were three teams: our Negus mines team, the Con mines team, and the Yellowknife town team. Con started vying for the best team in the league by transferring some of its good players from Trail to Yellowknife. This was a simple matter for Consolidated Mining and Smelting, since it had hundreds of employees at Trail and Kimberley. During the Depression years, all the mining towns had great hockey teams, the reason being that the mines were the only place a young fellow could get a job that let him earn what we considered then to be big money, and so all the championship teams, such as the Trail Smoke Eaters, Kimberley Dynamiters, and Sudbury Wolves came from mining centres. Yellowknife was no different. Soon Negus was importing hockey players from the Prairies—we had players from the Prince Albert Mintos, Saskatoon Quakers, and Edmonton Superiors. Our star player was Lloyd Goundry, who should have made it to the National Hockey League.

During my boyhood, I had never learned to skate well because I didn't have decent skates to wear or a decent skating rink to skate on. However, in the winter of 1937 I became a good enough skater to play goalkeeper for the Royal Canadian Corps of Signals team in Fort McMurray and managed to become fairly adept, probably because I had very fast reflexes. I tried out for the goalkeeper position on the Negus team and to my joy was accepted. This was in the days before goalies wore masks, and we usually played at night since the men worked during the day. I often wonder how I didn't get killed, considering the poor quality of the lighting, which was provided by sets of ordinary incandescent lamps strung on wires across the rink. The disadvantage of playing goal was that your feet usually froze because you didn't get a chance to skate very much. Our rink was on Great Slave Lake, just below the camp, and there was usually a cold wind blowing off it, but we didn't play if it got colder than -40°F (-40°C).

I don't know how the fans stood the cold, but they were always there en masse. Our fellow workers were rabid fans and bet what I considered huge sums of money on the games, especially during the playoffs in the spring—as much as five hundred dollars. In those days, that seemed like a fortune and it put a lot of strain on me as the goaltender. I'd wonder whether they'd want to run me out of town if I let in a soft goal. However, we managed to win the championship and were the first hockey champions of the Northwest Territories in 1939–40. ∎

The Negus Mines Hockey Team, spring 1940. We were champions of the Northwest Territories that year. I am the goalie in the centre of the picture.

PART THREE

THE WAR

Joining Up

*I*n the spring of 1940, George Hamilton came to Negus as the mine engineer. One of my duties as the mine's sampler was to help him survey the various drifts and stopes underground. George was impressed with my lack of fear of heights—we were often nearly 100 feet (30 m) in the air, clambering around empty stopes. He became, and was to remain, one of my lifelong friends. George was in the Reserve Army and was called up to receive his commission with the Royal Canadian Engineers. He left in May 1940 for Calgary. Up until this time, the war had been called a "phony war," but when the Germans began overrunning Europe in 1940, people began to get concerned and realized that time was running out for our side. I was eager to join up and had gone to Edmonton in March 1940 to join the Royal Canadian Air Force (RCAF) but was turned down because of my size. When George suggested that the army signals corps might accept me since I was a trained Morse code operator, I told him I wanted to enlist but was afraid I would be rejected because of my weight and height. The army's requirements were the same as those of the air force as far as height and weight were concerned—you had to be at least 5-foot 4-inches (1.6 m) tall and weigh 135 pounds (61 kg). George said he would look into my getting accepted in the Royal Canadian Corps of Signals (RCCS).

About a week after George left Yellowknife for Calgary, I received a telegram from him. He instructed me to come to Calgary and said that, provided I passed the medical, I would be accepted into the RCCS. I got Dr. Stanton in Yellowknife to examine me, and he said I was fit. I gave my notice to Negus and bought a ticket on a Canadian Airways flight to Edmonton. I flew out on a Barkley-Grow twin-engine plane, piloted by Grant McConachie. Grant had his own airline, Universal Air Service, but at that time was leasing this plane to Canadian Airways. He asked me how I liked the flight, and I told him it was much smoother than the single-engine planes. He said, "That's what I've been trying to tell them. These are the types of planes of the future—the day of the single-engined plane for passenger traffic has passed." Grant later became president of Canadian Pacific Airlines. I think he had a great deal of vision and the aviation industry in Canada owes him a great deal.

From Edmonton I took the train to Calgary, where I arrived with only twenty-five dollars left in my pocket after I had paid my fare. George and his wife, Doris, met me in Calgary and George took me down to meet George Eckenfelder. Eckenfelder was an engineer working for Calgary Power who had just received his commission as a lieutenant in the RCCS and been given the task of recruiting a section—thirty-odd men—for the new Third Canadian Divisional Signals. This was to be a unique unit, and sections for the division were being recruited from every province in Canada except British Columbia. Why it was left out I don't know, since there was even a section from Quebec.

After meeting Eckenfelder, I was escorted by George Hamilton to Mewata Barracks in Calgary to have my medical. First, I was measured and weighed. My height was 5 feet 2 inches (1.57 m) and my weight was 116 pounds (53 kg)—2 inches (5 cm) shorter and almost 20 pounds (9 kg) below the minimum requirements. George, who by then was wearing his lieutenant's uniform, came with me to the room where a corporal was weighing and measuring the recruits. George whispered to the corporal, "I'll give you a buck if you add an inch to his height." The corporal said, "Sure," and slipped the dollar into his pocket. Then he told me to keep my shoes on and said my height was just 5 feet 4 inches. He weighed me, and my weight (with shoes) was 119 pounds (54 kg).

A photograph of me upon joining the army in June 1940.

It was then time for the doctors to examine me. At that time, medical officers were still in civilian clothes. Their offices in Mewata Barracks consisted of blankets hung up on wires strung across the barracks, so I could hear everything they said when they were discussing my case. One said, "Well, he's physically fit, but only weighs 119 pounds, when he should be 135." Another said, "Eckenfelder really wants him. He's a trained radio operator, and they're pretty scarce." Then yet another doctor spoke up and said, "Well, he comes from away up north; he probably hasn't had enough to eat. The army food will soon fatten him up. Let's pass him." So, with George's influence, I was promptly signed up and on 11 June 1940, I became M44411, Signalman Thomas E. Morimoto, known in the army as "Toc Eddy," which at that time was the signals' phonetic alphabet for my initials, T. E. We stayed in Calgary for approximately a month while George finished recruiting "G" Section of the Third Canadian Divisional Signals.

Our section was filled with all kinds of characters. The sergeant was a short, corpulent beer-drinker named Innes; our orderly room corporal was a great guy named "Hash" Gofsky; and our corporal, Chuck White, was a good fellow but inclined to spout off bullshit. The other fellows who began to join us, or had already been recruited, were Jimmy Milne, who had been an accountant in the Imperial Bank of Commerce and later became the sergeant in charge of the section; the three Tatro brothers, who became good friends of mine; and John Mullan, who had been a butcher and became known immediately as "Moon" from the comic-strip character of the day Moon Mullins. There were also a few veterans who had been operators in the First World War. One was "Goody" Goodwin, a great guy but an alcoholic who did not stay with us for more than a couple of months. The surprising thing about him was that, although he hadn't used Morse code since the First World War, it came back to him very quickly. Another recruit was Art Layzell, who came from a well-known Calgary family. Then there was "Limey" Philips. Although he came from Wales, he was immediately named "Limey" and was called that throughout the war. The ironic thing was that his mother had brought him to Canada in 1939 so he wouldn't get caught up in the war, and here he was joining the Canadian army to get into it. His regimental number was M44414. We used to repeatedly ask him what his regimental number was because we got such a kick out of hearing him say, "Em foe foe foe one foe. What do you want to know foe?"

Our commanding officer, Lt. George Eckenfelder, was very capable and fair-minded, which is more than can be said of some that we had.

He should have become a colonel because of his capabilities but ran afoul of some of the higher-ups and never rose above the rank of captain. After the war he returned to his job as a civil engineer, specializing in designing and constructing dams, and became one of the most outstanding hydro-engineers in the world. He was made a vice-president and one of the principals of the large Montreal Engineering Company. George is a man I was proud to know then and one who has proved to be a good friend in the years since. When he celebrated his ninetieth birthday in Victoria, British Columbia, in 1999, I was delighted that my wife and I were invited to attend the party arranged by his daughter. It was wonderful to see how healthy he was and that his mind was as sharp as ever. At the party George told me his version of why I had been given a pass by the medical officers back when I was trying to sign up for the war. He said that when the doctors told him I was too small, he told them, "Stretch him. I want him."

In July 1940 we left Calgary via the Canadian Pacific Railway (CPR) for Barriefield, Ontario, near Kingston, where the rest of the Third Canadian Divisional Signals was gathering. We were to stay there until early January 1941. For me it was exciting to be travelling to eastern Canada, as I had never been out of Alberta. While we were crossing the prairies of Saskatchewan, with wheat fields stretching as far as the eye could see, there was a bit of excitement when Art Layzell ran amok and jumped off the train. The emergency cord was pulled and the train shuddered to a halt. Several of our men were detailed to chase Art across the prairie and bring him back. Moon Mullan finally caught him, and he was dragged back on board. This was when we discovered that Layzell was an alcoholic.

The train ride gave me an idea of the vastness of our country, travelling through the endless wheat fields of the Prairies and then the miles of forests through Northern Ontario. In addition to the natural beauty of the country, a memorable sight to all us young fellows was the vision of hundreds of girls at Kenora, Ontario. This was in July, at the height of summer vacation, and it seemed that all the beautiful girls from Winnipeg had come there, to wave at us troops.

147

On arriving at Kingston we were installed in a hut in Barriefield that we shared with the E, or "Eddy," Section from Prince Edward Island (PEI). There were catcalls and arguments between the two sections about western "stubble-jumpers" and eastern "herring chokers" far into the night. Despite this, we got along well and became good friends with the PEI boys. This is when I discovered that Maritimers had a different accent from other Canadians—for example, a fellow from PEI would say, "Where's me poyp [pipe]?"[1]

Every morning, right after our seven o'clock breakfast, we had to be shaved and have our shoes shined and our uniforms spic and span to go on parade, at which time the roll would be called. And every morning, right on schedule, having been called to attention, we would be standing erect and looking straight ahead when Art Layzell would promptly puke. It became quite a joke. Our sergeant would then be ordered to send Layzell on sick parade. It got so that Art had to go on sick parade every morning, and the medical officer (MO) began to hate the sight of him. The medical people gave Art all the tests they could, but could find nothing wrong with him. Finally, one day the MO said, almost crying, "Layzell, either you'll have to go or I will." Layzell got a discharge and was sent back to Calgary.

With sections drawn from all across Canada, I think the Third Canadian Divisional Signals must have been the most representative regiment in the Canadian army, as regiments were usually recruited from one specific area. This gave us a chance to meet fellows from all the other provinces in Canada, and I became good friends with some of the French-Canadian lads. It was a good experience for someone like me who had come from a small community in the bush country of northern Alberta and the Northwest Territories.

While training in Canada, the Third Canadian Divisional Signals was kept together as a regiment. (Once overseas, however, the regiment was split up, with some sections going to infantry brigades, others to artillery regiments, and still others to the Third Canadian Division headquarters.) As anyone who has been in the army and undergone basic training will know, life became an endless round of parade-square drilling, which included marching and rifle drill. We also endured countless lectures, which were given in big marquee tents. It was hard to stay awake in Ontario's hot, humid summer weather while listening to a lecturer droning on about the makeup of the various units, the number of vehicles, and so on.

While in training, we also had Morse code practice. Compared with most of the operators, who had obtained their training while in the militia, I was an experienced operator. Morse code takes hours of practice and a long time to become proficient at it. As a result I had quite an advantage over the others. We also went on what are known in the army as "schemes," which are practice operations. When we were issued our wireless sets, I was astounded and dismayed at what we were given—they were from the First World War and were called No. 1 Sets, which was quite appropriate as they must have been the first radio sets ever built! In order for these sets to operate on the same frequency, they had to be "netted," which required placing two vehicles rear to rear so that the operator could listen to the receiver of one while tuning the transmitter of the other. This was then repeated with all the other sets on the network. I was the only one in our section who knew how to "net" the sets. Adding to their deficiencies, the sets could only transmit Morse code and not voice transmissions. I couldn't believe this was the equipment we were taking with us overseas.

In addition to schemes and lectures, we were subjected to vaccinations and inoculations, with endless numbers of jabs. At that time there were separate injections for each disease; the single multiple-injection had not yet been developed. I had been vaccinated for smallpox years before in Fort McMurray but, possibly because the vaccine was too old, my vaccination never took. When I was vaccinated at Barriefield, I got the customary red sore on my arm, but it grew quite large and angry looking. Several days later, I received two other inoculations in one day and that night was taken to the hospital with a temperature of 103°F (39°C). I don't remember being taken to the hospital but woke up the next day to discover that about twenty other signals' personnel were in the beds around me with the same problem. Although by this time we had all recovered and felt perfectly okay, we weren't let out of the hospital for several days, and the nursing sisters had a difficult time keeping order with a bunch of young bucks in perfect health but being kept in bed. The nurses must have been glad to get rid of us. The needles proved to be too much for a couple of men, and they received discharges when they refused to take any more inoculations. One fellow used to pass out before they even jabbed him.

Our training camp was only a short distance from Kingston. At that time, the people of Kingston were mostly of old United Empire Loyalist stock and looked down their noses at what they considered riff-raff—rowdy army men. They frowned on soldiers unless they were army cadets training to become officers at the Royal Military College, which was located in Kingston. Kingston was also the seat of Queen's University and we regularly received challenges from its students to come and fight. There were a few times when we were confined to barracks over the weekend, forbidden to go downtown because of these challenges. Although Kingston's residents didn't seem to welcome our presence, this didn't prevent me from enjoying the beauty of the surrounding countryside. I loved looking at the boats and the beautiful homes on some of the Thousand Islands and certainly envied what we considered to be the rich people who owned them. There were apple orchards in the Kingston area, and I delighted in seeing apples growing on trees. Being from northern Alberta, I had never seen fruit growing on trees before!

Guard duty was normally rather a boring assignment, but one night we were ordered to go on a hazardous mission. Our corporal, Chuck White, who was the NCO in charge of the guard at the gate, came around and said, "We're going out to get some chickens." So half a dozen of us set out in a truck and raided a hen house several miles away. We used palliasses—cotton bags that were usually filled with straw for use as mattresses—to gather up about a dozen chickens and returned to camp. The cooks cooked them the next day and we all had a feast. It just seemed like a prank then, but I've thought since that it was a stupid thing to do, robbing some poor old farmer who could probably ill afford to lose those chickens. Besides which, we could have gone to jail if we had been caught. At the time, though, it seemed perfectly all right, since our corporal had told us to do it. I guess that's the way young fellows sometimes get into trouble, from being easily led. This is especially so in the army, where you have to obey the orders of your superior.

One day I discovered that a trade-test examination was going to be held. It was primarily intended to allow the sergeants to earn some extra money, but I asked to be allowed to take the radio operators' trade test and was granted permission. I was the only signalman to do so, as the others taking the test were all sergeants. There was a written exam on radio theory and operation, as well as a code test. I managed to pass and so received an extra fifty cents a day as trades pay. This bumped my pay up to the beautiful sum of $1.80 per day. Receiving this extra money was like manna from heaven.

As Christmas 1940 approached, we were all granted leave to go home for the holidays. I had been saving my money for the trip since at that time soldiers didn't receive free fares on the railways—we were required to pay half the ticket price. When it came time to go home, instead of storing our equipment, the army forced us to take it all with us. I had to lug my kit bag, big haversack, small haversack, small respirator (gas mask), and rifle with me all the way from Kingston to Alberta. It was certainly a nuisance carrying all this gear across the continent and back when it could easily have been stored until we returned. I travelled via the CPR to Calgary, then on to Edmonton, and from there to Fort McMurray via Northern Alberta Railways.

Ever since then, I have harboured resentment toward the CPR for the way it treated us on that trip. Although we had paid half of a full fare, the servicemen were separated from the other passengers and forced to ride in the old nineteenth-century colonist cars, which CP had resurrected and pressed into service. These had hard, wooden seats and no heating except for a coal stove at one end of the car. We felt that the railway officials, and especially the conductors (who must have received their orders from higher up), treated us in a very arrogant and cavalier manner, even though we were paying passengers and not riding gratis.

After my leave was up, I returned to Barriefield via the Canadian National Railway (CNR) from Edmonton to Toronto, rather than take the CPR through Calgary to Toronto. The treatment I received from CN was in marked contrast to that meted out by CP. I was treated courteously and rode in relative comfort on cushioned seats in a regular coach. I was almost broke but had enough money left over to rent a pillow for myself and a fellow soldier who was sitting beside me. I fell asleep and dreamt that the conductor had come along and told us to move back to the old colonist cars, so I yelled at him to "F— o—." At this, I woke up and realized I had yelled out the words in my sleep. Heads had popped up everywhere, and I ashamedly hid my face in my pillow and didn't surface again until we reached Toronto.

During our stay in Barriefield, whenever we could scrape together enough money we went to Montreal for the weekend, using our thumb to hitch a ride. During the war years it was relatively easy to hitchhike, especially if you were in uniform. People were not yet afraid of being murdered or raped by someone they had picked up. Montreal was a vibrant city, its French influence making it much more interesting and lively than Toronto, which we considered dull and stodgy. Everything was astoundingly cheap when compared with today's prices. During one trip to Montreal, I remember meeting Sergeant Blouin from our Quebec section. We became good friends and after doing the rounds of the city were both almost broke. He said, "I'll take you to a place where we can get a meal for thirty-five cents." It was a pretty fair meal, but when the proprietor tried to charge us forty cents each, Blouin had a terrific argument with him, threw down seventy cents, and said that was all he was getting—in French, of course—and we walked out.

In January 1941, the Third Canadian Division moved from Barriefield to Debert, Nova Scotia. This camp, near Truro, had just been built and we were the first troops stationed there. The camp was built as a staging point to house troops on their way overseas via Halifax. I was surprised at the amount of snow that fell in Nova Scotia, as I had thought it was relatively balmy in the Maritimes. When warm, moisture-laden air coming up from the Caribbean hits cold Arctic air, though, it turns into snow, sometimes several feet of it at a time. However, when spring came we found the Nova Scotia countryside lush and green. A lot of strawberries were grown near Debert, and we enjoyed eating them.

On weekends we hitchhiked around the province. Sometimes we had difficulty getting back to camp in time for our Monday morning parade, but we always seemed to make it. In the spring the Fourteenth Field Regiment of Artillery, to which our signals section was to be permanently attached, went to the firing range at Tracadie, New Brunswick, and for the first time we got a chance to work together. This is when I found out that our section wasn't the only one issued with out-of-date equipment—the guns the artillery were using on the firing range were First World War eighteen-pounders.

The move allowed us to see more of the Maritimes, as we drove up through Chatham, New Brunswick, to Tracadie. At that time, Tracadie was one of the most depressed areas in Canada. One could see why—the timber had been logged out, so the livelihood that the area had depended upon had disappeared. The only thing left was fishing and some farming, though the soil didn't seem that fertile. The whole area reeked of the smell of dead fish, which were used as fertilizer. Tracadie also had something that few Canadians were aware of—the only leper colony in Canada. It was run by a group of Catholic nuns, who had dedicated their lives to serving the lepers and were committed to staying there for life. Many years later the colony was closed when the modern treatment of leprosy eliminated the disease in Canada. While at Tracadie, I went to Bathurst, a pulp and paper town in northern New Brunswick. It impressed me as one of the most attractive places I had seen in the Maritimes—besides which, it boasted a lot of pretty girls.

Before leaving for overseas, we were given another medical. Referring to my height and weight that was noted in my file, the MO who gave me my physical said, "These figures don't look quite right." So I said, "They may be out a little bit." He just laughed and let me go. Not everyone was as willing as I was to see service, however. Any serviceman who passed the medical could ask for a "reboard" if they felt there was something wrong with them. A friend with whom I often played table tennis did this, claiming there was something wrong with his eyes. Although Ken was slightly cross-eyed, there was nothing wrong with his eyesight—as I could testify, having seen how well he played table tennis. He was sent to the eye specialist, who tested him several times in a period of some weeks. Ken would usually come to me quite elated after each of these tests and say, "Well, I'll be back in Calgary soon, with my discharge," only to be disappointed. Then one week he came to me, looking down in the dumps, and said, "Oh, I think he's caught me. I wonder if they'll court-martial me?" When I asked what he meant, he explained how the MO had been puzzled at the difference in his eyesight during his several visits. Apparently the MO had moved an object to different spots and asked Ken when he could see it and then said, "That's strange, you could see it last time." In the end, however, Ken obtained his much-sought-after discharge, and I have never heard from him since. Meanwhile, I, along with thousands of young men like me, was off to war. ■

A Taste of Britain

*I*n July 1941 we embarked at Halifax for England on the SS *Orion*, a P&O liner that had just come from South Africa. We left in beautiful weather, which continued all the way across the Atlantic. We were in a large convoy, with destroyers and corvettes escorting us. When I saw how the little corvettes tossed up and down in the waves, I felt lucky I wasn't on board one of them and was glad I had joined the army instead of the navy. I didn't get seasick during the crossing but always felt a dull headache. Seasickness is, I suppose, in some cases psychological, because some of the men were seasick as soon as we boarded at Halifax. I found out later that I was prone to it during rough weather.

During our North Atlantic crossing, there was a tremendous amount of gambling on board. The main army game was blackjack. There were a couple of professional gamblers amongst us, and they cleaned up several thousand dollars. One gambler had come to Canada from Scotland and then joined the Canadian army. I think he joined up so he could rook all the suckers in the army. He had a Scottish brogue so thick you could cut it with a knife and so was known as "Scotty."

The meals on the *Orion* were not what we were used to, and as usual among troops there was a lot of complaining. I didn't mind the food and even found it interesting. For example, we had tripe, which I had never eaten before. I rather liked it, although most of the men didn't and expressed their dislike at having to eat it.

The sleeping accommodations were something else. As you can imagine, with thousands of troops on board, space was at a premium. Although the officers had quite comfortable quarters in cabins in the upper decks, we ORs ("other ranks") had to find a place to sleep in the stuffy, smelly quarters below. The stench from people getting seasick drove a lot of us onto the open decks where, fortunately, we were able to sling hammocks. A hammock took some getting used to, but once we'd got the hang of it (pun not intended), it proved comfortable enough. Luckily, the weather held and we were able to sleep on deck for most of the voyage.

We came down the Irish Sea from the north and could see Ireland, which looked as green as it was purported to be. We did not land at Liverpool, as most of the ships did, but went south to the Bristol Channel and disembarked at Bristol. It was a sunny day when we came ashore, and my first impression of England was "what a beautiful place." The countryside was green and the houses looked quaint. What really struck me was how small the railway cars on the freight trains seemed—the goods wagons, as they were called, looked like toys compared with our Canadian boxcars. The whistles of the locomotives also sounded like the tooting of toy trains when compared to the drawn-out, lonesome wail of the steam-engine whistles on our Canadian trains. It was a short ride to Aldershot, where we were to be stationed in Mons Barracks for a couple of months. These ancient barracks must have been over one hundred years old, and they well looked it.

The food at Mons Barracks left a lot to be desired, and we discovered that the English did not eat nearly as much as we Canadians did—what was sufficient for English soldiers was never enough for us. At mealtime the food was brought to each table in large platters, which were passed around. There being eight men at each table, it was often the case that the eighth man got little or nothing. When we protested, the men waiting on tables, who were soldiers like us on fatigue duty, just shrugged their shoulders and said there was nothing they could do about it. Each table had its quota of food, and that was it. As a result we were always hungry and spent what money we had in the Navy, Army & Air Forces Institute (NAAFI, pronounced "Naffy") canteen, eating buns and sandwiches. The sandwiches were made with reddish-coloured sausages—guaranteed eight percent meat—dubbed "horsecock" by the Canadians. I remember feeling rather despondent, thinking I wouldn't be able to last long on these rations if the war was prolonged for several years. Fortunately, we moved out to the field within a couple of months. We didn't move very far, only to Farnham, 10 miles (16 km) or so from Aldershot, but we were finally attached to our artillery regiment, the Fourteenth Field Regiment. As the signals section for this regiment, we were based at regimental headquarters and so came under the artillery regiment for our messing and other services and duties. The food became more plentiful, and we finally had enough to eat.

One of the men in our signals section was a young lineman named Melvin Butler. He had joined up at the age of fifteen and was only twenty-one when the war ended. He was a good-looking, short, stocky lad with a lot of self-confidence, although he likely had never gone past grade three in school. He could read, but his massacring of the English language was something that had to be heard to be believed. We called him the "Dead End Kid," after the character in the movies. I regret not keeping a record of all his Mrs. Malaprop sayings, as they would have filled a small notebook. One evening when we were returning to camp on the bus after having gone to a movie in Aldershot, I asked Butler to call to me when we had reached our bus stop, as I wasn't sure where it was in the dark. As usual the bus was crowded, with everyone practically standing on each other's toes. Finally, I heard a yell from Butler somewhere down the bus, "Come on Tommy, it's time to get off. We've reached our destiny!"

Our commanding officer, Lt. George Eckenfelder, liked young Butler and wanted him to qualify for trades pay as a lineman. Eckenfelder would take Butler into his hut each night and try to teach him arithmetic. Once they were working with fractions and George said, "Butler, if I had a pie and cut it into four equal pieces and took three pieces away, what would I have left?" Butler said, "Dat's easy. A piece of pie." I think George gave up after that, but he still asked the testing officer to go easy on Butler and not test him on the technical side. As a result Butler got his trades pay, and he just took it as a matter of course that he had passed the test on his merits. When we asked him how the test had gone, he said, "Aw, nuttin to it. Easy as pie."

At the end of the war Butler stayed in the army and went to Korea during the Korean War. I looked him up many years later in Montreal, but regretted seeing him, as I would have liked to remember him as the good-looking brash kid he had once been. By then, he was a gap-toothed alcoholic who soon put the touch on me: "Could you lend me ten bucks?" So I gave him twenty dollars. I never saw him again and understand he died in Montreal a few years later.

In England we soon became accustomed to the blackout, and it seemed that it had always been with us. However, it could cause problems, as it did when we were moved to Purley, near Croydon. There we were billeted in a large, four-storied house, with the signals section situated on the top floor. This meant groping our way down the stairs in blackouts whenever we had to relieve ourselves, as the toilets were on the ground floor. However, there was a little alcove with a small window and some of the fellows would pee out the window when they didn't want to make the long trip down and back up the stairs in the dark. One night, Sergeant Hepburn of Artillery Regimental Headquarters was mounting the guard when, all of a sudden, he felt something spraying down on him. When he realized what was happening, he went charging up the stairs in a rage and caught one of our linemen, George C., buttoning up his fly as he came out of the alcove. "You pissed out of that window just now," roared the sergeant. George admitted he had, and Hepburn said, "You pissed all over me, you son of a bitch," and immediately put him on charge. Poor George got seven days CB (confined to barracks) and a notation on his crime sheet for "urinating out of a window on a sergeant."

Soon we were moved to Chichester on the south coast and were billeted under the stands at the famous racing course Goodwood Park, a miserable place mired in mud. Although Goodwood Park is now quite a posh place, then it was a ramshackle wooden affair and the quarters were no better. At that time, December 1941, the Germans were reported to be gathering an invasion fleet across the channel in France, and we had to be on alert. I remember how cold it was standing guard at night with the chilly wind blowing in from the Channel. We were glad to finally leave Chichester.

One thing that sticks in my memory arose from a church parade we had at Chichester Cathedral. We were paraded into this beautiful cathedral and sat listening to one of the most inane sermons I had ever heard. It seemed to me that repeated over and over again was the admonition "Good [pronounced with the *oo* sound] is good, and Eevill is eevill." However, we then heard the most beautiful voices I had ever heard. I had never heard boy sopranos sing before, and to this day I can recall the thrill of hearing the boys' choir. If there are angels, that is what they should sound like.

In 1941 the Canadian army divisions in England—the First, Second, and Third—were the only ones with any equipment, the British having lost most of theirs in France in 1940. Someone in the upper echelons decided that the Canadian divisions should be moved around the country to delude the Germans into thinking the British had more fully armed divisions than they actually had. As a result we had to move to a new base every few weeks. I think Great Britain (and Canada) was lucky that Germany didn't invade England in 1940 or 1941. Our Canadian divisions were still equipped with First World War armaments—the artillery had obsolete eighteen-pounder guns and our No. 1 wireless sets quit working if the weather got damp. I am sure the Germans, even if they had suffered heavy losses in the Channel crossing, would have been able to walk through us. Thank heaven they didn't invade then.

As a result of being constantly moved from base to base, we were stationed all over the south of England—mainly in Sussex but also in Surrey. Although this is a lovely part of the country, being young fellows and wanting to see the nightlife in the cities, we did not fully appreciate the beauty of the countryside. England is beautiful in the spring, when the rhododendrons are in bloom and the daffodils and other spring flowers come out in all their glory. I had never seen rhododendrons before and could not believe the masses of blossoms like those we saw in Horsham Park in Sussex.

In March 1942 we went up to the mountains in Wales with the artillery to fire on the firing range there. We drove up through Cardiff and small Welsh towns such as Merthyr Tydfil, which had been one of the most depressed areas in England during the Depression. One thing that astounded me was the playgrounds in Wales. On Sundays the seesaws, swings, and other children's recreational facilities were locked up with chains to prevent them from being used. It was my first encounter with the narrow-minded fundamentalism of Welsh church goers.

When we first arrived at our army camp in Wales, a place called Sennybridge, we heard soldiers in English uniforms speaking a strange language, which we finally realized was their old Celtic tongue. Then on going to town, we were fascinated by the beautiful lilt of the women's voices. However, what made Wales special was that we were able to order eggs when we went to a café or restaurant. For some reason, there didn't seem to be rationing of eggs in Wales. Having fried eggs was a wonderful treat. We eventually began our artillery shoot in the Welsh mountains, where the only inhabitants were grazing sheep. This was the first shoot with live ammunition that our artillery regiment had performed in the United Kingdom. As the signals section for the regiment, we supplied communication from regimental headquarters to the three batteries. In the damp and wet weather of the Welsh mountains, our No. 1 Sets were quite unreliable and we had to rely on our telephone system, using insulated cable laid by our linemen.

In early 1942 we took part in the largest army manoeuvres that the British and Canadian forces had participated in to that date. (One good thing had happened before this exercise: we received new wireless sets made in Canada, the No. 11 Set, which was much better than the No. 1 but still underpowered.) The exercise was code-named "Spartan" and was meant to toughen up the troops. Each man was issued three cans of bully beef and three packages of hardtack as rations for the day. The exercise started on the south coast and ended up near Oxford. We rode in our eight-hundred-weight trucks—the army's version of a pickup truck. However, the poor infantrymen had to march all the way, and throughout the march the foot soldiers discarded half-eaten cans of bully beef along the roads from Worthington to Oxford, trying to get rid of excess carrying weight. It must have distressed English civilians to see all this wasted food when they couldn't get bully beef at all.

Although we operators did not have to march, the exercise put quite a strain on each of us. Each truck was manned by an operator-driver and an operator. Since we were constantly on the move, the driver was not able to do much operating, as he had to be in shape to drive. Because our moves were usually at night, the driver had to be awake and get what sleep he could snatch during the day. Therefore, the operator had to do practically all the operating, and the only chance he had to sleep was when the vehicle was on the move. After a week of this, I was almost out on my feet from lack of sleep. After the Spartan exercise, the brass realized we were understaffed, and a driver and two operators were assigned to each vehicle.

Exercise Spartan gave anyone with a motorcycle an opportunity to play hooky, as any absence could be accounted for as having been captured by the enemy. During Spartan, our two dispatch riders, Dick MacKenzie and "Gyp" McDonald, went missing, as did Melvin Butler, our mounted lineman. These fellows were quite a threesome and would roam around the country on their motorcycles. Dick had been in the Permanent Force with the Lord Strathcona Horse before the war, while Gyp was a former jockey who knew all about horse racing. The three of them finally showed up at the end of the manoeuvres and said that they had been "captured." I am sure they went to Brighton, where they had girlfriends.

Soon after Spartan, we lost our commander-in-chief General Andy McNaughton, presumably because General Bernard Montgomery didn't think he was capable of leading the Canadian army. I think most of us felt the loss, as McNaughton was beloved by all the men. General

Montgomery was General Officer Commanding (GOC), Southern Command, and was therefore in command of the Canadian divisions. He was a fanatic about physical fitness and ordained that everyone from the top down had to do physical exercises each morning. He also decreed that every man had to be able to march 6 miles (10 km) in an hour, *not* 6 miles an hour but 6 miles in an hour—no rest breaks, all this to be done in our heavy army boots. The only way I could do it was to run in order to make the distance in the required time. As a result of this order, we lost quite a few men who were sent back to Canada. Some of the older ones—especially our First World War veterans—couldn't meet the requirements of what we all considered a ridiculous order. I think physical fitness could have been accomplished without such draconian measures.

Just before Christmas 1942 I became quite ill and thought I had the flu. I was sent to a Field Ambulance Unit where I was given aspirins and slept on a cot. The Field Ambulance Medical Corps sergeant asked me if I wanted to go back to my unit, as I probably didn't want to spend Christmas on a cot in the Field Ambulance, so I went back to the section. I dragged myself around for about three months and gradually got my strength back. After the war I developed pneumonia and realized that I had had pneumonia in 1942, because the symptoms were exactly the same. I still wonder how I recovered from pneumonia in the days before penicillin, without any treatment whatsoever.

All servicemen in the Canadian army received a week's leave every three months, with a free railway ticket to anywhere in the United Kingdom. I had gone to Edinburgh, Scotland, for my first leave and was very impressed with the city. The castle on the hill above Edinburgh's main street seemed like a castle right out of a fairy tale. While I was exploring the city, I got into a conversation with the man sitting beside me on the upper deck of a bus. He pointed to a street and said, "Dinna go down that street. It's the wuckedest street in Edinburgh." This was Leith Street, and I immediately headed there when I got off the bus. However, it was only a street lined with pubs, and since I couldn't drink—I am severely allergic to alcohol—it wasn't of much interest.

On my other leaves, I went to Aberdeen, Scotland, to visit relatives of Scotty Morrison from Fort McMurray. They welcomed me with open arms and made me feel right at home. The Ramsays had a cottage about 30 miles (50 km) inland from Aberdeen, and one weekend Mrs. Ramsay, Scotty's sister, and I went out to their cottage. After getting off the bus, we had to walk 3 miles (5 km) to the cottage so stopped for a rest at a farmhouse owned by Flora and her husband "Heery." Flora, a buxom woman in her forties, bustled about making tea for us, chattering away to Mrs. Ramsay, while her six-year-old son kept trying to get her attention. When there was a lull in the conversation, the little lad yelled out, "Wumman, am I gettin' to Daffodil tea or ain't I?" Flora stopped and putting her hands on her hips barked out, "No, you little buggar, you'll get run over by the goddom motorkeers. Heery, take him out and find some bird's eggs or something." I had a hard time keeping a straight face, especially since at that time with petrol-rationing there were only a few lorries and delivery vehicles per week on the roads in the country. Following this, Flora said to her seventeen-year-old son, "Come on, entertain the sojerlad. Play the grammyphone." So the lad played cowboy songs sung by "Big Bill Combull" (Campbell), a Canadian I had heard on the BBC. I had to endure this as he played record after record, until we finally left to complete our hike to the cottage.

At the cottage we met the "fairmer" from whom the Ramsays rented their cottage. Being in the Home Guard, he had an army rifle fitted to fire 0.22-calibre bullets for target practice, and he lent it to me, along with some 0.22 ammunition for shooting rabbits. I shot two rabbits to Mrs. Ramsay's delight, as they were very welcome in practically meatless Britain. Though there were a lot of them, the rabbits in Scotland were much more difficult to shoot than the ones back home. For one thing they seemed to be a lot smarter. As soon as they heard anyone approaching, they would immediately go into hiding in one of their many holes in the ground and would not show themselves for fifteen or twenty minutes. I had to sit patiently, not moving, in order to pot one.

Everyone wanted to go to London on leave at least once. I don't suppose there ever was, or will be again, a city like London during the Second World War. The city had been pounded by German bombers but, although there was some damage elsewhere, most of the damage had occurred in the poorer East End. Most of the West End, where all the action occurred as far as the servicemen were concerned, was relatively untouched.

At night the West End, from Hyde Park to Piccadilly Circus and Leicester Square, was teeming with people. In the blackout it looked as though the air was filled with hundreds of fireflies, but these turned out to be the glowing cigarettes held by prostitutes to identify themselves. One could hardly walk in Hyde Park after dark without stepping on a couple on the ground. All the theatres were operating and if you had the money—which we didn't—you could get an excellent meal. The buses and underground stopped operating at midnight, leaving many—mostly soldiers—stranded somewhere in the outskirts of the city.

One weekend when my friend "Irish" Knowles and I were in the city, we escorted two girls home to the North End and, of course, discovered we were stranded. We were at a place called Manor House, miles away from our hotel in the West End. We stopped to get a cup of tea and a biscuit at a tea wagon operating in a large square called Manor House. While we were drinking our tea, a gang of about eight young fellows, aged from about fourteen to seventeen, congregated. Some were bragging about having beaten up on a Yank soldier. Then they spotted us, and one of them started spitting in our direction. They were obviously looking for trouble, so we decided to leave. It was a bright moonlit night, and as we began walking across the broad square the gang came running toward us. I thought they were just cavorting until they came at us and tried to attack us.

One of them started to grapple with Irish, while I crouched and started circling in a fighting stance. Fortunately, they did not seem to know much about fighting. They came in trying to kick me and as a result were off-balance, so I managed to hit a couple of them, which caused them to back off. I then went over to help Irish. I hit the fellow he was struggling with in the mouth, and I think I broke some of his teeth, because he let out a scream and ran off. At that point a bunch of

RAF men came along and said, "If you fellows are going to fight, fight one at a time." I said, "Great!" and started to pound one of the punks until he begged me not to hit him any more, saying, "Me pants are falling down." By this time I was really angry and yelled, "Okay, come and get it, one at a time or any way you want it." A crowd of people had gathered, and since none of the young punks came forward, a civilian handed me my forage cap and said, "You'd better leave now. The police are coming, and you'll get the worst of it, because you've been drinking." I said I hadn't been drinking, but he said, "Anyone can tell you've been drinking, challenging the whole crowd like that." I guess in my rage I thought everyone was against us.

We left the scene, and as we wandered about trying to find a place to sleep, we gathered up half a dozen other stranded Canadians. Every place we went, we got the same answer: "No beds." There wasn't even room at the police station, which someone had told us was a good place to sleep for the night. Eventually, I got separated from Irish and found a hostel where they gave me a blanket and let me sleep on the floor. The lady who looked after me suggested I go to the washroom and clean up first. Until then I hadn't realized I was covered in blood from the brawl.

In 1942 George Eckenfelder left our section to take over a sister section, F ("Freddy") Section, which was attached to a sister artillery regiment, the Thirteenth Field Regiment. All the operators in the signals section had to man the telephone switchboard, which was tied into the headquarters of our division and to the civilian General Post Office (GPO) switchboard. (The post office ran the country's telephone system.) We would receive air raid warnings through the GPO lines and relay the message on to the duty officer of the artillery regiment. Each warning had a code word. There were code words for various situations, such as the different types of air raids and the anticipated "invasion." This list of code words was kept in a prominent place by the switchboard so the operator could refer to it.

One night, the operator on duty in "F" section, George Eckenfelder's new signals section, received an air raid warning "Red" from the south coast, looked up the code word for it, and gave the code word to the artillery duty officer at regimental headquarters. Unfortunately, the sleepy operator used the code word for "invasion" instead of the word for air raid warning "Red." The artillery duty officer immediately called divisional headquarters and gave the code word for the invasion, and inevitably the whole of South Eastern Command was on the move to repel the invasion! It took hours to countermand the orders and stop the process. George Eckenfelder, through no fault of his own, had to take the brunt of the blame for the debacle and was sent to North Africa as an observer with the Eighth Army. However, he returned to Third Canadian Divisional Signals in time to take part in the Normandy invasion.

Eventually, around 1943, we received new wireless sets, the No. 19 Set, which proved to be quite reliable and had enough power to ensure communication using radiotelephone (RT). Instead of Morse code, this became the standard for all forward units. In 1943 we were stationed at Christchurch, near Bournemouth, on the south coast. We enjoyed this location, especially since we were billeted in a house right across the street from a pub, which seemed to be the social centre for the area. We got to know the local people and made many friends there. It was the first time we had been billeted in a town and been given an opportunity to become acquainted with the local people. We also got to know the children who lived near our billets and they, of course, loved chocolate, which we gave them from the parcels we received from home. I remember one little girl telling us her sister had been to Canada. The sister had been evacuated to Canada at the start of the war and had lived there for a number of years before being brought back to England. The little girl said, "When she came back she didn't talk arf funny." So much for our Canadian accents.

From my time in England during the war, I gained an affection for English people that has remained to this day. I think most of the Canadian servicemen felt this way. Needless to say, many Canadians married British girls. I suppose there were lots of tall tales told about the big ranch the soldier owned back in Canada. I can imagine the sinking feeling some of the war brides must have had when they got off the train in some lonely spot on the Prairies. I think I felt sorriest for the women who married French Canadians from Quebec, where no one spoke a word of English. It is no wonder that some of the war brides gave up the struggle and went back to Britain. However, most of them stayed and became real Canadians—although it seems as though most of them had to make one trip back home before they finally decided that Canada was home. Our country is all the better because of them.

I've previously mentioned how I taught myself to box by reading the book *How to Box* back in Fort McMurray. It turned out that my interest in boxing continued beyond my boyhood years. I was an avid reader of the bible of boxing—*Ring* magazine—and knew the history of all the early fighters. I was a fan of Joe Louis, Sugar Ray Robinson, and our Canadian fighter Jimmy McLarnin. All three were true exponents of what I called "scientific" boxing and they were beautiful to watch as they threw their various punches. I don't suppose it is proper to call boxing a science as it is probably more of an art, but there is a correct way (and many wrong ways) to throw a punch.

After I joined the army, some of us often sparred with each other and it was evident that I was a much better boxer than most of the other fellows. I was talked into joining the Fourteenth Artillery Field Regiment's boxing team by Sergeant Eddie Lee. Eddie had been quite a prominent middleweight pro fighter before the war and had fought one of the best middleweights of that time, Ace Hudkins, in New York's Madison Square Garden. The team from the regiment entered the individual championships to represent the Third Canadian Division in the Canadian Army Championships in 1943. I had to box as a bantamweight—under 118 pounds (54 kg)—since this was the lightest class in the Canadian army, although I was really a flyweight—under 112 pounds (51 kg). I won my elimination fights and was scheduled to fight in the championships when I was notified that I had to go to the Isle of Man on a signals security course. I tried to get out of going and even had our artillery lieutenant colonel, Harold Griffin, try to intercede for me so I could go to the boxing finals. However, I was told I had to go on the course.

After the war I discovered why I was sent on the signals security course. Apparently, every few months a memo would come down from Canadian Military Headquarters (CMHQ) in London asking, "Who is this Cpl. Morimoto? Is he loyal? Should we not send him back to Canada?" My company commander, Major Henry Patterson from Calgary, consulted with my former section commander, Capt. George Eckenfelder. They were both quite indignant at CMHQ for questioning my loyalty, and so they put their heads together and came up with an idea: "Let's get the Brits to clear him!" Thus they had me sent on the signals security course with the British army. Henry Patterson, who later served as a judge on the Alberta Court of Queen's Bench, became a very close friend of mine after the war, and he told me how he and George had stopped the desk-bound bureaucrats at CMHQ from questioning my loyalty any further.

Even though I had tried to get out of it, the course on the Isle of Man turned out to be very interesting. To qualify to remain on the course, we had to pass a Morse code test of twenty words per minute in five-letter groups—five letters chosen randomly. Groups like this take considerably longer to send in Morse than plain language, because the five-letter groups have so many more long letters, such as "Q" (dash-dash-dot-dash) and "Y" (dash-dot-dash-dash). In plain language, there are a lot of short letters, such as "E" (dot), "T" (dash), "A" (dot-dash), and "N" (dash-dot). Twenty words per minute in five-letter code groups is equivalent to approximately twenty-four words per minute in plain language. I passed the entrance test, and the instructors then began to train us to print letters in a certain manner so we could print much faster. As a result we were soon reading and printing thirty five-letter groups a minute, which was the equivalent of thirty-six words per minute in plain language. We were also taught various means of maintaining security while using radiotelephone on our wireless sets.

During the war, the Isle of Man was used as a detention camp for interned civilian Italians in Britain. Most of the peacetime resort hotels and lodgings in Douglas, the main town on the island, were used for this purpose. I didn't get to see much of the Isle of Man during my three-week stay there, as I was concentrating on my studies for the course. Also because of the course I didn't have time to train, though there didn't seem to be much point in training, as the army boxing finals were to take place during the weekend my course ended. However, in the last week I received a letter telling me that if I could make it to Epsom by a certain date, I could still fight in the championships, as my replacement had not been able to make the weight.

I went to the officer in charge of the course and explained my situation. He said that since I had done well in the course and since the last two days were only a scheme, I could leave early. The next morning I left camp, not eating breakfast since it was only fried bread, and took the ferry to Liverpool across the Irish Sea. I'm not a very good sailor and it was quite rough, so I didn't feel too healthy when I got on shore. I caught the train to London, hoping to get something to eat when I got there, but somewhere en route the track was bombed and we had to sit for eight hours while it was repaired. I finally arrived in London, where I was unable to get anything to eat; it was 1:00 AM and I was lucky to find a place to sleep. At 6:30 that morning, I caught a train back to my section in Christchurch in the south of England, where I learned that I had to catch a train back to Epsom, near London. I finally got to Epsom at 6:00 PM and found out I had to fight in two hours. I won that fight and the one the next day and advanced to the finals. Unfortunately, I lost the final fight on points—I was out of shape because I hadn't been able to train and ran out of gas in the last round—and won the silver medal. ∎

The Invasion
of Europe

*P*rior to D-Day we made many practice landings with LCTs (Landing Craft, Tank), which carried several tanks. I was an operator in one of them. The Third Canadian Division had been made an armoured division for the assault landing, and all the vehicles, including tanks, were waterproofed. For the assault landing, the Artillery was supplied with American Self Pre-Propelled 105-mm guns rather than the 25-pounder guns that they normally fired. The guns were to be fired from the landing craft on their way to shore. We used Studland Bay, near Poole, as the practice landing beach and would sail around the English Channel for hours. Whenever I picture the Isle of Wight bobbing up and down, it almost makes me seasick. The flat-bottomed LCTs really bounced around in the choppy seas, and even the young sailors were seasick (most were boys, some fourteen to sixteen years old).

In early May 1944 we were put in camps in the south of England, where we were confined and not allowed out except for some dire emergency. The whole of south England had millions of men concentrated in it, along with thousands of vehicles, tanks, armaments, and supplies. Fortunately, the German Luftwaffe was not in control of the air and did not pose much of a threat. Also very fortunately, the Germans had not perfected their v-1 and v-2 rockets in time to deal with the beautiful targets that we must have presented. It was only when we embarked and were given money in French francs that we knew we were going to France. Not until we were at sea were we given maps and told that our destination was Normandy. I embarked at Southampton on an LST (Landing Ship, Tank) and was to land with a Jeep on Sword Beach, the British beach, but actually landed on Juno Beach, the Canadian beach. After taking a signals security course on the Isle of Man, I was transferred from my original section, which was attached to Artillery, to take over a section at divisional headquarters. We were due to land on 5 June but, because of bad weather, stayed in port an extra day and finally set out to land on 6 June 1944.

On the way across, we were given anti-seasickness pills, which we were told had been developed by Dr. Frederick Banting, the great Canadian doctor and co-inventor of insulin. We were assured that none of us would get seasick as the pills had had a ninety-five-percent success rate. Seasickness was no laughing matter. During our training some men became so incapacitated by it that they had to be carted off the ship like sacks of grain upon landing. These men had to be replaced by others for the D-Day landing simply because they became incapable of performing the most ordinary tasks in bad weather. On 6 June the weather was quite rough, and I soon began to feel queasy. I felt ashamed of myself because of the reported efficacy of the pills we had taken. I went to the head and there I saw some big military policemen puking their guts out. After that, I felt relieved I wasn't the only one who had become so seasick and let everything go.

When dawn broke on 6 June, it revealed an unforgettable sight: thousands of ships, seeming to reach forever across the sea, with their barrage balloons hoisted to keep off low-flying enemy aircraft. It was with a mixture of excitement and fear that I approached the beach on D-Day. I think what keeps every soldier going is that he doesn't think he'll be hit— it's the other unfortunate guy who is going to get it. To top it all off, I was still feeling a bit queasy and wanted to get my feet on dry land again.

The listing of my name on one of the monuments at the Canadian memorial
on the beach at Corseulles-sur-mer, Normandy.

Our landing was relatively easy as we weren't to land until H+1—
one hour after the first landing. However, there were a lot of problems
for some of the other landing craft. The craft that were to launch
rockets to blow up mines on the beaches were unable to arrive on
schedule because of the stormy weather and as a result a lot of vehicles
were disabled by mines once they hit the beaches. When we landed, we
were fortunate. We didn't even get wet, as our Jeep was able to
disembark in fairly shallow water. We eventually headed inland and set
up headquarters at a location near the present-day Canadian cemetery
at Beny-sur-Mer. We had a fairly small beachhead that was only several
miles inland from the beaches because of the stubborn German
defences. Our Third Canadian division, commanded by Major General
Rodney F. L. Keller, was still under the British Second Corps, which
was under the command of General Miles Dempsey. Our division,
along with the British Third and Fiftieth divisions, faced the bulk of the
German Panzer divisions. About two weeks after D-Day, a violent
storm caused havoc with Mulberry Harbour, which had been
constructed offshore to allow transport ships to unload, so the
escalation of troops and supplies coming ashore was delayed by several
weeks. Because of this we were on short rations for several weeks and
our division had to remain in the front line, with all the brigades in
action, for two months without a break. Usually, only two brigades

were kept in the front line at one time, with one brigade held to the rear in reserve.

Several days after D-Day we were bivouacked in what remained of some French barracks. Our vehicles were parked on an asphalt tarmac, and I was reluctant to dig a slit trench through that hard surface. However, I decided to dig one and we toiled all day, because it turned out there was hard limestone beneath the asphalt. This was true of most of the Normandy coast, and it was back-breaking labour to dig even a few feet. We had just finished digging shallow slit trenches, when a German aircraft flew over us just after dark and started dropping anti-personnel bombs. These bombs made the most piercing, wailing sounds and it felt like they were coming straight at us. The next morning we found an unexploded bomb not 10 feet (3 m) from our slit trench. These anti-personnel bombs were ideal for using on asphalt tarmac.

Soon after D-Day, George Eckenfelder, now a captain in charge of the signals section attached to the Thirteenth Field Artillery Regiment, was taken prisoner by the Germans. He and some other Canadian prisoners were kept in a cave a short distance inland from the beach. George could speak German and told the German officer in charge that the Canadians would soon overrun their forces and it would be prudent to surrender to prevent unnecessary bloodshed. He finally convinced the Germans to surrender and thus single-handedly captured 119 prisoners! On his way back to the Canadian lines, he met one of the signals corps personnel who had a Jeep and asked him for help in transporting the captured German weapons. George ended up coming back to his regiment escorting 119 prisoners and commandeering a Jeep full of captured weapons.

Looking back, I realize our tanks were hopelessly outclassed by those operated by the Germans. The German Tigers, with their 88-mm guns, were far superior to the American Sherman tanks with which our forces were equipped. The Shermans did not have heavy enough armour and caught fire very easily, so they were knocked out by the German Tigers like sitting ducks. If the guys inside were lucky enough to crawl out, they were usually badly burned. Apparently, some dunderheads in the upper echelons of the military believed quantity was superior to quality, so all that counted was that we had more tanks. But more is not always better and despite the thousands of Shermans produced and shipped from the United States and Canada, they still made wonderful cannon fodder for the German Tigers.

The summer of 1944 was hot and dry, so at least we didn't suffer from having to get wet in the rain. In the hot weather the many cattle and horses that had been killed by artillery or mortar fire putrefied and became masses of crawling maggots. The Normandy fields were divided by hedgerows that must have been centuries old and so fighting was difficult, going from hedgerow to hedgerow. Probably the scariest times were when we were bombed by our own aircraft. We were first hit by high-altitude American bombers in a daylight attack in which I lost several friends. Then, about a week later, the RAF Bomber Command, with a thousand heavy bombers, was set to bomb the enemy in a low-level, close-support role. However, because of poor liaison between the air force and the army over the significance of yellow smoke signals, bombs were dropped on our troops. It was the first time I had ever been so close to a Lancaster bomber that I could see the bomb-bay doors open and the bombs dropping. This was near Falaise, and I remember seeing men on bicycles pedalling as hard as they could down the road back to Caen.

We lost our divisional commander, Major General Rodney Keller, when he was wounded by the American bombs. He was replaced by Major General Dan Spry, the youngest major general in the army. After the closing of the Argentan-Falaise Gap, during which thousands of Germans were killed, our division came under the command of the First Canadian Army, under Lieutenant General H. D. G. (Harry) Crerar. Our Third Canadian Division was delegated to clean up the pockets of Germans left in the coastal cities of Boulogne and Calais. Then it was north to the Scheldt Estuary in Belgium.

The battle for the Scheldt Estuary, and for control of the port of Antwerp in Belgium, took place in the autumn of 1944 and was the most miserable campaign. The low-lying land was flooded with water by the Germans in an attempt to hinder our advance. It was next to impossible to find an inch of dry ground. One night, a friend of mine, a lineman who had a cable-laying vehicle, asked me to go to the city of Ghent with him. "Blackie" had several British "compopacks" of food and he wanted to sell them. These compopacks were carried as emergency rations, and the food in them was horrible, the most unappetizing conglomeration of tins of stew and other tasteless vegetables that you could imagine. The tea was a mixture of tea, sugar, and powdered milk that had to be mixed with water and boiled. The only good items were canned peaches, which seldom got to us anyway, as the personnel in the Army Service Corps would steal them first.

We drove down the main road to Ghent, which was only some 10 to 13 miles (15 to 20 km) away. We went into a café and Blackie had a deep discussion with the owner, following which we went out to the truck and lugged two compopacks into the courtyard behind the café. Blackie helped the owner hide them in a secure place and after getting his two thousand francs we left. As soon as we were out of sight, however, we stopped and Blackie climbed over several walls and snuck through several courtyards to the hiding place and retrieved the compopacks. We then went to another café, where he resold them to another proprietor for another two thousand francs. Blackie was a born con man. The last I saw of him was in Brussels, sometime after v-e Day. He told me he had been in a hospital in Brussels for something—I think for a rash on his arm that he kept irritating—and he had a half-dozen army blankets under his arm, which he was going to sell. Army blankets were in great demand after the war, as they made excellent wool coats for women.

Following the completion of the Scheldt Estuary campaign in late 1944, which brought the port of Antwerp into our hands, we pursued the German army through Belgium, where we were greeted as liberators. Then it was on to the Nijmegen area, where we were sent to relieve the American 81st and 101st Airborne Divisions, which had taken part in the ill-fated Arnheim operation known as Operation Market Garden. We were to remain dug in on the west bank of the Rhine near Nijmegen for the rest of that very cold winter. Most of us dug trenches, which we covered over with anything we could find to try to keep warm. We spent Christmas there and for the first time became acquainted with Saint Nicholas and his black servant who brought presents to the Dutch children. There was a sanatorium close by operated by Catholic nuns, so we got to know them and the inmates. We gave them what we could of our rations and of what we received in parcels from home, for which they were very grateful.

In the spring we finally crossed the Rhine River into Germany, using vehicles that had been developed to travel both on land and water. Once a bridgehead had been established, the engineers installed Bailey bridges, so our vehicles were soon streaming across.[1] As soon as we were across the Rhine, we set about establishing a command post. We were setting up in a farmyard and I had been digging a slit trench, but when some chickens started to run about I started chasing them, trying to hit one with my shovel. While I was doing this, Bruce Haeberle, who had been helping me dig the trench, was hit by mortar fire. He took a piece of shrapnel that went up through his throat and came out of his cheek below his eye. I tried to stop the bleeding with a field dressing and drove him to a nearby Field Ambulance. The tent was full of wounded men groaning and moaning, so I got out of there quickly. I never saw Bruce again but heard that he did recover. Those chickens had saved my life; if I had stayed at the slit trench, I would very likely have been hit by shrapnel.

After I had returned to the command post, a lieutenant came by and told us to stop chasing the chickens, but that evening I took one of my men and crept into the henhouse nearby. All the chickens were roosting and were easy to snatch. We grabbed a chicken under each arm and snuck back to our truck. On the way, one of the chickens squawked and a sentry called, "Who goes there?" but we just kept running. (I later learned that the way to nab a chicken is to quickly grab it by the neck, tuck it under your arm, and tightly hold the neck so it can't make a sound.) The next day one of the hens laid an egg, and when we killed it there were several more eggs inside, so we had eggs for the first time in a couple of years. We then took our chickens and using vegetables from a German garden made a delicious chicken stew.

In April 1945, toward the end of the war, I was sent to Catterick in Yorkshire, England, on a course to learn about the No. 9 Set, which was higher powered than the No. 19 Set that was standard issue for army use. The No. 9 Set had a longer range and was used for communications between the army and the rear. We understood that our division was going to send a brigade on a swift thrust across the north of Germany toward Denmark. At this time, I was promoted to lance sergeant and was to be in charge of a set to communicate with our headquarters. We had visions of oodles of eggs and butter and pretty girls in Denmark. I left from Ostend, Belgium, on a small ship, landed at the mouth of the Thames, and then took a train to Catterick in Yorkshire. For one week we took instructions on the No. 9 Set and then went on a scheme to the Lake District. We had a wonderful time in the mountainous area of the Lake District. On Saturday night we went to a dance at the local community hall and I was surprised to see everyone doing reels and dances that seemed so similar to our square dancing back home. Thinking back on it now, I shouldn't have been so surprised at the similarities given that so many Hudson's Bay Company personnel came from this part of the country. A very kind lady took me home and let me sleep in her son's room. Her son was in the army in the Far East. In the morning she cooked me a wonderful English breakfast.

After the course, I left to return to Germany but had a week's leave before going back. I arrived in London on V-E Day amidst the most riotous celebration. Since the war was now over, I did something I had never done before. I took my leave pass and added a "1" in front of the return date, granting myself an extra ten days leave. When I arrived back at my unit, my commanding officer said, "Oh, here you are. We wondered what had happened to you." That was all that was said. With the end of the war—by which time we were in northern Germany, near the port of Hamburg—we were sent back to Holland, to the city of Utrecht.

Before being assigned to billets in Utrecht, we stayed in a local park. When we arrived there, our kitchens were set up and the cooks prepared our evening meal, which was ladled out onto our mess tins as we queued up as usual. However, we found ourselves surrounded by dozens of kids hungrily eyeing the food with such big eyes that I couldn't eat and gave my dinner away to some of them. We had never seen starving people before, and it really shook us. As the days went on, food was brought in and gradually the situation was rectified, but we were always surrounded by kids looking for chocolate or anything else we could give them.

Our unit was eventually placed in some army barracks, and we settled into the boredom of army routine. This was offset to some extent by sightseeing trips to other areas. As lance sergeant, I was put in charge of sports and I had to turn in a report on the various activities for each day. I tried to organize softball and soccer games, but in the warm summer weather no one wanted to do anything. It got so that when I tried to get a game going, everyone would tell me to FO. Needless to say, it was a frustrating assignment.

It was about this time that we were told that the combined Allied Command in Europe planned to stage a huge boxing tournament late in 1945, which was to involve all of the Allied armies. Accordingly, our Third Division established a boxing training camp in Utrecht, and as I was the divisional bantamweight champion, I was invited to attend the camp. I was so fed up with trying to organize sports among the signals sections, it was with great relief that I jumped at the offer in July 1945. I lived in the sergeants' quarters and ate in the sergeants' mess at a Medical Field Ambulance unit. We would start training at 9:00 AM and finish at noon, have lunch, and then do roadwork in the afternoon. In the army there was no distinction between professional and amateur boxers, so there were a lot of ex-pros either instructing or training to fight. I learned more about boxing during the two months I spent there than I had ever learned before. Among the pros who were instructing us were Billy Macrea, who had been the welterweight champion of western Canada, and Maxie Spoon, a Jewish middleweight from Montreal. There is a certain kind of camaraderie between boxers that I can't explain or quite describe. I noticed this afterward in civilian life when I met fellows like Tiger Fischer, who had been a good professional middleweight before the war. We became instant friends and remained so for many years.

Some years after the war, I and my young son drove to Prince Albert, Saskatchewan, to see Tommy Settee, a Métis who had been with the Regina Rifles in our division and had become welterweight champion of the Canadian army. He had spindly legs but the upper body of a much heavier man and a terrific punch. After the war he became a pro in Calgary and was western Canadian welterweight champion several years from 1946 on. He had been wounded at Caen in Normandy and was receiving a pension, so he changed his name to Deschambeault because he thought the government might question him about receiving a pension when he was able to fight professionally. He had become a barber in Prince Albert and was really pleased to see me. He asked me, "Are you handling any boys?" Meaning, was I managing any boxers? It was a natural enough question for one boxer to ask another. I replied I didn't have anything to do with the fight game any more. Although I loved boxing, I realized it was a dangerous sport and I had been fortunate not to have sustained any brain damage. Blows to the head can cause serious injury to the brain and because of this, when I became a father I didn't allow my son to box.

Soon after the Americans dropped the atomic bombs on Hiroshima and Nagasaki and the announcement of V-J Day, my number came up to return to Canada and I arrived back in England to await the sailing of the ship that would take me home. The sailing date was determined by the number of points I had accumulated. All personnel were awarded points based upon the number of months they had been overseas and whether they were married or single. I had been overseas for sixty-two months. The Canadians who were still languishing in Holland and England were quite miffed that the Americans, who had been away from home for a much shorter time, were getting the bulk of the shipping. The Canadians in England were given leave until their time for departure came. However, they soon ran out of money and became quite restive. Many of them resented the shopkeepers in the town of Aldershot because they felt they took servicemen for everything they could whenever they shopped there. At any rate, a bunch of Canadians rioted one evening and looted the stores in Aldershot. Some were sentenced to five and ten years in prison. I was thankful that I was in London at the time, especially since I believe the Canadians who were arrested were just picked at random. I'm sure if I had been there, I'd have been picked out quite easily.

While in camp in England we were subjected to a "rehabilitation course" for a week, which was supposed to prepare us for our return to civvy street. All it consisted of was lectures with graphs and tables showing that about nine hundred thousand men would be demobilized, all of whom would be fighting for jobs, and that it just stood to reason that there weren't nine hundred thousand jobs available. The solution? "Stay in the Army."

At the end of the course each soldier was interviewed by an officer. I met with a young lieutenant who asked me what I intended to do when I got back to Canada. I told him I was going to university. He did everything to try to dissuade me, telling me that at twenty-seven I would be too old and would be at least thirty-one when I graduated. When I insisted that I still intended to attend university, he said, "Well, you may not be able to get in because of your race. They might not accept you." I had discovered during my time in the service that you can say almost anything to an officer as long as you follow it up with "Sir," so I replied, "I don't give a damn what you say sir. I intend to go to university." Thus ended the interview. I've often wished I could have met that lieutenant years later, but I didn't even know his name. If I had met him, I would have revelled in telling him that I had received my Master of Science degree in chemical engineering despite his trying to dissuade me.

Finally, in September 1945, my turn came up to return to Canada on board the Cunard ship the *Scythia*. The crossing was very rough, and I was quite seasick the first two days but then felt fine and enjoyed the rest of the trip. I, along with many others, landed at Halifax and began the long train ride via the CPR to Calgary. This time we did not have to ride in colonist cars, so I enjoyed the trip across Canada. It was a treat to get ice cream and order eggs for breakfast. I especially loved hearing the women and children speak. I hadn't realized how much more nasal our Canadian accent is than the English. I guess that's how we sounded to them. I could better understand why that little girl in Christchurch said her sister "didn't talk arf funny" when she came back to England from Canada. It was the first time in almost five years that I had heard the voices of Canadian women and children.

On arriving back in Calgary I received a month's leave and immediately went to Fort McMurray, where my father and younger brothers still lived. It was wonderful to see my father again. Only my two youngest brothers were living with him, as the others had left home. I was pleased to hear that my family hadn't suffered the same treatment as that encountered by Japanese-Canadians in British Columbia. Since Fort McMurray was inland, the authorities did not force them to leave their homes and go to camps. However, I was surprised to find that men in my own outfit, the Royal Canadian Corps of Signals, were still based in Fort McMurray and receiving several times the pay I had received overseas—all for the "safety" of Canada. Needless to say, I took a dim view of this, but there wasn't much I could do about it. During the war the top echelon of officers in the Signal Corps was predictably made up of permanent force men, and they jealously guarded the monopoly they had on northern communication. This was presumably because they wanted to return to it after the war. This was also understandable, since the allowances for northern service were several times the regular army pay and undoubtedly accounts for the Signal Corps maintaining the status quo of the Northern Radio System throughout the war. What is more difficult to understand is that able-bodied soldiers stayed in Canada during the war to perform a civilian function, while their brothers-in-arms fought overseas—all with the blessing of the corps's hierarchy. Eventually, in 1959, the Signals Corps lost the NWT and Y Radio System to the Department of Transport. I think this was long overdue and should have occurred during the war years.

Another thing disturbed me: presumably on the instructions of the Mounties, the warrant officer in charge of the signals station, who had been my teammate on the signals hockey team, used to make periodic visits to my father's house to inspect the remains of my old radio equipment, which I had gathered when I had been a radio "ham." There were no radio receivers or transmitters, nothing but a lot of old junk, like coils and condensers. My father knew nothing about radio anyway, and so even if there had been receivers and transmitters he wouldn't have known what to do with them. Any radio man would have known at a glance that there was nothing there to worry about. How they could ever imagine that my old father could fashion together anything out of this junk to communicate with the enemy, I could not—and still cannot—fathom. All this took place while I was risking my life overseas and about to land in France on D-Day and go through the whole Northwest Europe Campaign until V-E Day. And all the while these signals personnel were sitting safely at home in Canada.

I would not have been too surprised at this happening in British Columbia, where there was considerable hysteria during the war about the supposed threat that Japanese-Canadians posed to security. However, this occurred in Fort McMurray in northern Alberta, where my family was well known and there seemed to be less anti-Japanese feeling than on the coast.

I am pleased to say that I encountered very little racial prejudice because of my Japanese origin while in the army. I suffered none whatsoever in my own unit and can recall only two minor incidents that occurred during the whole war. One was with an old fogey medical officer while we were stationed at Barriefield, Ontario. While I was waiting to get a medical test, I could hear him yelling, "What the hell's that Jap doing in the Army?" The other incident involved an operator in another section, who one evening after he had been drinking asked me in a sneering tone, "Have you got any relatives over there?" I had never had any contact with him before this and don't know why he said it, other than he may have been jealous of my operating ability—he was an excellent operator himself and was perhaps feeling a little competitive. Later on, especially after the war, he became a friend. The only big problem I had—one that I was not aware of at the time—involved the inquiries about my loyalty from a pencil-pusher at Canadian Military Headquarters in London, as I have previously mentioned. All in all, I encountered more prejudice after the war than I did during the war. I think this illustrates the fairness of the men who were my comrades and justifies my pride in having served with them.

I have been asked what my thoughts were on the atom bombing of Japan by the Americans in view of my Japanese heritage and that my parents must have had relatives living in Japan at the time. I don't think my father had any relatives in Japan at the time of the bombing, since he was an only child and his mother had died some years before the war. As far as I know, he wasn't in contact with anyone in Japan. My mother had a brother and a sister who immigrated to Formosa (now Taiwan) before the war. She also had a sister who immigrated to the United States.

As for my feelings regarding the A-bombs, I believe that the militaristic regime in Japan had to be ousted and that dropping an A-bomb may have been the only way to convince them to surrender. However, I feel that the bomb could have been dropped on a military target, rather than on the civilian population of Hiroshima. I also think that more time should have been taken before deciding to drop the second bomb on Nagasaki; I believe that second bomb strike was unnecessary.

I should point out that I enlisted as a volunteer during the dark days of 1940, when the German army was overrunning Europe, and I felt that our whole Western world was being threatened by Hitler's Nazis. Although Japan was not in the war when I enlisted, it became an ally of Germany after Pearl Harbor, thus becoming my enemy as well. ■

PART FOUR

ESTABLISHING A CAREER

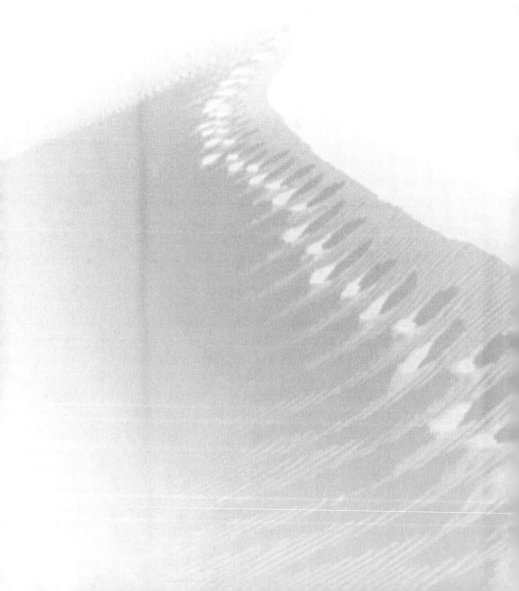

Back to
Civvy Street

*A*fter a few weeks back home in Fort McMurray and a trip to Yellowknife, I got my discharge in Calgary on 31 October 1945. I then went to Edmonton and made arrangements to enrol in engineering at the University of Alberta. Under a program of the Department of Veterans Affairs, I was able to receive a month's free tuition for each month I had served in the military. Contrary to what my army rehabilitation officer had tried to cram down my throat, I was welcomed at the U of A because of my good marks in high school. The term was to start in January 1946, rather than in September. This was a special class to accommodate returning vets and allow us to catch up to the regular class that had started in September 1945.

Before entering university I attended a refresher high school course held at the old Technical School in Edmonton. To my pleasant surprise, two of my old teachers from Eastwood High School were teaching there, Mr. Sim and Mr. Younic. I had been out of school for over eleven years, so I had a lot of catching up to do. I had always intended on going to university but was unable to do so after I left high school because it was too expensive. It was a godsend to receive the free tuition under the Veterans Act.

In 1946, the U of A campus was still quite small when compared with the present-day maze of large buildings, with their sophisticated equipment, and a student enrolment of some 28,000. The enrolment in 1943–44 had been only 2,023, but the influx of veterans after the war more than doubled that number, peaking student enrolment at 4,865 in 1947–48. With this student influx the campus became overcrowded. To compound the physical drawbacks caused by this overcrowding, there was a shortage of capable professors, especially in chemical engineering. It was a good thing that Dr. George Govier, having received his doctorate from the University of Michigan (where he had worked under the great Dr. Donald L. Katz), returned to Alberta during my third year. Listening to Dr. Govier, I began to comprehend what the science of chemical engineering was all about. Soon afterward, two great chemical engineers, Dr. Donald Robinson and Dr. Donald Quon, arrived to round out an outstanding staff. We were fortunate to have three such brilliant men as our mentors.

Getting through first-year university was the most difficult thing I had ever done, and I felt like giving up several times. However, I kept going and each year got easier. On New Year's Day 1946, an event happened that changed my life: I met the girl who became my wife. My father had known her father years before when he lived in Edmonton. So, I went to visit him and there I met Kim Iriye, who was teaching school north of Edmonton and was home for the Christmas holidays. We went to see a movie on New Year's Eve, and I fell for her hook, line, and sinker. We got married during the Easter holidays and rented a room from the parents-in-law of my army pal "Mac" Macdonald. This Scottish couple, "Mom" and "Pop" Browning, became like a mother and father to us, and we lived with them for a year before we were able to buy an old house in East Edmonton. While I was going to university, Kim got a job at a correspondence school in Edmonton, which gave lessons to children in outlying districts by mail. My first year of university was followed by my second year with a break of only about two weeks in between, allowing my class to catch up with the September 1946 class in September 1947.

Following my second year of university, I got a summer job with Jimmy Mason, doing plane-table geological mapping at Yellowknife. Jimmy was the manager of some gold mining prospects a few miles north of Yellowknife—the Lynx and the Crestaurum properties. I had known him during my early days in Yellowknife and was pleased to get a summer job, as they were not too plentiful. We spent a delightful summer mapping the two properties. Plane-table mapping is used to make extremely detailed topographic maps on site, using surveying techniques. I had not used a plane table before, but Hugh Baker, who operated the other plane table, and I quickly became experts at using them.

During that summer we lived in tents with floors and walls made from lumber and were quite comfortable. We had a wonderful cook, and the meals were excellent. Our boss was a geologist named Rye Casselman, whose wife, Marg, and young baby son were living with him in a tent. It must have been pretty tough for Marg living there through the winter, but she seemed to thrive on it.

It was a pleasure to discover that some of my old Negus friends— Charlie Botham, "Gentleman" Jock Mackinnon, and Sam Daigle— were operating the diamond drill rig on the Lynx property while we were doing the mapping. They were working for my old friend Jim Kelly, and it was a real delight to meet up with them again. Unfortunately, the Lynx property didn't seem to carry any ore, even though it had large quartz veins. After completing our work on the Lynx claims, we moved on to map the Crestaurum property that was just to the north. These claims seemed to have the makings of a mine. We saw a considerable amount of free gold in a trench across the main vein and also discovered some new veins during our mapping. However, I'm not sure whether any further development work was ever carried out on the property.

By September 1947 I was back in Edmonton to begin my third

year of university. At that time, engineering students took all the same courses in their first two years, but then had to decide by their third year what discipline to follow. I chose chemical engineering and have often been asked why I chose it as a career. From the time I was a boy, my father had wanted me to become a doctor, but after viewing mangled bodies during the war, the idea of working in such an atmosphere did not appeal to me. Because of my background as a radio operator, I thought that perhaps electrical engineering would be a good fit. During first year, though, I soon discovered that electrical engineering would be very boring for me. Since I did well in my chemistry course, it seemed that chemical engineering would be a good choice, although later I learned there is a lot more to chemical engineering than just chemistry. In chemistry, you learn how chemicals react or behave. In chemical engineering, you utilize this information in a practical way by employing processes called "unit operations" (e.g., distillation) to produce a desired product. It was fortunate that even in my ignorance I ended up choosing a career I enjoyed.

Following my third year of university, I got a job with the construction company that was building the Imperial Oil Refinery at Edmonton. Because of the shortage of material following the war, Imperial had purchased the Canol refinery at Whitehorse in the Yukon. This refinery had been built during the war to process crude oil from Fort Norman in the Northwest Territories. A pipeline from Fort Norman to Whitehorse had also been constructed to supply crude to the refinery. However, with the end of the war there was no need for the refinery. With the discovery of oil at Leduc in 1947, Imperial Oil needed a refinery at Edmonton so it purchased the Canol refinery, dismantled it, and shipped it to Edmonton.

My first job was as a ditchdigger at various areas around the site that required hand-digging. I found it hard work at first, because I had not done any hard manual labour since before the war. However, I soon toughened up and enjoyed getting in shape again. Several weeks later I was promoted to be welder Jack Rusk's helper. Jack was a superb welder and, unlike most of the welders, could do acetylene welding as well as electric-arc welding. I spent a most enjoyable summer working with him and learned something about pipefitting and welding, which helped me later on.

In September 1948 it was back to university for my final year. I graduated in the spring of 1949 "with distinction"—but so did eleven or so others out of the class of fifty-eight students. Our class contained outstanding men who became leaders in the Canadian business world, people such as Dick Reid, who became president of Imperial Oil; Jack Stabback, who became head of the National Energy Board; Doug Craig, who became head of the Alberta Conservation Board; and Vern Horte, who became president of Trans Canada Pipelines. Almost all of the members of our class were veterans. I believe the Veterans Act was one of the best investments ever made by a Canadian government (in addition to free tuition for each month served, qualified veterans got sixty dollars a month), as the success of the graduates from the University of Alberta must have been duplicated in every university in Canada. They improved the fabric of Canadian society in every respect.

Before I graduated I had an interview with Dr. George Govier, the head of the chemical engineering department at the University of Alberta (and later the head of the Alberta Conservation Board). George had one of the finest engineering minds I have ever encountered. He had the knack of being able to grasp what the problem was and come to the heart of it. He asked me what I intended to do after graduation. I replied that I wanted to go into industry and use my chemical engineering. Although he had no racial prejudice whatsoever, he was afraid others might not feel the same way. He urged me to consider doing research work since I had a logical mind and would probably do well in that area. I told him that I'd been a lance sergeant in the army with a section of men under me and had never had trouble getting people to do what I asked, so we left it at that.

None of this was of much consequence after I graduated, though, because I couldn't get an engineering job anywhere and it didn't have anything to do with my cultural background. There was a recession in

Canadian Pacific

AIR LINES

LIMITED

MUNICIPAL AIRPORT.
EDMONTON, ALBERTA

February 10th, 1948.

<u>TO WHOM IT MAY CONCERN</u>

<u>THOMAS E. MORIMOTO</u>

        I have known Mr. Morimoto since 1929 and take great pleasure in highly recommending him as to his character and ability.

        Mr. Morimoto worked for me at Ft. McMurray off and on for two or three years before he joined the armed services at the beginning of the war. He spent 5½ years in the Signal Corps and obtained the rank of Sgt.

        He is now going through for a chemical engineer in his third year. I am thoroughly convinced from past experience that he will be an asset to any organization requiring his services.

                        W. R. MAY
           Director of Northern Development

WRW/MA

The letter of recommendation Wop May wrote for me in 1948 when I was nearing the end of my engineering degree.

1949, and there were very few engineering positions available. I went across the street from our house on the south side of Edmonton (we had sold our house in east Edmonton and moved to the south side) and got a job as a carpenter's helper with Aldritt Construction, which was building houses in the area. After two weeks, I got a new job with the City of Edmonton engineering department as a draftsman. The city's sewer maps were a hodgepodge, with different maps for each area and with a different scale on each one. My job was to go through all the old records and consolidate them into standard drawings with a standard scale. I started at the east end of the city and worked west.

Meanwhile I had applications in for several positions, and after several months at the drafting job, I received three offers almost at once. One was from the Defence Research Board in Ottawa. Another was from the Standard Chemical Company in Toronto, through Dr. J. R. Donald, who was probably the foremost consulting engineer in Canada at the time. Dr. Donald was very kind to me and I appreciated his efforts in getting me a job offer. The position I finally accepted five months after graduation was from the Research Council of Alberta, right at home in Edmonton. I was pleased to get this position as a research engineer as there were twenty-six applicants from all over Canada vying for it. In addition, it allowed me to use my research work as the basis of my thesis for my Master's degree in chemical engineering.

I soon settled into the routine of working at the Research Council. My research project was on the "cleaning of coal," which meant reducing the ash content of coal. Alberta coal has a high content of ash, and we wanted to lower this percentage to produce a much better quality fuel. The chairman of the Research Council was Dr. Robert Newton, who had just retired as president of the University of Alberta. My real boss was Mr. W. A. (Bert) Lang. He had been with the Research Council for many years under the tutelage of its original head, Mr. Edgar Stansfield. After hearing the stories about Mr. Stansfield, I could understand Mr. Lang's attitudes and actions. He had been schooled during the depths of the Depression by a man who used to save string, which he would wind into a large ball, and used envelopes, which he would slit and use for scratch pads. Mr. Lang was no different from his stringent mentor. During his summer vacation, I was delegated to take his place and had to do various analyses. One day, a leak occurred in the copper tubing of a small vessel used for analysis and I was using a soldering iron to repair the leak when Mr. Lang came by and asked what I was doing. I told him about the leak and he said, "Why don't you just use chewing gum or something to plug it?"

After considerable reading about the different methods used to clean coal, I decided to use a hydraulic cyclone separator for my research to try to remove ash from fine coal. Because I had been told there were only limited funds available to spend on the project, I set about building most of my own equipment. However, near the end of the year I discovered the ways of civil servants. The Research Council was given a certain amount of money to spend on equipment each year. For most of the year we had to pinch pennies, but as the end of the year came we were told to come up with things to purchase as we had a surplus that had to be spent, otherwise our appropriation for the following year would be cut. I am sure this same procedure is followed in all civil service departments and explains why our governmental spending has ballooned to such astronomical amounts and why we sometimes have such huge deficits.

Our research quarters were on the second floor of the old North Lab building on the U of A campus, with the mining department occupying the first floor. The head of that department was Dr. Karl Clark and Ewold Lilge was his assistant. I had first seen Dr. Clark in Fort McMurray when he was building a tar sands research plant on the Clearwater River near Waterways. When I told him I was from Fort McMurray, he seemed to take a fatherly interest in me and became my mentor and a treasured friend. Whenever I wanted some advice or to talk over a problem, I would go and talk it out with him.

Dr. Clark was one of the most clear-thinking men I've ever known, and I'm pleased that he has been recognized for his achievements in the field of tar sands technology. I had taken an undergraduate course in metallurgy from him and received valuable advice about writing engineering reports. He impressed on me the importance of writing clear, straightforward reports without any gobbledygook. He said, "The people who will be reading your reports when you get out into the real world will most likely be presidents or vice-presidents who

Me in 1952, after graduating with my Master of Science degree in chemical engineering.
I had also just become a father to our son, Dana.

won't understand technical jargon, so you have to make your reports
understandable to men like that." I never forgot what he said and later
tried to teach my young engineers the same thing.

While working at the Research Council, I took several post-graduate
courses in chemical engineering toward my Master's degree from Dr.
Govier, Dr. Don Robinson, and Dr. Don Quon. I found studying after
working during the day to be a real chore, and it was further

compounded by the birth of our son, Dana. Kim had left her job at the correspondence school to be at home with him. It was a relief to finally be done my oral exam and receive my Master of Science degree in chemical engineering in 1952. The oral was not as bad as I had feared. I think it's a nerve-wracking ordeal for anyone to go through—it isn't easy facing a panel of professors from several disciplines who can theoretically question you on anything you have taken at university.

The year 1951 was an important year for Kim and me. It was the year our son, Dana, was born. We were overjoyed and were indeed fortunate to have him, as we later discovered that Kim couldn't have any more children. I happily donned my new role as a parent, enjoying this new experience. It was a delight to watch Dana progress as he was so bright (he was tested with an IQ of 160 during his young school years). However, within a few years we had another child in our family. My brother Bob and his wife divorced and he was left with his daughter, two-year-old Beverly. Since he obviously couldn't give her the care she required while working at his job in Uranium City, Saskatchewan, we assumed the responsibility. At first Dana reacted quite jealously, but he eventually got over it. Both Kim and I are pleased with how Beverly has turned out. She has a wonderful husband, Len Brown, and two children, Duncan and Kimiko. After a career as a top-ranking pastry chef with a prestigious hotel in New York City, she and Len now own a successful inn on Salt Spring Island, British Columbia.

In 1952, the Celanese Corporation of America—its Canadian subsidiary was Canadian Chemical Company Limited—started building a large petrochemical complex just outside the Edmonton city limits at Clover Bar. Since I was not interested in continuing with coal research and wanted to begin doing process-design engineering, I jumped at the opportunity that Canadian Chemical seemed to present. I applied for a position with the company and was happy to be accepted as a process engineer. I first began working as an inspector on construction. The plant was being built by the large American firm Brown & Root, which was based in Houston, Texas. The complete design was done in its Houston office and comprised process design, civil, electrical, and instrumentation engineering. Each week we would receive large batches of engineering drawings from Houston. My job was to see that the construction complied with Brown & Root's drawings.

After a year, the plant was completed and start-up was begun. Most of the engineering staff was sent into the plant to help with the start-up, but I was kept in the office. Although I was bitterly disappointed at not getting the start-up experience, the engineering experience I gained was probably much more valuable, even though I didn't know it at the time. Since I was the only engineer in the office other than the chief engineer, the chief process engineer, and the chief mechanical engineer, the chief process and chief mechanical engineers fought over my services. I was given not only process engineering (chemical engineering) projects but also mechanical engineering projects to execute. As a result, I gained valuable mechanical engineering experience that I would not otherwise have acquired. We had a wonderful mentor in the chief engineer, Dave Keck, as well as in the assistant production superintendent, Clint Wurzback. These two believed that a process engineer should be an all-round engineer and should know mechanical engineering as well. I learned a lot in those few months and did all sorts of engineering jobs that helped me later on.

When the plant was finally started up, the rest of the engineering staff came back into the office. However, a part of the formaldehyde concentration unit was having problems—the recovery of formaldehyde was only at fifteen percent. Formaldehyde was one of many chemicals that formed during the oxidation of propane in the reaction furnace of the primary oxidation unit at Canadian Chemical. The main function of the formaldehyde concentration unit was to separate formaldehyde from the other chemicals present. Formaldehyde is used as the basis for other chemicals, especially alkyd resins. I was sent with two other engineers into the plant on night shift to see if we could straighten out the problem. I was finally getting my operating experience. We were on night shift for three months, and as far as I could ascertain we didn't do anything to account for any change in the operation. However, we were told that we had done a terrific job and had brought the recovery up from fifteen percent to ninety-two percent. I think that the operators on night shift, all being new, had been playing with the dials on the instruments and causing upsets in the towers. Since there were so many towers in the series, an upset in one tower carried over to the next, so the whole system was affected.

I was glad to get out of the night shift job, especially since our clothes got so smelly from getting wet when we drained some of the chemicals. The process developed by Celanese consisted of oxidizing propane and butane with air in a furnace. The resultant products were a hodgepodge so diverse that no one knew what all of them were. The main products we wanted to recover were alcohol, acetaldehyde, and formaldehyde. The methyl alcohol, or methanol, was sold as a finished product. The acetaldehyde was used to make acetic acid, which was then combined with cellulose to manufacture cellulose acetate. The formaldehyde was also employed to form pentaerythritol (used as a paint solvent) and sold to other companies to use to manufacture alkyd resins. The materials left over from the formaldehyde concentration unit were sent to a pressure vessel from which they were periodically drained into the sewer. I mentioned that our clothes got smelly from these foul-smelling liquids, so smelly that we didn't dare ride home on the bus!

The waste chemicals were drained into a sewer that ran directly into the North Saskatchewan River. During the plant's construction, I had noticed in the drawings that these chemicals were going to the river, but when I questioned whether this should be done I was told to keep quiet and not discuss the matter. The Americans at that time must have thought that Canadians didn't know anything and what they didn't know wouldn't hurt them. The North Saskatchewan River's stream flow varies tremendously from summer to winter, with the flow in winter dropping to about a tenth of the maximum summer volume. As a result, when winter came, the concentration of the chemicals in the water increased tenfold and the water downriver at Prince Albert became undrinkable. John Diefenbaker, the future Canadian prime minister, was then an opposition Member of Parliament for Prince

Albert and raised such a fuss in the House of Commons about the pollution that the federal government finally sent some people to investigate. The attitude of the management was, in my opinion, idiotic and put us in a very difficult position, as we were told not to say anything to the investigators.[1]

Within a few months the management capitulated and a program was set up to impound some of the more evil-smelling compounds and limit the amount of chemicals drained into the sewers going to the river. To this end, the company's chemical engineers had to take periodic samples of the sewer effluent and test them for odour. Each sample was diluted until no smell could be detected. For example, if a sample had to be diluted by a ratio of 1:100, the odour number was 100. If a ratio of 1:1,000 existed, the number was 1,000. In effect, the higher the odour number, the more unacceptable the sample. A limit was set on the odour number that would be acceptable to Alberta's department of health, and a panel of three chemical engineers from our company decided on the odour number for each sample. Each sample was tested by both the company's panel and the provincial health department. Although I had never realized it before, I found out I had a very poor sense of smell and, happily for me, was kicked off the panel.

After working on various routine engineering jobs involving plant operations at Canadian Chemical, I was given a project to manufacture a chemical called methyl ethyl ketone. The manufacturing process was based upon a Shell patent that had expired, and I was instructed to prepare a process design using what information I could glean from it. The project necessitated the complete grassroots design of a unit (a miniature plant). It entailed process design of the unit, mechanical engineering, which included making scale drawings of the required piping and control instrumentation, civil and electrical engineering to manufacture the catalyst, and the construction and start-up of the unit. It was an interesting and valuable experience for me, designing something from scratch (even manufacturing the catalyst), utilizing existing equipment in an operating plant, overseeing the construction, and then starting up the unit. All my work paid off in the end—the new methyl ethyl ketone unit worked perfectly from the beginning.

Canadian Chemical was having a difficult time, however. Because there was such a small margin of profit in the chemicals it produced—sometimes only one or two cents per pound of product, I discovered—it was difficult for the company to compete given the high freight charges from Edmonton to eastern markets or to foreign markets via rail to Vancouver. I was one of only two engineers who got a raise of twenty-five dollars per month after two years of working for the company. I couldn't see the situation improving in the future, so when Polymer Corporation from Sarnia, Ontario, came west to recruit engineers, I applied for a job with it. The artificial rubber business would prove more profitable than the petrochemical business.

When Polymer Corporation made me a job offer, Kim and I decided to leave Alberta, moving to Sarnia in the summer of 1955. We were advised by my friend Bob "Chooch" Geddes, one of my fellow process engineers at Canadian Chemical, to take the combined train-boat trip from Calgary to Toronto. He told me that the CPR ran a train from Calgary once or twice a week that was met by a boat at Fort William, Ontario. The boat would take us to Midland on Lake Ontario, where we would disembark and then go by rail the short distance to Toronto. I should mention here that Chooch was given that name because of his love of trains. He knew the schedule of every train that operated in North America. He loved trains so much that he used to take the train from Edmonton's south side Strathcona Station over to the north side, rather than take the bus. Once when he was late for work at the plant, he went to the railway station and got a ticket to the siding near the plant site. He had to help the ticket agent find the ticket, as the agent had never heard of the stop. When I told Chooch that our ticket agent had said we would not have to change trains between Calgary and Fort William, Chooch said the agent was wrong and that he was sure we had to change at Winnipeg. I thought the ticket agent probably knew what he was talking about and disregarded Chooch's warning. Sure enough, though, while we were sitting in our train car at Winnipeg, some train men came running to tell us we had to change trains at once.

Our suite on the train was a real treat. Travelling with two small children is no picnic (Dana was four and Beverly was five), but because of the suite we had no problems with them bothering other passengers. The CPR meals in those days were world class and we ate like royalty. The boat ride on Lake Superior and Lake Huron was also a perfect holiday. I regret that the CPR no longer has this service, as I would have liked to take that trip again.

We arrived in Sarnia at the beginning of July in the midst of a heat wave that was the most severe they'd had in years. Coming from Alberta's dry climate, we were really affected by the heat and humidity and wondered whether we'd ever be able to take the hot weather. We finally settled into Sarnia, though, and had a house built and started to enjoy living there. At work I was a process engineer in the Butyl Rubber Plant and enjoyed the work. In contrast to the narrow profit margins at Canadian Chemical, this plant made a profit of over one hundred percent on the cost of production—for a production cost of about ten cents a pound, we obtained twenty-two or twenty-three cents a pound. Added to this was the production rate of eighty to one hundred tons a day. The plant had originally been designed during the war to produce fifteen tons a day, but through various innovations and additions of auxiliary equipment, the rate had been upped to eighty tons a day by the time I arrived. When I left a couple of years later, it had reached one hundred tons a day.

While working at Polymer in the butyl rubber plant, I discovered chewing gum was made from butyl rubber. (I've never chewed gum since.) We ascertained that the reaction underlying the production of the chewing gum was being poisoned by the presence of certain components. By eliminating a small stream and sending it to another unit in the plant for purification, we immediately increased production by five tons a day. Polymer obtained a patent for this process change, and I received fifty dollars for having my name on the patent, which became the property of the Polymer corporation.

My job at Polymer was probably not much different from a typical civil service job. We started at 8:00 AM and finished at 5:00 PM. Since we were working in a plant that was producing almost one hundred tons of butyl rubber a day, with a profit of twelve cents on every pound, and since this went on whether we worked hard or not, there was no incentive to work our butts off. In the chemical engineering department, our role was to see that the plant was operated efficiently and to try to increase production without spending too much money to achieve it. My two-year stint at Polymer was the most leisurely time of my working career. During the summer, my family and I enjoyed the lovely warm water of Lake Huron and spent a lot of time at the beach, as well as going camping in various parts of Ontario and Michigan. During the winter, I joined the Sarnia Curling Club and curled twice a week.

Sarnia's winter weather was gloomy and dismal compared with the sunshine and clear skies of winter in Calgary. In addition, there was usually a chemical odour in the air from the various chemical plants in the area. Whether or not this atmospheric pollution contributed to the health problems that my wife, Kim, and our son, Dana, incurred, I don't know, but they both had colds and chest problems during the winter. Kim also suffered from polyps in her nasal passages. As a result, in 1957 when I was offered a position as a process engineer with Brown & Root, the engineering construction company in Calgary, I accepted the offer and we moved back to Calgary. As soon as we arrived back there, Kim's polyps disappeared and neither she nor Dana had any further chest problems.

We drove back to Calgary via the northern U.S. states in mid-September. As we reached the northwestern states, we realized we had forgotten how big the sky is in the west. In the eastern provinces, you can't see for miles like you can in the west. We left warm, practically summer-like weather in Sarnia and hit winter in Shelby, Montana, where we ran into a terrific snowstorm. It was quite a shock as we were still in light summer clothing. I bought snow tires and we finally made it to Calgary.

Soon after starting working with Brown & Root, I became its chief process engineer. Our manager was Wayne Williams, who had come from Brown & Root in Houston. He was an ardent sports fan and a great supporter of the Calgary Stampeders football team. Back then, football players had to augment their salaries by getting jobs with employers who were willing to give them time off during the football season. Wayne hired several of the players, and one of them was Harvey Wylie, a native Calgarian who came from a very athletic family and had been a star with the Montana State University football team in Bozeman, Montana. He had graduated in mechanical engineering and was hired as a junior engineer under the wing of Fred Ter Borg, a Dutch engineer who had formerly worked for Shell Oil in the oilfields of Venezuela and Indonesia. Harvey, who was eventually elected to the Canadian Football Hall of Fame, became a good friend of mine and this friendship has lasted over many years. Through Harvey, I got to know many of the Calgary Stampeder players. One of the guys I remember in particular was "Porky" Brown, who had biceps bigger than most men's thighs.

When I arrived back in Calgary, the boom in natural gas was just beginning and the first gas plants were being designed and constructed. Brown & Root was the Canadian arm of the giant Brown & Root construction company based in Houston, Texas. The Houston office was designing gas recovery units and compressor stations for the Pembina field, west of Edmonton. I had to learn (what for me) was a new area of engineering: gas-plant design. As a result I spent a good deal of time in the Houston office learning the ropes.

In those days gas-plant design was still in its infancy. Because a lot of data concerning the behaviour and physical properties of the various components of natural gas was not available, a great deal of these properties had to be estimated and methods for evaluating them developed. Today, design procedures have been computerized and young engineers use computers to obtain their results. They would probably look down their noses at our old methods, using slide rules, but many of the younger generation do not understand the principles underlying the data used in their designs. Spence Landes, one of my mentors while I was in Houston, still works as a consultant there and sometimes teaches classes on gas-plant design for young engineers. He tells me that when he gives young engineers a problem in design, they're astounded that he can come up with approximately the same answer as they do with their computers in the same amount of time using his slide rule.

During one of my stays in Houston, I left my motel one evening and went out for a hamburger. I stopped at a drive-in place, and while I was getting my order two young Mexican-Americans came and asked me if I could give them a ride home, as they had missed the last bus. I said, "Sure," and bought them each a hamburger. I drove them where they asked me to take them, which was in an alley. I got out of the car and was going to bid them good night when one of them pulled out a switchblade, stuck it in front of my stomach, and said, "Give us all the money which you got."

Instinctively, I grabbed the blade in my left hand. Immediately I regretted doing so and thought, "What the hell do I do now?" The only thing I could do was hold onto the blade, which I did while the other fellow tried to grab me from behind and even bit me on the back. Eventually—I don't know how—as I fought and kneed the one with the knife in the groin, I succeeded in getting the knife. Brandishing the knife in my right hand, I said, "You bastards are going to get it now." They took off like scared rabbits. A pickup truck came by and I yelled for help, but the driver didn't stop. I was indignant that this fellow didn't stop to help, but I realized later that he must have thought I was a murderer—I was covered with blood and waving a switchblade at him. I got in my car and drove to a service station, where they ordered a taxi that took me to the Jefferson Davis Charity Hospital Emergency Ward. I couldn't believe all the cases that came in during the short period I was there, including a woman who had been shot, several people who had been knifed, and others who had been beaten up. The police came and interviewed me and confiscated the knife for evidence.

When the hospital staff found out I worked for Brown & Root, they advised me to go to Hermann Hospital, probably the best hospital in Houston at the time. There, a wonderful surgeon operated on a tendon in the little finger of my left hand that had been severed in the attack. The operation was a success. Apparently, a tendon like that should be operated on within eight hours of being severed for it to have a chance of mending properly. Other than having to exercise the finger after the cast was off, I have had no problems with it since.

During another one of my trips to Houston, which usually lasted several weeks at a time, the run-up to the 1960 U.S. presidential election was taking place. Practically all the engineers I worked with were Republicans, and some were members of the right-wing John Birch Society. Surrounded by them, my reading of who would win Texas in the election was completely skewed and, as it turned out, wrong. It seemed to me that most Texans were Republicans, so I was quite surprised when Texas went Democrat and John F. Kennedy won the election against Richard Nixon. Lyndon Johnson was running for vice-president under Kennedy, and during the campaign he travelled around in a four-engine aircraft owned by a subsidiary of Brown & Root—this airline was really Brown & Root's private air service. When I flew in one of their smaller aircraft from Calgary to Houston, the pilot told me that none of the crews liked Johnson because he treated them all like servants.

Through the tutelage of Houston engineers like Spence Landes and Don Kemendo, I eventually became familiar with gas-plant design and was able to form an efficient design team in Calgary. At that time practically all the engineering services for the burgeoning gas industry in Canada were performed by American companies in the United States. We were the only Canadian engineering company actually doing the work in Canada. Most of our draftsmen, whom we trained to become piping designers, had come from Holland after the Second World War. Probably because Canadians had liberated Holland and formed a fraternal bond with the Dutch, many of the Hollanders immigrated to Canada. They made excellent draftsmen, and although this may only be my opinion, I attributed their skill to their natural artistic ability.

One of the young Hollanders whom we hired had never done any drafting, but I could see he was very intelligent and hired him as an assistant. He caught on very quickly and became invaluable at developing mechanical flow sheets from the process flow sheets that were given to him. This was Gerry Sloof, who later came to work with me at Mon-Max Services after I had left Brown & Root. Another invaluable individual was Peter Timmermans, who was made chief draftsman. He could spot errors immediately and was probably the most important man in the organization, as he ensured there were no conflicts between the piping, electrical, civil, or instrumentation installations. His keen eye saved us thousands of dollars during the construction of the various gas plants that we had designed, when any errors in the drawings could have resulted in very expensive alterations.

The soft eight-to-five work regime I had had in Sarnia with Polymer came to a sudden halt when I moved back to Calgary. Because we had deadlines for turning in bids for gas plants, we often had to work long hours, sometimes all night, in order to meet bid-closing dates. Even though I was under more pressure at work I enjoyed it, especially when we were successful in procuring a contract as a result of our efforts.

At that time, during the late 1950s and early 1960s, competition in the gas industry was cutthroat. Whenever an oil company decided to build a gas plant, it demanded what were known as "turn-key" bids. A turn-key bid was a fixed-price bid, meaning that the contractor had to take all the risk and build the plant for a fixed price. Engineering contractors like Brown & Root were hungry for work and there was no shortage of companies willing to bid on a project. I felt that demanding turn-key bids from contractors was an unfair practice. These contractors had to perform free engineering, complete a process design, and go through the whole operation of designing the plant in order to make takeoffs of material and labour that allowed them to estimate the cost of building the plant. It was also a risky business. Contractors had to contend with the vagaries of the weather, labour disputes, and possible increases in the cost of materials before the project was completed.

Despite these challenges, I probably gained more design experience in one year with Brown & Root than I would have in four or five years with an oil company. I had to design eight or ten plants per year, even though we might only get the opportunity to build two of them. We had to ensure that our design worked and that it would produce the quantity of gas and liquids that were specified. If the plant did not perform in accordance to the owners' design criteria, it would cost us money because we would not have lived up to our contract. This served as a great incentive for us to get our design right. While with Brown & Root, I designed several successful plants for some of the major oil companies, which gave me some recognition in the gas industry. After five years with Brown & Root, during which time I had become the chief process engineer, I received an offer to become chief engineer of a new Canadian company that was being formed to break into the gas-plant design and construction business. ■

The Mon-Max Years

I had been with Brown & Root for four years when, in 1961, I was offered a position as chief engineer for a new engineering-construction company that was just being formed. Mon-Max (which would eventually become Mon-Max–MHG International) was to be a joint venture between the largest construction company in Canada—Mannix—and the largest Canadian engineering company—Montreal Engineering. As I've stated earlier, up to this time the engineering for gas plants and related facilities for the gas industry was performed in the United States. This new company was being set up to try to break into this field. Mannix had tried several years earlier with a company called Mannix-Gill, which had not survived. Originally, the new company was not incorporated; it was simply a fifty-fifty partnership between Montreal Engineering and Mannix, called Montreal Engineering-Mannix. It all sounded grand, but we had no employees other than the general manager, Roy Sorrenti, me, and a female secretary, who was beautiful but couldn't spell. To my delight, I found that George Eckenfelder, my commanding officer during the war, was the manager of Montreal Engineering's Calgary office. However, he did not stay with us very long. Within a few months, he went on assignment to a huge hydroelectric project in

Brazil and his place was taken by Larry Carey.

Once we began setting up operations, I received the impression that neither of our owners really understood what was involved in designing and building a gas plant. They seemed to think that all that was required was for me to turn out a process design, which I would then turn over to the Montreal Engineering group in Montreal, which would crank out the final design. Finally, after a lot of pleading, I was allowed to hire a draftsman, Gerry Sloof, who had worked with me at Brown & Root. By this time Gerry was much more than an ordinary draftsman. I would turn over the process design to him, and he would produce the mechanical flow sheets and the equipment layout. The drafting of these items still had to be done, though, and this was to be accomplished by the personnel in Montreal.

I soon discovered the limitations of using the Montreal Engineering personnel to do our engineering design work. In 1962, we had finally received an offer to bid on a gas plant, and I completed the process design based on the criteria we had been given by the oil company. I calculated the sizes of the various items of equipment, and Gerry Sloof drew up a rough penciled sketch of a mechanical flow sheet. We then went to Montreal to get Montreal Engineering draftsmen to draw up the mechanical flow sheets, copying Gerry's penciled drafts. However, we soon discovered they had never drawn up flow sheets for their steam-power plants, let alone gas plants.

Montreal Engineering's mechanical engineering department operated in a much different manner than we did. Their main design work was in the field of steam-power plants, and their practice was to have the manufacturer of a boiler or a water-treatment plant supply drawings of their packaged units. From these, they would then design the piping and electrical equipment to tie all the components together. I broached the subject of designing steam plants in the same manner as we designed gas plants with their vice-president of mechanical engineering. (This meant first preparing a flow diagram and then a mechanical flow diagram with the major pieces of equipment connected by any required piping. Next would be the preparation of a to-scale layout of the major equipment and detailed to-scale drawings of the piping, showing all the equipment and pipe fittings, such as elbows, tees, and flanges.) The vice-president replied, "We'd never be able to design them that way for five percent of the capital cost." This was the reimbursement that Montreal Engineering received from utility companies owned by Mr. Isaak Killam. Previously, the reimbursement had been on a rather haphazard basis, since there was so much interchanging of personnel between the power companies and Montreal Engineering, but once instituted, the percentage system had never been changed—Montreal Engineering had a captive market for doing the engineering for these utilities, so no one paid attention to the reimbursement system. What no one seemed to realize, however, was that although the engineering was done for a comparatively low price, the construction might be much more costly. We at Mon-Max had drawings that were as correct as we could make them, and it paid off in lower construction costs.

Although my opinion may offend some of the old Montreal Engineering hands, I truly believe their mechanical engineering method was what led to the demise of the company. When Calgary Power was taken over by ATCO in 1981, Montreal Engineering no longer had a lock on the engineering because they were no longer competitive. The company was finally taken over by Agra, another engineering company, and disappeared. This was truly regrettable because Montreal Engineering's other disciplines, such as civil and electrical engineering, were first class. The main reason for the shortcomings of its mechanical engineering department was, I believe, that none of their personnel were grounded in modern plant design—most of them had come from Britain, where they had not been exposed to modern American methods of design, such as those used by engineering contractors such as Bechtel, Fluor, and Brown & Root.

When I got back to Calgary from Montreal, I discussed matters with Roy Sorrenti, the general manager of Mon-Max, and persuaded him that we had to form our own design team in Calgary. If necessary, we could move some of the Montreal Engineering personnel to Calgary and train them. Roy agreed with me and eventually was able to persuade our two parent companies to allow us to build up our own staff. We gradually built an engineering design group in Calgary and within three years had a staff of over one hundred people.

During the first year in my new post, I spent most of my time trying to convince the managers and engineers of the various oil companies in Calgary that we were capable of designing and constructing any facilities that they might require. It was an uphill struggle. Most of the oil companies were American and, naturally, went to the well-known American engineering contractors with whom they were familiar and had faith in. To most of the gas and oil people, we were just upstarts who had yet to prove ourselves. Of course, this was an impossible task if we couldn't get a job to demonstrate our skills. I was well known in the industry from my days at Brown & Root, and this sometimes helped us get a foot in the door. Finally in 1962, we obtained a contract from Texas Gulf Sulphur to build a small liquid-sulphur storage tank at its plant in Okotoks, Alberta. It was only a minor project, but we were grateful to Jim Estep, the manager, and his assistant, Fred Roniker, for giving us the opportunity.

In 1963 we won a contract to build refrigerated-propane storage facilities for the Greater Winnipeg Gas Company in Winnipeg, Manitoba. This was the first installation of its kind in the country. During the winter months, whenever the temperature drops during a cold snap, gas utility companies have difficulty meeting the demand for gas. Greater Winnipeg Gas had decided to augment its gas flows with propane during these peak periods. The cost to store propane in normal propane pressure vessels, which are designed for pressures of 250 pounds per square inch (114 kg per 6 cm^2) or more, is quite costly. Therefore, tanks with 24 inches (60 cm) or more of pearlite insulation are employed for large quantities of propane, and the propane is chilled to -45°F (-43°C) so the pressure is reduced to almost zero.[1] Thus, the tank can be designed with a much thinner shell at a much lower cost.

The plant we designed for Greater Winnipeg Gas consisted of a refrigeration plant to chill the propane to -45°F (-43°C) and the necessary piping and valves to pump the propane into a large 125,000-barrel storage tank. After we had completed the design, we discovered to our horror that the small amount of ethane that was normally present in commercial propane would concentrate in the top of the tank and cause the pressure in the tank to build up. As a result, the relief valve in the tank would actuate and we would be continually losing ethane and propane to the flare. The plant was already scheduled for construction, and I lay awake nights wondering how to cope with this problem. One night it finally came to me. The next day we started working on the design of a de-ethanizer—a small distillation tower filled with ceramic rings that would concentrate the ethane at the top and yield ethane-free propane at the bottom. To make it work, I used cold propane to condense the overhead and heat from the compressor piping to supply the re-boiler heat at the bottom. The ethane that concentrated at the top of the tower was channelled into the Greater Winnipeg Gas pipeline. Luckily, we were able to install this unit while the rest of the plant was being constructed. Although its additional cost cut into our profit, it was a lifesaver.

To ensure that our plant started up properly, Greater Winnipeg Gas brought up a supervisor from a refrigerated-propane storage facility in Alabama. When he saw our de-ethanizer, he said, "Oh, you're lucky to have that. We didn't have anything like that in our plant in Alabama, and we had a terrible problem with losing propane to the flare. You won't have any trouble at all."

We started up the plant in Winnipeg in 1963 without a hitch and thought we were out of the woods. However, one more matter arose to plague us before we could hand the facilities over to the owners. The ground on which we had built the plant was clay. This blue clay was like jelly—it was so unstable that we had to put concrete pilings down 60 feet (18 m) into a hard-pan formation for our main storage tank. The concrete foundation on which the tank sat rested on these pilings, but we had not provided similar support for our compressor foundations. I had conferred with Dr. R. M. Hardy, dean of engineering at the University of Alberta in Edmonton, and he had not thought it was necessary to do so. However, when we started up the reciprocating compressor, it shook the piping and everything in the building. I had Hardy come and look at it, and he recommended that we drill two holes down to the hard pan, fill them with concrete, and tie them into the compressor foundation. As we could not drill vertically beneath the compressor foundation, we had to slant-drill the holes. Thankfully, this solved the problem and we were finished with the project.

Building the plant in Winnipeg helped us become recognized in the industry—we now had a project that we could point to. With that recognition came an invitation to bid on a 7,300-barrel-per-day fractionation plant for Imperial Oil in Devon, Alberta.[2] This new plant was to work in parallel with the existing plant, which had been installed following the discovery of oil at Leduc in 1947. We competed for the project with American engineering firms and were successful. This was a real breakthrough for us, and I have always been grateful to Stu Mason, the Imperial Oil engineer in charge of their gas plants, for giving us the opportunity to bid and for having the faith to award us the contract. I'm sorry to say that there were other Canadian engineering managers of Canadian oil companies who weren't as supportive—like the one who said to me, "I'm sorry, but we use [a certain American engineering company] because they are the best."

My pleasure at having secured the contract for the Devon plant was tempered by the fact that at this time, August 1964, my father passed away at the age of eighty-four. I had not seen very much of him in his final years as he had been living in Uranium City, Saskatchewan, with two of my brothers. However, his passing left an empty spot in my life. He was responsible for any of the success I had ever had, and I was thankful that he had at least seen me complete my university degrees and then become the chief engineer at Mon-Max. We had his body cremated and my brothers and I took his ashes to Fort McMurray, where we had a memorial service and interred his ashes in a plot next to our mother's in the Fort McMurray cemetery. Practically the whole population of what was still a small town came out to pay their respects.

After we won the contract to build the extension of the fractionation plant at Devon, we were invited to bid on practically all the gas plants being built in Canada (previously, we could not even get on the bid list). Most of the oil companies in Canada at that time were American, with the senior managers or engineers almost all from the United States. They naturally had a preference for established American contractors such as Fluor, Bechtel, Stearns-Rogers, and Pritchard. As well, since the industry at that time was small, most of the oil companies' higher-echelon personnel knew their contractor counterparts and in some cases were good friends. This meant we had a built-in bias to contend with, in addition to being newcomers to the game. Gradually, however, as we bid on and in some cases won contracts, we began to design and erect gas-processing and compression units throughout Canada. We designed and constructed gas plants for many companies, including Home Oil, Imperial Oil, Shell Oil, Amoco Oil, Chevron Standard, Gulf Oil, Greater Winnipeg Gas, Trans Mountain Pipe Line, Trans Canada Pipelines, Texas Gulf Sulphur, Pacific Petroleum, and Cities Services.

With the competitive climate that prevailed during the 1960s and 1970s, along with the scourge of the turn-key fixed-price bid process, engineering contractors only placed a very small profit margin in their bids and made minimum provision for contingencies. This meant that if there was some error in the design or if construction was slowed by bad weather, the contractor could easily lose his shirt. However, we were fortunate to not lose money on any of our contracts. We were gradually able to throw off the yoke of having to use Montreal Engineering personnel, with the attendant communication problems of dealing long distance with people in Montreal. We were able to hire our own people in Calgary and eventually ended up with a staff of some two hundred. Although this may not seem like a large number, to us it was huge, especially considering our lowly beginnings with a staff of three. Once we had built up our capabilities in Calgary, our engineering was accomplished much more proficiently and efficiently. In 1962 we were incorporated as a separate company, Mon-Max Services, which was still owned fifty-fifty by Montreal Engineering and Mannix.

In 1965, we obtained the contract to build a refrigerated-propane storage installation for Trans Mountain Pipe Line, near Vancouver,

British Columbia. It was an interesting project as it entailed liaising with the Japanese Mitsubishi Engineering people, who were going to build the tankers that would be used to take the propane to Japan. This meant that I, along with some of the Trans Mountain personnel, had to go to Japan to meet with the Mitsubishi personnel. The meetings were unlike any I had ever attended. During these meetings, we met with between twenty and thirty Japanese representatives—each company that had any interest in the project was represented. Whenever I would propose some technical requirement, there would be much discussion amongst them, in Japanese, of course. Although I cannot speak Japanese, having forgotten most of what I knew from speaking to my mother, I seemed to always know what their attitude was and whether or not they agreed with us. Almost invariably, they would tell us through the interpreter that they would let us know what their decision was at a later meeting. Presumably they had to confer with a superior before answering us. It was interesting to note how often they would return agreeing with my proposal, when originally they had seemed to be against it.

At some of our meetings, there were American engineers from Gulf Oil, which was to supply some of the propane in Canada. I wasn't impressed with their attitude toward the Japanese. One young engineer in particular spoke to them in a condescending way, with an exaggerated, simplified English, as though he were speaking to young children.

I enjoyed my first visit to Japan. Originally I wondered whether the Japanese would treat me with contempt because I couldn't speak the language. However, I was treated with the utmost respect and several of the people with whom I dealt became friends. One of them told me that after my wife, Kim, left (she had come with me for a week's visit), he would take me on a tour to sample the nightlife where the Japanese went. This we did and I found the prices were a third of those in the tourist-frequented Ginza district.

In 1965, Japan was still a rather chauvinistic male society, and Kim wasn't invited to the entertainment I attended in the evenings. However, she enjoyed the trip immensely, especially the beautiful pearls she was able to buy. Prices were still low, and she got some real bargains. Unfortunately, circumstances didn't permit us to explore my family roots. My mother's relatives lived in the south island of Kyushu, which was too far from Tokyo for us to visit, so I never got in touch with them. I had never been in contact with any of them, although my younger brothers Harry and Bill were able to locate some of them several years earlier while on a trip to Japan. Looking back, I can see that I missed another opportunity. In 1965 no one in North America had ever heard of Japanese cars, or Sony or Seiko watches, or Nikon or Canon cameras. When I saw these things, I thought what a good idea it would be to get an agency to sell them in Canada. However, at that time my knowledge of anything other than engineering was limited, so I never did anything about it.

Montreal Engineering and Mannix Construction were leaders in their fields in Canada in the early 1960s. To understand how these two firms played a role in the development of Mon-Max, I've included a brief history of their origins and beginnings. Each of them played a significant role in the development of Canada in the twentieth century.

Montreal Engineering was founded by William Maxwell Aitken, who later became the famous Lord Beaverbrook of England. He eventually sold the company to his protege Izaak Killam, under whom it blossomed and eventually became one of the largest engineering firms in the country. Aitken was born in 1879 in a village near Toronto, but at the age of one he moved with his family to Newcastle, New Brunswick, where his father, a minister in the Church of Scotland, had taken up a parish. The future Lord Beaverbrook grew up in Newcastle and tried to enter Dalhousie University in 1895, but failed the entrance examination in Latin. He then returned to Newcastle and started working as a clerk in a law firm in which Richard Bedford Bennett, who would become Canada's eleventh prime minister, was a junior partner. He and Bennett became very good friends, but Bennett soon moved to Calgary and Aitken enrolled in the St. John Law School in 1897. When it soon became evident that he was not cut out for academics, he decided to go out west to join his friend Bennett in

Calgary. After being involved in several business ventures in Calgary and Edmonton and on the advice of another friend, James H. Dunn (who later became Sir James H. Dunn, one of the wealthiest entrepreneurs in Canada), Aitken moved back to New Brunswick.

Once back in New Brunswick, Aitken acquired an insurance agency and began selling bonds, getting a start in the financial market. He moved to Halifax in 1902, where he met and became a protege of John F. Stairs, the president of the Union Bank of Halifax. In 1903 when John Stairs, his brother George, and several friends formed Royal Securities Corporation, with John Stairs as president, they placed Aitken in charge as its manager. The company was involved in the sale of corporation bonds and was a huge success, as it provided a financial service at a time when the electrical generating and transmission industries were in their infancy. Most of Aitken's energies were devoted to financing electric facilities in Trinidad, British Guiana, Puerto Rico, and Cuba, as well as for the coal and steel industry on Cape Breton Island that eventually became the Dominion Steel and Coal Company.

John Stairs died in 1904, and his brother George succeeded him as president of Royal Securities. However, Aitken was, in effect, running the company and when George Stairs died in 1908 was named president. In 1906 he moved the company's headquarters from Halifax to Montreal and began organizing the formation of several companies that would become major enterprises in Canada. Among them were Calgary Power, the giant Canada Cement Company, and the large pulp and paper company Price Brothers and Company.

In 1909 Aitken established a Royal Securities office in London, England, and in 1910, looking for other fields to conquer, he and his wife moved to England. He immediately made a forceful impact on British politics. He became a Member of Parliament five months after leaving Canada, was knighted in 1911, and became a member of the House of Lords as Baron Beaverbrook of Beaverbrook, New Brunswick, and Chertsey, Surrey. He obtained control of the *Daily Express*, one of the leading newspapers in the United Kingdom, and befriended Winston Churchill. During the Second World War, he was put in charge of aircraft manufacture and raised the level of production, especially of the Spitfires and Hawker Hurricanes that played such a great role in defeating the German Luftwaffe.

When Aitken opened the Royal Securities office in London, he placed Izaak Killam in charge of the operation. The two had met when Killam was a neophyte seventeen-year-old employee of John Stairs's Union Bank of Halifax. Aitken took a liking to Killam and in 1904 hired him as the second employee of Royal Securities. Most of the Canadian companies in which Aitken was involved obtained capital in the London market through Royal Securities, so Killam acquired a thorough grounding in international finance during his sojourn there.

With the outbreak of war in 1914, the London office was closed and Killam returned to Canada. In 1915 he succeeded Beaverbrook as president of Royal Securities, but it was not until 1919 that Beaverbrook sold his controlling interest in Royal Securities and its subsidiary Montreal Engineering to Izaak Killam and Ward C. Pitfield. Also included in the sale were Beaverbrook's interests in Calgary Power and Camaguery Electric (Cuba). Beaverbrook, however, kept his assets in the Canada Cement Company, Price Brothers and Company, and the Steel Company of Canada.

In 1928 Ward Pitfield left Royal Securities to form his own company, which became the large brokerage firm of Pitfield Mackay Ross. Killam proceeded to follow in his mentor Beaverbrook's footsteps and began to carve out an industrial empire that would become one of the largest in Canada and make him one of the wealthiest men in the country. His interests covered the whole of the nation, from the Maritimes to western Canada, and ranged as far south as the Caribbean and South America. Most of his interests involved electrical-power generation and transmission. Montreal Engineering, which had been formed in 1907 by Aitken and Royal Securities, played a major part in his acquisitions and in the organization and management of his companies. Soon after Killam took over Montreal Engineering, Denis Stairs (the son of George Stairs and nephew of John Stairs) and Geoffrey Gaherty (John Stairs's stepson) joined Montreal Engineering. They were to play a pivotal part in the development of the company. Geoffrey Gaherty was made chief engineer in 1920, and Denis Stairs, chief engineer in 1930.

In the early years of Montreal Engineering, Killam used the capability of its personnel, including Denis Stairs and Geoffrey Gaherty, to assist him in building his empire, which included Calgary Power. (Incidentally, the president of Calgary Power in those early days was R. B. Bennett, who had been placed there by his old friend Max Aitken.) In 1954 Killam, who died suddenly a year later, sold his shares in Montreal Engineering to its senior employees, and Montreal Engineering became an employee-owned company. Soon the company began to branch out into outside consulting engineering projects.

The four leading lights of Montreal Engineering were Geoffrey Gaherty, Denis Stairs, Frederick Krug, and Harry Thompson. Thanks to the ability and integrity of these men, Montreal Engineering acquired a worldwide reputation for its engineering excellence and expertise. Although I've mentioned them by their first names, no one in the organization referred to them as anything but Mr. Gaherty, Mr. Stairs, Mr. Krug, and Mr. Thompson. In fact, when I first joined the group in 1961 everyone in Montreal Engineering seemed to speak of these men with awe and reverence.

I never met Mr. Krug or Mr. Gaherty. While I saw Mr. Stairs in the office in Montreal whenever I went there, I did not get to know him other than to say hello. However, Mr. Thompson had moved back to Calgary by the time I joined Montreal Engineering-Mannix and was chairman of the board of Calgary Power and in overall charge of Montreal Engineering's western operations. Mr. Thompson was originally from Calgary and had joined Calgary Power in 1925 and then risen rapidly to become general manager in 1930. He then moved to Montreal and became supervisor of the Northern Properties. Mr. Krug was supervisor of the Southern Properties (the Caribbean and South America) and the general manager of Montreal Engineering.

Mr. Thompson took over as manager of Montreal Engineering in 1947 and began a reorganization of the engineering department. Up to this time, the relationship between the various Killam companies had been quite loose, and personnel had moved back and forth from one company to another. In fact, even before he was named Montreal Engineering's general manager, Mr. Thompson had been left with the responsibility of running the engineering department—Mr. Krug spent most of his time dealing with the Southern Properties, while Mr. Gaherty was mainly concerned with Calgary Power and Mr. Stairs was in Ottawa during the war years. As part of his reorganization efforts, Mr. Thompson formed departments of civil, electrical, hydraulic, and mechanical engineering, with department heads for each. When he moved back to Calgary, Mr. Thompson was instrumental in the formation of my group, Montreal Engineering-Mannix, with the view to designing and constructing plants and facilities for the growing oil and gas industry in the West.

An interesting sidelight that demonstrates the high regard in which Montreal Engineering was held is the assignment given to it by C. D. Howe, the minister of Munitions and Supply, during the Second World War. He asked it to evaluate the hare-brained scheme of building a floating iceberg airport for the mid-Atlantic. The project was the brainchild of Geoffrey Pike, who was part of Lord Louis Mountbatten's combined operations staff. Pike had made a convert of Mountbatten, and Lord Louis, in turn, had convinced Churchill that the idea should be looked at. The Americans vetoed the idea, so Churchill called on the Canadian government to see what could be done. Canada at once complied—in those days, Great Britain still ruled the roost and Churchill's wishes could not be denied. Montreal Engineering at once began studies and testing to determine the feasibility of the "Habakkuk" (the code name for the secret project). In August 1943, four months after the investigation, Mr. Gaherty submitted a report demonstrating the impracticability of the scheme.

The original idea of going to the Arctic and cutting off an iceberg that measured 2,000 feet (600 m) long, 2,000 feet (600 m) wide, and 200 feet (60 m) thick and then towing it to the Atlantic to act as a runway was impractical, so the focus was on building a structure out of ice. This artificial iceberg would have to have 50 feet (15 m) of freeboard, be continually refrigerated, and be protected by an insulating skin. A model 60 feet (18 m) long by 30 feet (9 m) wide, with an overall depth of 20 feet (6 m), was constructed on the ice surface at Patricia Lake in Jasper National Park. Tests showed that ice alone would not have enough strength. However, Geoffrey Pike, a professor at Brooklyn Polytech, had discovered that the addition of wood pulp made the ice mixture (which came to be referred to as "Pikecrete") quite tough and resistant to explosives. Mr. Gaherty's report was completed in time for the Roosevelt-Churchill conference in Quebec City in August 1943. It outlined the gigantic material-supply problem—the amount of wood pulp required would exhaust most of Canada's annual production and the requirement of refrigeration equipment was tremendous. There were many other drawbacks as well, such as the necessity to supply self-propulsion for the floating mass. The project was simply too impractical and Mr. Gaherty's report shot it down.

With old age creeping up on the four senior members of Montreal Engineering, a new crop of eminent engineers came to the fore to take over the management of the company in the 1960s. Many of these men came up through an apprentice engineering program in which young graduates were given employment and training, and tribute should be paid to Mr. Gaherty and Mr. Thompson for exhibiting their faith in the future of the companies and the young engineers they hired during the Dirty Thirties. Some outstanding future leaders in both Montreal Engineering and Calgary Power were members of this apprenticeship program, including Chris Ritchie, Bert Howard, George Eckenfelder, Kent Carruthers, and Harold Hurdle. Other notables who were hired earlier were Howard McLean, Jack Sexton, and Bill Davis. Most of these men were graduates of the University of Alberta in Edmonton.

Mannix Construction was owned by Fred Mannix. He became and has remained a legendary figure in Calgary, paradoxically because he was so little known by the general public. He shunned publicity because he feared becoming the target of the acts of violence and kidnapping that were becoming more prevalent. As a result very few people even knew what he looked like—there were never any photographs of him in newspapers or magazines. Although he could be hard and determined in his business deals, he was a warm-hearted, lovable guy who always pretended he didn't know very much. He had flunked out of his first year of engineering at the University of Alberta in 1931, but, as Dean Bob Hardy of its engineering faculty told me, "The most successful engineering alumnus of the University of Alberta was Fred Mannix, who didn't make it past Christmas in his first year."

Fred probably flunked out because he was such a wild, untamed character in his youth, so intent on enjoying life that he didn't get much studying done, much to the despair of his father. However, in 1939, he persuaded Margaret (Margie) Broughton, after relentlessly pursing her, to marry him. Margie, with her beauty, magnetic yet feminine personality, and astuteness, contributed to a remarkable turnaround in Fred's life. He became so successful that in 1951, with the guidance of his triumvirate of managers, Everett Costello, Brock Montgomery, and Eric Connelly, he was able to buy back Morris Knudsen's interest in the company to become the sole owner of Mannix Construction. This was to be the pattern of his future career—he always wanted to control any project he undertook, even though it might be joint-ventured with another firm. Eventually he built an empire that included Pembina Pipelines (a veritable money-making machine), Western Decalta, an oil company, and the largest coal mines in the country. This was in addition to his construction company, which became the largest in the country in the 1960s. Since his death in 1995, his sons Ronnie and Freddie have increased his considerable fortune to several billion dollars.

When I was involved in Mon-Max, the Mannix empire was run by the triumvirate of Fred, Everett Costello, and Brock Montgomery (Eric Connelly had left the company). Ev Costello was a lawyer who came from a pioneering family in Calgary, and Brock Montgomery was a burly, tough engineer who had grown up around Trail, British Columbia. Brock served with the Royal Canadian Engineers in Italy during the war, surviving a wound to his leg and ending up as a major. I got to know Brock very well; we became ski buddies and often went on ski trips together—including one to Val D'Isere, France, and another to Verbier, Switzerland. I was also privileged to get to know

Fred quite well and he became a very good friend. One time, when Kim and I were having problems with our son, Dana, Fred took him out to lunch for a heart-to-heart talk. Dana later told me that the talk had had a real effect on him, as Fred spoke to him as one who had been through the same mill.

I think one of the main reasons Fred and Brock took a liking to me was because of an incident that occurred in 1962, soon after I joined Mon-Max. Roy Sorrenti, the company's general manager, had asked me to bring his car over to pick him up at the Petroleum Club. The car was parked on the street but was boxed in by a pickup truck, which was illegally double-parked. I tried to manoeuvre the car out of the spot but couldn't make it, so I tried to push the pickup. While I was doing this, the driver of the pickup came running out of a nearby building and started cursing me, so I got out of the car to try to tell him he had no business being parked illegally. When he continued cursing and then used some racial epithets, I lost my temper, hit him several times, and managed to knock him down. He moved his truck and left. I picked up Roy and told him what had happened—he thought it was hilarious.

We returned to the office, and I went to the washroom to clean off the blood from my knuckles and clothes. I was chewed out by Montreal Engineering's vice-president for "getting into a brawl on the street." I meekly retreated to my office. I had been there only a short time when Roy Sorrenti called me and said that the Calgary Police had just phoned him and asked if he was the owner of a car with a certain licence number. Upon admitting that he was, they said he was being charged with assault for attacking a man who said he had been beaten up by a 6-foot (1.8-m), 200-pound (90-kg) assailant. In reply, Roy chuckled, "No, that wasn't me. That was Tom Morimoto, who is 5 feet 2 inches (1.57 m) and weighs 115 pounds (52 kg)." When the police called back, Roy transferred the call to me. The police officer explained why he was calling and asked how big I was. I told him, and he said, "God! You must have looked huge to this fellow!" I gave him my side of the story, and he said, "Well, it looks as though he was asking for it, but unfortunately if he lays a charge, we must pursue it."

When I got home and told Kim what had happened, she became distraught at the thought I might have to go to court and might even go to jail. She was in tears and insisted on calling Henry Patterson, who had been my company commander in the Royal Canadian Corps of Signals overseas and had become a very good friend when I returned to Calgary. Henry was now a judge on the Court of Queen's Bench and a member of the Calgary Police Commission. He told Kim to bring me to his house, so we went to his place, where Henry had a lawyer waiting for me. I told them the story, and the lawyer said he would see what he could do. The next morning, Henry called to tell me that the lawyer had spoken to the police, whereupon they had brought the complainant in. After one look at the size of the complainant, the lawyer told him he would be laughed out of court if his statement were read and then I walked onto the witness stand. The guy reluctantly withdrew his charge, and that was the end of the case.

When the Mannix people heard the story, I immediately became a hero and got to know Fred and Brock quite well. It was rather interesting to note the different reactions to the incident by the two groups, Montreal Engineering and Mannix. I suppose it illustrates the difference between a staid group of engineers and a tough, hell-for-leather construction gang. The incident also provided a never-ending source of amusement for Henry Patterson, who would tell the story to anyone we met. He teased me about it for years and used to say, "Morimoto, I should have let you go to jail!" ∎

Trade Missions

uring my time with Mon-Max, I participated in four trade missions to foreign countries. The first was to the Caribbean and South America in May 1969. That trade mission was sponsored by the Canadian Department of Trade and Industry and featured representatives from the Canadian oil industry. It was organized in an attempt to obtain work in the oil sector in Aruba, Curaçao, Trinidad, and Venezuela. All five members of the mission came from Alberta, and I represented the gas-plant design-and-construction sector.

We first went to Aruba to visit the Shell Oil refinery that was located there. The visit was a waste of time as far as getting any work from Shell—the Aruba personnel told us they had no say when it came to selecting contracts, which were all awarded out of The Hague. Aruba was an interesting place to visit, however. When I was there, it was both a gambling mecca and a bit of Holland transported to the New World. On our flight from New York to Aruba, the plane was practically filled with gamblers from New York on a junket. Our Canadian contingent seemed to be the only passengers not with the group. The organizer of the gambling trip called himself a "junketeer," and when we left Aruba, he said to me, "I've been watching you Canadians. If you had been gamblers, I'd have called you up in Calgary and offered you a free trip down here, but you guys aren't gamblers. So what's the use?"

From Aruba we went to the island of Curaçao, another Dutch colony, where Standard Oil had their huge refinery. Here again we found the visit a waste of time, as all contracts for anything on the island were awarded out of Standard Oil's head office in the United States. We then flew on to Caracas, just a short distance away in Venezuela. Caracas was a vibrant city, with huge skyscrapers, but a tremendous contrast existed between the opulence of the wealthy in their grandiose edifices and the indigence of the poor in their miserable hovels. It seemed to me that such a situation was a powder keg waiting to explode at some future date. We went on to the oilfield at Lake Maracaibo, which was huge and the source of almost all Venezuela's oil at that time. Standard Oil had all their production onshore around the lake, while Shell Oil produced all their wells on the lake. So much oil had been produced that the shoreline had sunk some 10 feet (3 m) and berms, or dikes, had had to be erected to keep the lake from flooding the surrounding countryside. This was in 1969—I'm sure there has been more sinking since then.

Again, we found the trip to Venezuela a flop as far as getting any work from the oil companies—we got the same story there that we had heard in Curaçao and Aruba: that we would have to go to the head office to obtain any work. The mission thus ended up being merely a fact-gathering excursion. We were pleased, however, to see Frank Wood, who had previously been the superintendent at Shell's Pincher Creek plant in Alberta. Frank toured us around the area and gave us an insight into what it was like to operate in Venezuela. He had quite a responsible position as the manager of all services except the direct production of oil, and he told us some interesting stories about the situation in Maracaibo. The oil wells out on the lake were linked by electrical cables for power, and a guard boat would inspect each well every hour. Yet, despite these high levels of security, the very large and heavy cable between each well, which measured a quarter of a mile (0.4 km) in length, would often be cut and taken away by thieves. Shell had not been able to discover how such a heavy cable could be disposed of in such a short time. As well, it was impossible to keep insulation on any above-ground pipelines as it was constantly being stolen. On another topic, Frank said that if you ever got into an automobile accident in Venezuela, the best thing to do was speed away as fast as possible because a foreigner would inevitably be found guilty and likely receive a prison sentence, as well as a large fine.

After we left Caracas, we flew to Port of Spain, Trinidad, for a consultation with some of the oil companies there. Gas had been discovered offshore, but we had no more success with any of the contacts there. Yet again, we were told that we needed to speak to the head offices of the companies involved. All in all, our trade mission was a complete bust from a business perspective.

When our tour in Trinidad was completed, we had a very relaxing weekend on the adjoining island of Tobago. We stayed at a resort hotel on the beach and relaxed on the beautiful sand beach and swam in the lovely warm water. The air was so warm, even in the wee hours of the morning, that lovers spent the night on the beaches. The warmth of the weather was something we luxuriated in, because back in Calgary it was still rather cool in May. I will always remember going offshore to the coral reef, wading and snorkeling to view the myriad of multicoloured fish swimming there. It seemed unbelievable that there could be so many different and beautiful varieties of fish just below the surface of the water. However, I got a terrifically sunburned back from snorkeling for an hour or so.

When our Canadian delegation first arrived in Caracas, an article had appeared in a local newspaper, describing our mission, along with a photograph of all of us. Early the next morning I received a telephone call from a man with an Italian accent. He said he had seen my photograph in the newspaper and had recognized me, having previously met me in Calgary. He told me that his company, Altabend, had fabricated some piping for one of our gas-plant construction projects. He went on to say that he had a diamond property out in the hinterland of Venezuela and had some equipment there he would like me to check out for him. I said I would meet him for breakfast and then got hold of Scotty Grant, the president of Barber Machinery Company in Calgary, who was in the room next door. I suggested to

Scotty that he should come to breakfast to meet this fellow.

Scotty was interested, so we went down to breakfast to meet Antonio, whom I recognized and remembered. He was an Italian who had immigrated to Canada and married a Canadian woman in Edmonton, where he resided when I first met him. He told us that his diamond property was about 400 miles (640 km) from Caracas. In order to get there, we would have to fly to the city of Ciudad Bolivar, some 300 miles (480 km) away and then drive another 100 miles (160 km) to the site. He had a compressor and a mining jig mounted on a barge that he had arranged to have constructed at the site, and he wanted us to check out the equipment to see if it would work properly. He also said that if we were interested in staking for diamonds, all we had to do was to stake a claim and then register it with the government for a nominal sum.

If we agreed to go, he would pay the airfare and arrange for a car to drive us to the location. Scotty and I discussed the matter and decided that it might be interesting to see something of the interior of Venezuela. We told him that once we had finished our trade mission, which would take another week in Trinidad and Tobago, we would fly back to Caracas to meet him. When our stay in Trinidad and Tobago came to an end, Scotty and I flew back to Caracas and were met at the airport by Antonio, who was accompanied by a woman and two other Italians. Apparently, the woman was financing the diamond venture and the two other men were divers who were to do the actual work of bringing the diamonds up from the bottom of the river. We all boarded a Viscount aircraft—I suspected it was one of the planes that Air Canada sold off when it finally converted to jets in the 1960s. When we arrived at Ciudad Bolivar, we found that it was situated on the Orinoco River, which impressed us by its size. The river was navigable from the Atlantic, at least to Ciudad Bolivar, by ocean-going ships, one of which we saw at the river wharfs.

When we saw the beat-up Fiat in which they proposed that the six of us—Antonio, his Jewish lady friend, the two Italian divers, Scotty, and myself—would travel, Scotty and I objected that the car was too small. In the end, Scotty and I rented a Volkswagen and, with one of the divers riding with us, we set out. We headed for the village of La

Paragua, which was on the banks of the La Paragua River. The river was a tributary of a tributary of the Orinoco.

We drove along a paved road and were quite impressed that a road so far inland was paved. The country seemed to be quite lush, with tall grass as far as one could see. I thought that it must be wonderful ranching country, but we never saw any cattle. (When I wondered aloud about this back in Canada, I was told that perhaps it was due to the prevalence of vampire bats in that part of Venezuela, which could kill cattle.) About halfway to our destination, the Fiat's alternator broke down and we had to tow it. It made for a difficult trip, but we were thankful that we had at least rented the Volkswagen.

When we finally arrived at La Paragua, we found a village of houses with thatched roofs and white-plaster walls. Old men sat outside playing some sort of game with tiles. There was a large gasoline tank on stilts near the riverbank, and when I asked who owned it, we were told by the local people that it belonged to the priest. Apparently, this priest had a diamond operation somewhere on the river with some fifty or so men working for him. He also had an airplane, in which he arrived every two weeks to pick up his diamonds. I'm sure he must have been doing "God's work" on these flights.

The river was a surprise. I had thought it would be relatively small, since it was said to be a tributary of a tributary of the Orinoco. However, it was approximately a mile (1.6 km) wide and quite deep, as well as swift flowing. When we asked where the diamond property was, we were told it was about an hour's ride down the river. The diamonds were in the riverbed. Gathering them involved sucking them up, along with a good deal of sand and gravel, using the compressor. The components of the mixture from the riverbed were then separated, using a jig. After that, workers had to use various screens to pick out the diamonds by hand from the gravel. The divers were required to move the suction pipe along the riverbed.

At La Paragua—the village—we boarded our craft for our trip downriver. When we first saw it, we were astonished by the canoe in which we were about to make our trip. It was a huge, hollowed-out log, about 30 feet (9 m) long, with wooden seats acting as spreader bars. The motive power was a thirty-horsepower outboard motor, controlled by a swarthy "El Capitan." Shortly after we started racing downriver, though, we realized our craft was very seaworthy and our initial trepidation disappeared. The river cut through luxuriant jungle, and we saw large turtles lazing in the sun along the riverbanks, and profuse numbers of blossoms on the dense green foliage. We were told there were all sorts of animals such as monkeys in the jungle but didn't see any.

After about an hour, we came to an island in the river where the catamaran barge with its compressor and jig was moored. We had a look around the operation, which seemed to us to be rather hazardous, with the divers moving the big suction pipes around on the riverbed some 50 feet (15 m) below the water's surface in a very swift-flowing stream. Added to this, the divers' equipment was old fashioned, consisting of helmets hooked up to air hoses. After examining the barge equipment, Scotty told Antonio that the base for the equipment was too weak and should be strengthened by welding in some angle iron if it could be obtained. Otherwise, it seemed to be okay.

We told our host we were not interested in trying to mine diamonds from the bottom of the river and asked if there were any diamonds in a gravel bed on the surface. He took us to a Senor Santos in the village, who had a lot of old mining equipment in his yard. Though he could not speak English, he told us through an interpreter that he felt he was too old to do any more mining but had a property on an old gravel bar in which there were diamonds at a depth of 10 feet (3 m) or so. We suggested we would offer him a fifty-fifty deal if we were allowed to mine the property. He agreed to this, and we were told to get in touch with him through an agent in Caracas.

We asked for some evidence that there were diamonds in the area, and immediately people came out of the woodwork with rough diamonds to sell. The would-be dealer would show up with rough diamonds wrapped in an ordinary piece of stationery paper, folded to make a small package. He would open the package to reveal the diamonds, which looked like dirty pieces of glass. He would then bring out a small balance and with a pair of tweezers proceed to weigh each diamond by placing it on one pan and the appropriate number of weights on the other. The price was set at so many bolivars (Venezuelan currency) per karat.

Several of the dealers in the village were from Israel, which apparently at that time (1969) was becoming quite a thriving diamond centre. I did not buy any uncut diamonds as I would not have known what to do with them. However, once we got back to Ciudad Bolivar, I was introduced to a man who sold me some cut diamonds. I bought twenty-four small diamonds, up to three-quarters of a karat in size, for three hundred U.S. dollars, which was quite a bargain as they would have cost much more in Canada. Ciudad Bolivar was also a centre for gold jewellery. The gold was fashioned into ornaments on the spot in much the same manner as it was at the Soukh in Dubai, which we encountered years later. For sixty U.S. dollars, I bought Kim some gold bracelets, which in Canada were worth several times that price. My purchases turned out to be the only tangible results of our trip into the jungle. When we got back to Calgary, Scotty and I tried to correspond with Senor Santos but never received a reply. We did, however, get solicitations from numerous people trying to interest us in gold-mining properties.

I made three trips to Russia (at the time still a republic within the Soviet Union) in the early 1970s, two of them on government-sponsored trade missions and the third to present a proposal for building a gas plant. On the first government-sponsored mission, my goal was to persuade the Russians to buy a gas plant from Mon-Max. There were several other people from Calgary trying to sell various items that they manufactured for the oil and gas industry in Alberta. We travelled via Air Canada to Denmark and then on to Moscow.

There were very few good hotels in Moscow at that time, the main hotels being the National, the Metropole, and the Rossiya. We trade mission members stayed at the National, but we liked to go to the Metropole for breakfast as it was the only place we could get toast. (You had to sit at certain tables, though, as it seemed only one waitress would serve toast.)

The largest hotel—in fact, it was reputed to be the largest in the world at that time—was the Hotel Rossiya, a square building, some ten to twelve storeys high, which had about thirty-two hundred rooms and covered a whole city block. One evening at the Rossiya, I was going to meet some of our group at a certain location but I could not find them. The hotel was divided into four identical quarters, and I ran from one quarter to another, soon becoming hopelessly lost, and I never did find my fellow group members. In my travels around the hotel, I happened to be waiting for the elevator on one floor when a group of women got off, a bunch of middle-aged, broad-beamed, brawny ladies who were all drunk. They looked to me to be charwomen. One of them slipped and sat with her bum on the floor. She didn't seem to be able to get up, so I went and tried to help her. You should have heard the roars of laughter from the women as they watched me trying to lift a drunk 200-pound (90-kg) heavyweight. Although they couldn't speak English and I couldn't speak Russian, they seemed to want to adopt me and tried to get me to go with them as they got on the elevator.

Moscow was cold, at least when I was there in January 1971, around -20° to -30°F (-29° to -34°C). Our charming Russian guide and interpreter told us we had to cover our heads, so I bought a Russian fur cap, which kept me quite warm. The hotel's heating system was hot water from a central heating plant that supplied heat and hot water for the whole downtown area. The first time I ran my tap in my hotel bathroom, the water ran cold for fifteen minutes, so I reported to the front desk that there was no hot water. I was told it took quite a while for the water to get hot and I should let the tap run for a while longer. I ran it for about half an hour before finally getting some hot water. I could only imagine the terrific waste of water and heat this system created. I also remember that there was a huge outdoor swimming pool, which covered a whole city block. In the winter you could see nothing but a cloud of steam rising from the pool. The people of Moscow seemed to be very hardy, as there were always a lot of people in the water, even when it was -20°F (-29°C) or colder.

Leaving Moscow, we flew to the city of Tyumen, which was the centre of oil production in Siberia. We flew in a propeller-driven, four-engine plane that was loaded to the gills with passengers returning to Siberia from Moscow. Everyone seemed to be laden with bags of things they couldn't obtain in Tyumen, especially oranges. On this flight, we were accompanied by Ed Volsky, an oil ministry engineer who spoke excellent English and had been assigned to be our guide during our Russian visit. At Tyumen, we were joined by two of the resident oil ministry engineers, with whom our delegation boarded a helicopter to visit one of the large gas fields—the Midviziye. This field, we were told, contained 50 trillion cubic feet of gas, the equivalent of total Canadian reserves at that time. Midviziye was dwarfed by another field, approximately 62 miles (100 km) away—the Urengoye field, which the engineers told us held 200 trillion cubic feet of gas.

Most of the land in the Midviziye area is many feet below sea level. Characteristic of the taiga, it is blanketed by small spruce or fir trees standing only a few feet high. The area is one vast swamp, and in summer most of it is covered by water. At one point during our helicopter flight, I noticed a pipeline floating on the surface of a lake, so I asked through Volsky if that was how they laid their pipelines—floating on the water. The engineer was a bit embarrassed at having to explain that there had been a miscalculation in the weights that were required to hold the pipeline down and as a result it had floated to the surface. We weren't impressed with any of the gas installations, which, although this may not have been a fair interpretation, looked as though they were held together with baling wire. General housekeeping around the plants was poor, as well, with rags or sacking tied onto pipes or valves.

Back in Moscow we met with various members and engineers of the Russian oil ministry and were then invited to speak to members of their oil institute. The institute in Moscow consisted of approximately four thousand people, mainly engineers and scientists. When I gave my talk on gas processing, I was quite surprised to discover that the Russian engineers and scientists were woefully ignorant about this subject. This I determined from the questions they raised—they demonstrated a very limited knowledge of the treatment of natural gas. The two gas plants that I saw in the Midviziye area were built by foreign firms, and I gathered that the Russians had not yet built a plant themselves. One of the plants I saw was designed and constructed by a French company, and the other was built by an Italian firm. The latter had a very tall building—it must have been 70 to 80 feet (21 to 24 m) high—that totally enclosed the various towers. In Canada, the practice is to make the building a standard height, only high enough to enclose the piping and the various vessels, plus the bottoms of the towers. The top parts of the tower stick out of the roof, as it is a waste of building space to totally enclose it. It's also a waste of energy to have to heat an unnecessarily high building.

The Russians were very hospitable, and we were treated to several banquets, which lasted for hours and consisted of innumerable toasts. Each toast required downing a small glass of vodka. Since I am allergic to alcohol and can't drink even a small amount, I would fill my glass with water. No one objected to this except a large, dark-haired woman who seemed to have quite a bit of authority. She reamed me out for not drinking, but I managed to escape her scrutiny for the rest of the evening and didn't incur any further wrath.

In early 1970s Russia, everything was scarce. Clothing was drab, with little variety. In the large GUM department store, I saw a lady trying to buy a pair of shoes. Apart from the terrible service she received from the clerk, she was not able to try on the shoes—all the clerk did was stand the pair on end to show the woman that both shoes were the same length. I also saw brassieres made of rough material that looked to me like canvas, and the largest size they came in, size ten, was large enough to hold two medium-sized watermelons. I was going to buy one as a joke to take home to Kim, but I found out that a brassiere cost 100 rubles. At the official exchange rate of $1.42 Canadian to 1 ruble, the joke would have cost me $142 Canadian. So Kim didn't get her brassiere.

On my last trip to Russia in December 1975, I went on my own. Our company had put together a proposal to build a gas plant and we were anxious to present it to the Russian officials. They had tried to dissuade me from going at that time, saying that there were no hotels available except Russian ones, but I said I would stay at a Russian hotel. What a mistake! The room was okay, though spartan. However, in order to take a shower, you had to go to the basement, where there was a wooden walkway floating on the water that covered the floor. The place was so wet and dirty that I didn't take a shower and tried to have a sponge bath in my room. Luckily, I didn't have to eat my meals in my own hotel; I could eat at one of the international hotels, such as the Metropole, downtown.

On my last day in Moscow I had hailed a taxi to take me to the hotel, when all of a sudden a young woman was in the seat beside me. She spoke in English and asked me to trade some dollars for rubles. I told her that I didn't need rubles as I was leaving the next day. Then she offered to sleep with me if I would change some dollars. She was quite put out when I refused and finally got out of the taxi. Afterward I wondered if she might have been an agent, as not many Russian women spoke English.

Our efforts in Russia were to no avail, as we never received any reply to our proposal. However, about six months after we had submitted our proposal, which included a flow sheet showing our proposed design, an article appeared in a Russian magazine stating that the Russians had invented a new technology for recovering heavier hydrocarbons such as propane and butane from natural gas by using a turbo-expander. A turbo-expander employs energy from the high pressure at which the gas comes up from the wellhead to drive a turbine. The gas is thus reduced in pressure, which results in a lowering of the temperature and the liquefaction of the heavier hydrocarbons. We had coincidentally included a turbo-expander in our proposal and showed the design in our flow sheet. The only conclusion we could draw was that the Russians had claimed this as their own invention! Turbo-expanders had been used for several years previous to this, so the Russians' claim to having invented them at this date was rather ludicrous, to say the least.

In 1973 we at Mon-Max formed a consortium called Concanal, which brought together several companies to perform work in Algeria. The consortium partners included Montreal Engineering, Trans Canada Pipe Lines, and Canadian Pacific Railway. I'm not quite sure why CPR was included, but I believe some thought that if we obtained a contract to build a plant, transportation might be needed. At any rate, CPR had no input into any work we did there. However, I do remember going into the company's dark-panelled offices in Montreal for a meeting and thinking that they acted as though they were still rulers of the roost, as they had been back in the early days.

In an attempt to obtain work from Sonatrach, the Algerian government gas company, I made several trips to Algiers in 1973 to meet Mr. Boucharif, the Sonatrach department head, whom I found to be quite capable. Unfortunately—in my opinion, anyway—he was the only engineer in Sonatrach's gas department who had any knowledge of gas processing. On one of my visits, I was invited to accompany Boucharif to Hassi R'Mel, a gas field in the Sahara. We drove south from Algiers into the desert for several hours. For the first 30 miles (50 km) or so, the landscape was not entirely bare, as there were bits of vegetation such as might be seen in the Arizona desert, though much more sparse. However, the farther into the Sahara we went the sparser the vegetation, until there was nothing but sand.

We arrived at Hassi R'Mel late in the afternoon, and the hours passed by with no sign of dinner. Finally, at about 11:00 PM, there was great fanfare and a whole sheep was brought in. It had been roasted on a spit all day and had a sword stuck though its throat to keep it erect on its four legs. Apparently, the dinner was in honour of Mr. Boucharif, who was a sheik in his own right and had been a leader during the rebellion against France that led to Algeria's independence. Immediately, the Algerians began tearing strips of skin and meat off the sheep. One of the engineers tore off a strip of skin some 6 to 8 inches (15 to 20 cm) long and offered it to me—this was presumably a choice serving. In addition to alcohol, I am allergic to mutton fat and so wondered how I was going to cope with this situation. It would have been rude and a sign of disrespect to turn it down, so I managed to eat a morsel but soon after had to run to the bathroom to be sick. I managed to get through the rest of the evening without swallowing any more of the sheep, only pretending to eat. The next day I was so ill that I couldn't do very much. The medic came to see me and asked if I was allergic to anything, and I said, "Yes, to egg yolks." He said, "Oh! That's probably the reason for your being ill. There are eggs mixed with the brains." Apparently, there had been a side dish that contained the sheep's brains, but I hadn't eaten any of it since it didn't look too appetizing.

Me, skiing at Zermatt, Switzerland, in 1975. The Matterhorn rears in the background.

The following day, a strong persistent wind from the north—known as a "shamal," from the Arabic word for "north"—started to blow, and we experienced a Sahara windstorm. It was the most depressing phenomenon, with the wind howling and nothing visible because of the blowing sand. Indoors, the very fine red sand permeated everything—it came through all the cracks and openings in the building—and left a fine layer of sand in the showers, in the corners, everywhere. Because of the storm, we were not able to drive back to Algiers for a couple of days. When we finally did go, we travelled at night. On the way we came upon some shepherds and their flocks in the middle of the night. It was just as though we had come upon a scene from Biblical times, with the shepherds in their long cloaks and staffs tending their sheep.

Eventually we were fortunate enough to obtain a contract from Sonatrach to design a gas plant for Hassi R'Mel. The contract stipulated that we were to deliver certain documents on designated dates; otherwise, we would be in breach of contract. This meant I had to make numerous trips to Algiers from Calgary—in fact, I made thirteen trips to Algeria that year (1973). With considerable effort we were able to finish the design under the deadline, and I delivered the last of the documents on schedule. I was glad to see the last of the arduous chore of toting thirty-five large, hardcover books (seven copies of five volumes), plus my own luggage, from Calgary to Paris to Algiers.

Our Hassi R'Mel contract was a success. Concanal made a profit of about half a million dollars on a one-million-dollar fixed-price contract. Under the terms of the agreement governing Concanal, each company that carried out any project under its umbrella was responsible for doing all the work required to complete it—other than any assistance for any specific portion that might be requested from any of the partners. All partners were to share in the profits or losses. The next phase of the Algerian venture was the design and construction of a pipeline, which was effected by Trans Canada Pipe Line. Unfortunately, the company was bamboozled by the Sonatrach people and took the contract at much too low a price. For a contract value of less than one million dollars, they lost more money than we made in our Hassi R'Mel undertaking.

In early December 1975 I was honoured to receive an invitation to go as the Mon-Max representative on a trade mission to France with the Honourable Donald Jamieson, the Canadian minister of Industry, Trade and Commerce. The purpose of the mission was to expand two-way trade between Canada and France. This followed a mandate given by Prime Minister Pierre Trudeau and French President Jacques Chirac in November 1974 to ministers and officials of their respective governments directing them to develop and strengthen economic relationships between the two countries. The mission, made up of some thirty-five men, consisted of the elite of Canadian industry—presidents or vice-presidents of practically all the major industries in Canada, such as the Aluminum Company of Canada, Marine Industries (Canada's leading shipbuilder), BC Forest Products, BC Packers, Polysar, Canadair, Bombardier, CAE Electronics, Domtar, and National Sea Products.

I don't believe I contributed a great deal to the fostering of trade between Canada and France, mainly because our company was in the business of designing and constructing gas plants. We did not see much opportunity to do any projects in France, where we would have had to compete with the government-owned contractor Technip. However, the mission did prove beneficial to us. About two years previously, I had tried to obtain a licence for the process developed by the Institut Français du Pétrole for reducing the sulphur-dioxide emission from sulphur-plant stack gas. The licence had been granted to American engineering contractors such as Fluor, Bechtel, Ralph M. Parsons, and Stearns Rogers—companies that were all quite active in Canada. However, the French would not grant Mon-Max a licence, except as a sub-licensee to one of the American companies. This, of course, would put us in a non-competitive position if we were to bid on a project against one of these contractors. When I discussed it with the French representative in Calgary, I likened it to a situation in which five Canadian engineering contractors were licensed by an American company to use a certain process in France, but French firms were excluded from access to the licence in their own country.

241

Despite all our requests, plus solicitations from the Canadian Department of Industry, Trade and Commerce, we were totally ignored by the French. However, when I made the request in Paris for an interview with the licensors, the response was completely different from the seeming indifference of the French representative in North America. I was immediately granted an appointment with the president and vice-president of Technip and met with them in their penthouse office in the prestigious Paris la Defense building. They immediately granted me a licence and signed an agreement to joint-venture future projects, if any should arise. Such was the difference when one was under the aegis of the minister!

Mon-Max also courted Yugoslavia for work. This was Yugoslavia before it was chopped up into various states, now called Serbia, Croatia, Bosnia, and so on. As a matter of fact, when I was visiting there in the early 1970s, I had no inkling of the divisions and animosities that existed in the country. To assist me in my dealings in Yugoslavia, I was fortunate to obtain the services of an agent who became a very good friend. His surname was Putnik—I don't even remember his first name, as he was called "Flyo" by everyone he knew. I believe this name was bestowed upon him because of his having been a Grand Prix racing driver. Flyo could well have been a character out of a novel. In addition to his racing background, he had been an airplane pilot for Yugoslav Airlines and had been in three airplane crashes. His family had owned vast estates in Yugoslavia—including a parcel of land approximately 6 miles (10 km) square near Belgrade and huge homes in Dubrovnik. All this property had been confiscated by the state when Tito came to power.

On one visit when my wife, Kim, was with me, we had been staying at a hotel in Dubrovnik. When Flyo drove us to the airport, we discovered that we had forgotten to pick up our passports, which had been taken from us at the hotel and kept overnight. Flyo said not to worry—he would drive back to the hotel to retrieve the passports. We only had about half an hour before the flight was to leave and I didn't see how he could drive back the 20 miles (32 km) or so over the curvy road along the coast and return in time. He said, "They'll hold the flight for us." Away he went and was back with the flight delayed no more than ten minutes. I don't know how anyone could have driven that distance along such a winding road in the time he did. I also don't know of anyone else who would have had the clout to delay a scheduled flight for ten minutes. In any case, they hustled us on board and we were off to Rome.

Through Flyo's efforts, Mon-Max was finally put on the bid list for a gas plant that was to be constructed for NIS Naftagas, the government-owned gas company. During the meeting at which the bids were to be accepted, the Naftagas manager began by rejecting the bid from a German company because it was not accompanied by a bid bond. One of the requirements was that a bid bond of ten percent of the bid price had to be submitted with the bid. Since there was no way our company would supply a three-million-dollar bond (our bid price was approximately thirty million dollars), I gave Flyo a telex from the Export Development Bank in Ottawa indicating that if we obtained the contract to build the plant, they would finance it. Flyo gave this letter to his friend, the manager in charge, who then accepted our bid. The woman serving as the interpreter tried to interject that our bid didn't include the bid bond, but the engineer waved her aside and shushed her up. That showed how much influence my friend Flyo had! Unfortunately, before the contract for the gas plant was awarded, Flyo had a stroke and was placed in a hospital. He went into a coma from which he never recovered and died within a month. Thus ended our Yugoslavian project—without Flyo's aid, we were out of the running. ■

PART FIVE

DUBAI

Sunningdale Oils

*I*n 1976 I finally decided to leave Mon-Max when I was offered a new job opportunity by Wally Carlson, a former colleague. With his partner, he was doing maintenance and construction work for Fording Coal at Elko, British Columbia. He wanted to expand his operation and wanted my help. I was concerned about my future with Mon-Max as we had only been on their pension scheme for a few years, it being a relatively young company. I broached the subject with the management of Montreal Engineering and Humpheys & Glascow when they were forming the company Mon-Max–H&G Services (which later became MHG International). I told them that even if I worked until the age of sixty-five, my pension would only be about one thousand dollars a month, which I did not think was sufficient. I stated that something should be done for the people who had started Mon-Max and brought it to where it was at that time. Although they agreed that the pension was not very high, nothing was done about it. I decided I would have to go out and fund my own pension—which meant that at age fifty-eight, I would throw away a vice-presidency with a large company and start all over again. Everyone at Mon-Max tried to dissuade me, but I had made up my mind, and with Kim's backing I left. I could never have accomplished any of the things that I have done without her help and support. I took a large cut in salary, since I did not want to burden our new enterprise with a large overhead.

Wally and I rented an office from a friend, Arie Van der Lee, who was also trying to establish a new business. With my partners doing maintenance work for the Fording coal mine at Elko, our company— Cantraun Ltd.—was managing to keep its head above water. Soon after I moved into my office, I received information that there was an opportunity to submit a proposal for pumping stations on an oil pipeline in Ecuador. I made a trip to Ecuador and hired an agent named General Pico to promote our interests there. General Pico was a retired Ecuadorian air force general, a small man with a smile that lit up his face. He was very proud of the fact that he was the only Ecuadorian air force officer to have attained the rank of general. I soon learned that he hated Peru, with which Ecuador had a long-standing dispute over the territory that lay on the border between the two countries. During his military career, when the territorial dispute had erupted into warfare, Pico had flown over one of the Peruvian forts and dropped corn on it—the implication being that the Peruvians were chickens.

I eventually obtained the bid documents for the pipelines and returned home to Calgary to begin the monumental job of preparing the bid proposal. I was used to having a staff of dozens who could be called on to perform the necessary tasks to put a bid together. I hired my son, Dana, to help me and together we began the project. This involved putting together specifications for equipment, making flow sheets and layouts for the various pumping stations, and sending out specifications to suppliers for quotes. When we received the quotes back from the suppliers, we had to evaluate them and make a choice on what to use. Then we had to make estimates of the costs of equipment and labour to install and build the plant. Making estimates can be risky, as so many factors can affect the construction of a plant— weather, site conditions, labour, politics, and so on. Wally, who was an experienced construction man, handled the estimates for the labour and equipment that would be used to construct the pumping stations. Once all the information was amassed, we had to assemble all the material and have it translated into Spanish. Dana did a tremendous job, working some eighteen to twenty hours a day during the last few weeks to meet our deadline, and we finished the proposal in six weeks. I then travelled to Ecuador with our proposal, lugging several volumes of paper for each of the six stations. Then began the wait for the verdict on whether or not we had received the contract. To our disappointment we finally received word that the project had been postponed for a year—effectively dashing our hopes to the ground, as we couldn't afford to wait around for a year to try for the contract again.

One day in 1977, soon after I had submitted our proposal to CEPI, the Ecuadorian oil company, I received a call from Harvey Wylie, an old friend who had been a junior engineer with Brown & Root when I worked there. Harvey had gone to the United States to work for Pipeline Technologies, a pipeline engineering firm, and had risen to the position of president. He had then returned to Canada to become president of a newly formed company that was proposing to build the Mackenzie Valley pipeline from the Canadian Arctic to Alberta. When this project collapsed due to the failure to obtain governmental approval for the pipeline, Harvey had been recruited by the Canadian oilman Angus Mackenzie to become president of his company, Sunningdale Oils (which would later be renamed Scimitar Oils). The company was formed to recover the casing-head gas that was separated from the oil being produced by the Dubai Petroleum Company, 60 miles (100 km) offshore in the Arabian Gulf. (The rest of the world knows it as the Persian Gulf, but in the United Arab Emirates, this large body of water that defines the eastern edge of the Arabian Peninsula is referred to as the Arabian Gulf.)

Angus Mackenzie is a big, charismatic man who can charm anyone he meets. After all these years, I have never heard anyone say anything bad or detrimental about him. He had a storybook rise, beginning as a struggling land man[1] in Calgary and going on to become one of the richest and most respected oilmen in Canada. Angus served in the air force during the war as a pilot in the Coastal Command. After the war

247

he kept flying and did a considerable amount of aerial mapping. This led him into the oil business, first as a land man and then as a promoter of small oil and gas operations. His big break came in 1966 when he and a lawyer friend, Jim Palmer, went to Norway and were able to obtain a North Sea offshore lease in the Hemdahl Field, which became one of the most prolific oil producers in the area. I have heard stories about how the big producers were astounded at these two unknowns from Canada obtaining the lease, and one producer was heard to say, "Who are these guys anyway?"

In 1967, Angus moved from Calgary to Sunningdale, in Surrey, England, and named his company Sunningdale Oils. He eventually sold his holdings in the North Sea for seventy-five million dollars—a tremendous sum in the 1970s—to Kerr-McGee Corporation. Included in the sale were his holdings in Dubai. However, Kerr-McGee was not interested in the Dubai gas, so Angus was able to buy those rights back from them. He then negotiated with the Dubai government to obtain the rights to process the casing-head gas from the oil production offshore. The gas was originally the property of the Dubai Petroleum Company (DPC), which was controlled by the U.S. company Continental Oil. DPC had told the Dubai government that it was not economical to process this gas, so it was being flared. Angus persuaded the Dubai government—actually, he persuaded Sheikh Rashid, the ruler—that he could recover the casing-head gas and obtain propane, butane, natural gasoline, and dry gas from it.

This undertaking required building a large complex that consisted of offshore platforms and compressors, a pipeline 60 miles (100 km) to shore, and a gas plant on shore to separate the propane, butane, and natural gasoline from the methane gas. Also needed were refrigerated storage tanks for the propane and butane, as well as loading facilities for the refrigerated tankers that would transport these products to Japan. Angus offered to obtain the financing and assume all the risks associated with the project. The Dubai government would be the majority owner, with Angus's company, Sunningdale, retaining a minority interest.

Originally, Bob McBean, a young engineer from Calgary, lived in

Dubai as the Sunningdale representative and while there contributed a great deal to Angus's obtaining the rights to the gas. Bob moved back to London to work for Angus when Harvey Wylie became president of the company. Harvey offered me a consulting assignment to oversee the design of the gas plant that Sunningdale was building in Dubai. I had only a vague idea as to where Dubai was but accepted at once, as I was pleased to obtain some work.

The contract to design and construct the facilities in Dubai had been awarded to McDermott-Hudson in Houston. I began travelling from Calgary to Houston, where I would stay for a week at a time to audit McDermott-Hudson's engineering design. My old friend and mentor Spencer Landes, who had been chief process engineer for Brown & Root in Houston while I had been working for their Canadian subsidiary in Calgary, now had a consulting firm. He let me have a brilliant young engineer named Bob Smith to assist me in my work with McDermott-Hudson. Bob Smith worked in McDermott-Hudson's office daily to follow what they were doing, and I would visit for a week, off and on, to review with him what was being accomplished.

We found the members of McDermott-Hudson's staff to be very arrogant, particularly when it came to listening to any of our suggestions. I discovered the reason for their attitude when I went to Dubai to take over the plant the following year. McDermott-Hudson's representative in Dubai was Mahdi Al Tajir, who was Sheik Rashid's right-hand man and the United Arab Emirates ambassador to Great Britain. No one could do any business in Dubai without his permission, and so the McDermott-Hudson people thought they controlled all the offshore construction in Dubai and could do whatever they liked without brooking any interference from an upstart company like Sunningdale. In addition, I think they resented being told by someone from Canada—which they probably considered a third-world country—that they had made a mistake. Most people assume that large engineering companies have great knowledge and that anything designed by a large company like Bechtel, Fluor, or McDermott-Hudson should be above reproach. However, in the real world, the design is only as good as the engineer who performs the work. In many cases this work is produced by junior engineers who may lack the knowledge they need because it is not taught at university but instead comes later from sad experience, as I can attest myself.

After I had been commuting between Calgary and Houston for several months, Harvey Wylie asked me to join Sunningdale, offering me a position as vice-president, which came with a substantial salary and an interest in the company. I was to remain in Houston to oversee the engineering and then reside in Dubai and manage the operation, which was to be called the Dugas Project. Thus, late in 1977, I made a trip to Dubai to see what the place looked like and to get acquainted with the area prior to deciding whether or not to accept Harvey's offer. ■

History of Dubai

*U*ntil recently, the Western world knew very little about Dubai, because it was such a tiny emirate and considered to be an inconsequential state. However, in the past twenty years or so it has become fairly well recognized, particularly due to the activities of the ruling family, the Maktoums, in areas such as horse racing and golf. In England, the Maktoums—especially the crown prince, Sheikh Mohammed (the current ruler of Dubai)—practically control racing, owning hundreds of horses and promoting a prestigious race, the Dubai Stakes. In Dubai, the Maktoums have a large racing facility where they fund one of the richest—if not the richest—horse races in the world and horses from all over the world run in this race. Dubai now also has three wonderful golf courses and stages a European PGA golf tournament that lures the best European and American players, such as Tiger Woods. Ultra-modern hotels and building complexes have recently been built, one of which consists of islands formed in the shape of a palm tree, just offshore where some of the world's wealthiest people have constructed luxurious residences. A bizarre attraction on the Dubai landscape is an indoor ski hill, which generates snow and a wintry climate when the outside temperature may be 113°F (45°C).

It was recently reported that one third of all the building cranes in the world were operating in Dubai and that the total capital expenditure was over ninety billion dollars. What a contrast to the Dubai I first saw in 1977!

Dubai is a small state, approximately 40 miles (65 km) square, at the southeastern end of the Persian Gulf. The southern side of the gulf is now known as the United Arab Emirates (UAE), of which Dubai is a part, while the country of Iran lies on the opposite side of the gulf. The UAE is composed of seven emirates—Abu Dhabi, Umm al-Qawain, Sharjah, Ajman, Fujairah, Ras al-Khaimah, and Dubai—each ruled by a sheikh or an emir.

In the early nineteenth century, the south Persian Gulf area was referred to as the Pirate Coast because of the piracy carried out by the Qawasim tribe, which owed its allegiance to the Sultan of Oman, who in turn controlled Sharjah and Ras al-Khaimah. The British asked the Sultan of Oman to end the piracy but he was unable to do this, so in the end the British navy destroyed the pirates' main base at Ras al-Khaimah in 1819. The British had no desire to take over the area along the gulf, which they regarded as desolate; they merely wished to prevent the piracy that threatened shipping to and from India. When the Sultan of Oman could not control the pirates, the British concluded a series of treaties with various tribal leaders. The treaties guaranteed the integrity of the emirates in the area and the British promised not to interfere in their domestic affairs in return for a commitment to cease piracy.

The Qawasim pirates were mainly centred in Ras al-Khaimah, Ajman, and Sharjah, all of them small ports along the southeastern gulf coast. The treaties, however, included Dubai and Bahrain, which, although not hubs of pirate activity, were locations where the pirates would sell their booty and buy supplies. As a result of these treaties, the Arab side of the gulf came to be known as the "Trucial Coast." The Exclusive Agreement of 1881, drawn up by Great Britain, specified that these Trucial States could not make any international agreements or deal with any foreign countries without British consent. This, of course, meant that these states (the present UAE) were essentially British colonies and accounts for the British influence that still exists in the UAE to this day.

The British presence eliminated piracy, and pearl fishing became the main livelihood for the inhabitants of Dubai and the other Trucial States. With the advent of competition from Japanese cultured pearls in the 1930s, the industry declined to almost zero. However, Dubai prospered as a trading centre, with dhows (Arab boats) plying their trade to Persia (now Iran) and India. In the 1960s, oil was discovered offshore in Dubai, and this led to the state's modern-day prosperity.

In 1971 six of the emirates formed the UAE—Abu Dhabi, Dubai, Sharjah, Ajman, Fujairah, and Umm al-Qawain. They were joined in 1972 by Ras al-Khaimah to make up the present-day seven-emirate federation. There are very loose ties between the various emirates. Abu Dhabi is by far the largest and richest, with the most extensive reserves of oil. Dubai, although much smaller in size and with much less oil, was—and probably still is—as politically powerful as Abu Dhabi, primarily because of the leadership of its ruler Sheikh Rashid bin Saeed Al Maktoum and, since his death in 1990, his four sons. Each of the emirates has its own ruler. While I was in Dubai from 1978 to 1987, Sheikh Zayed bin Sultan Al Nahyan was the ruler of Abu Dhabi, and he and Sheikh Rashid of Dubai were the two most influential sheikhs. The lesser emirates tended to fall under the protection of these two more powerful and influential states.

It is interesting to note how tribal warfare was still the norm as late as 1939, when Sheikh Rashid was wedded to his one and only wife. At that time Rashid's father, Sheikh Saeed bin Maktoum, was the ruler of Dubai, which is on one side of Dubai Creek, the inlet that intersects the most heavily populated area of Dubai. The father of Rashid's bride was the ruler of Deira Dubai, on the opposite side of the creek. Sheikh Saeed, Rashid's father, had been quarreling with members of his "Majlis," a council of some of the leading members of his emirate. He dissolved the Majlis and ordered a group of Bedouins who were in Dubai for Rashid's wedding to attack and disperse these council members. During the ensuing melee, the father of Rashid's bride was killed. Because of this tragedy, Sheikh Rashid's sons are said to have promised their mother that they would never fight with one another. This is probably a primary reason for the stability of the ruling regime in present-day Dubai, plus the fact that Rashid had only one wife and therefore his four sons are all full brothers. This is in stark contrast to the scenario in Saudi Arabia, where the ruler had several wives and innumerable sons, who are only half-brothers and form competing factions, vying against each other for power. ■

Starting Out
in Dubai

*W*hen Harvey Wylie persuaded me to join Sunningdale Oils as vice-president of operations, I accepted the offer with some trepidation. My previous experience had been almost completely in the design and construction of gas and chemical plants—not in their operation. However, it was an exciting challenge and a great opportunity for me, with the possibility of a very substantial monetary return if we were successful in recovering the hitherto wasted hydrocarbons. I have often heard men deploring a change they made, or did not make, in their lives. Perhaps it has been merely good fortune, but I have never had any regrets in this respect, as everything has always worked out for the best whenever I made a career move. In this case, joining Harvey Wylie at Sunningdale was the best career move I ever made.

I first visited Dubai when Harvey kindly allowed me to visit there when I was still deciding whether or not to join him. When I encountered Dubai at that time—November 1977—the emirate was just emerging from being a relatively undeveloped, though quite bustling, port town to taking on the trappings of the thriving metropolis it was to become in a few short years. It must be remembered that only six years earlier it had been one of the Trucial States, a protectorate of Great Britain. Most of the city roads, except those in the downtown area near the creek, were unpaved, dusty tracks. The port of Jebel Ali, which would become the largest man-made port in the world, was still being carved out of the gulf 22 miles (35 km) southwest of the city of Dubai. Sunningdale's Dugas plant was to be built near Jebel Ali, ensuring excellent loading facilities for the tankers that would haul our products overseas.

I went back to Calgary and told Kim that I wanted to accept Harvey's offer and move to Dubai. Kim said, "Okay, you do whatever you think is best." I have been blessed with a wife who has backed me in every undertaking. Kim was even ready to move to a country she had never heard of! She had no idea of what life would be like in Dubai, other than the climate would be hot. It says a lot about her adventurous soul that she was unhesitating in her decision to accompany me to Dubai. Before moving to Dubai, however, I had to continue auditing McDermott-Hudson's engineering designs in Houston—in effect, pursuing the same work I had been doing as a consultant. So in early 1978, we wound up our company (Cantraun), and I moved to Houston. Kim joined me a few months later. We stayed in Houston for a year before leaving for Dubai.

The construction of the plant in Dubai began in late 1978, but I remained in Houston to receive treatment for my "frozen shoulder." I had been unable to lift my right arm to more than shoulder height and had gone to a doctor who said that I had bursitis and gave me a cortisone shot. When no improvement occurred, I went to see an orthopedic specialist who said that I had "frozen shoulder." He sent me to the athletic trainer at Rice University, who immediately began to manipulate my arm. Everyday for half an hour, he would try to rotate my arm in several directions, which would result in a hot, searing pain, accompanied by the sound of a little click, as an adhesion broke loose. The pain would last for half an hour or so after each treatment and then subside until the next session. After a month I could raise my arm to almost its full extent, so I left for Dubai. I was ready to leave Houston and especially the McDermott-Hudson engineering group.

We arrived in Dubai in early July 1978, the hottest time of the year, but we did not find the heat oppressive as we had become used to the climate in Houston, which is very hot and humid in July. Temperatures in Dubai in the summer months range from 100 to 113°F (38 to 45°C), with the average high during the day usually somewhere between those temperatures. If you were not working in the sun, the conditions were not too onerous, as we drove air-conditioned cars and lived and worked in air-conditioned houses and offices. However, not everyone was as fortunate. For the fellows working in the hot sun on construction, it was quite enervating until they finally got used to the heat. So, although these temperatures may seem unbearable to anyone from Canada, we gradually became acclimated to them. People who had lived in Dubai for some time maintained that their blood had become thinner, allowing them to withstand the high temperatures. In my own case, I played golf regularly in 100 to 110°F (38 to 43°C) temperatures, which I would never do in Canada.

Before we moved to Dubai, we worried about how we would fit into the local scene. However, the culture shock was minimal—mainly because there was a sizable European and American community that had been there for several years. Perhaps only ten percent of the city's 250,000 residents were Arab; the majority of its inhabitants were Indians and Pakistanis who had come to Dubai, in most cases, to get away from the poverty in their countries. The Pakistanis, being Muslim, were probably more accepted by the Dubaians and many of the personnel in Dubai's armed forces were from Pakistan. I'm sure the lifestyles of the émigrés from India or Pakistan were considerably better than what they had experienced at home. We soon grew used to the sight of Arab men wearing a *dishdasha*—a long, white cloak covering the whole body down to the ankle—and a headdress known as the *ghutra*—a square scarf of cotton held in place by an *igal*, a doubled, black cord that sits on the top of the head. The Arab wives of devout Muslims wore veils, but unmarried women and girls went about with their face uncovered. Many of the Arab women we knew did not wear veils.

Moving to Dubai probably didn't induce as much culture shock as relocation to a country such as Saudi Arabia might have. For one thing, expat women had much more freedom and fewer restrictions in Dubai than in any other state in the Middle East. For example, they could drive cars, travel unaccompanied downtown to shop, and go into a hotel restaurant for a meal, things that they would not be allowed to do in Saudi Arabia. In Dubai, expatriates like us were allowed to purchase 275 dirhams worth of alcohol per month, the equivalent to more than 100 U.S. dollars a month, which was a considerable amount, considering the low cost of liquor in Dubai. As well, drinking was allowed in the hotel bars. This, of course, was in contrast to the practice in other Arab countries, where alcohol was strictly forbidden. As a result, many Arabs came to Dubai from Saudi Arabia and other neighbouring Arab states for recreational visits. Although Muslims were also forbidden to drink liquor in Dubai, they found ways to get around this taboo. I understand that at this date things haven't changed in this regard. ■

The Dugas Project

*T*he Dugas Project was larger and considerably more complex than the gas plants we were accustomed to in Alberta. First, there were the offshore platforms that had to be installed in the gulf. Dubai Petroleum (DPC) was producing oil from two fields in the gulf—the large field was known as "Fateh" and the smaller field was called "Southwest Fateh." The fields were named by Sheikh Rashid. According to the DPC, *fateh* means "good fortune." In each field, DPC had a platform on which separators were installed to treat the oil from the various wells.

Oil is a mixture of hydrocarbons that is at a high pressure underground. When brought to the surface, the mixture is sent to a separator where the lighter components (the gas) are separated from the heavier components (the oil). The oil can then be stored at atmospheric pressure and shipped around the world in tankers. We installed platforms at both the Fateh and the Southwest Fateh fields to capture gas that had previously been flared by DPC. On these platforms were centrifugal compressors powered by gas turbine engines that compressed the gas to a sufficiently high pressure to force it through a pipeline to our onshore plant. Included on the platforms, which were connected by bridges to the DPC platforms, were pressure vessels, piping, and instrumentation, plus a control room where the instruments were housed, living quarters for the operators, and a helipad for helicopters.

Once onshore, the compressed gas was put through a processing plant, where it was refrigerated to remove propane, butane, and heavier liquids called condensate. (This condensate is natural gasoline and could be used as such, but is normally sent to a refinery to be processed into marketable gasoline.) Once the propane and the butane were separated, each of these products was sent to a refrigerated storage tank that kept their vapour pressure near zero and allowed them to be stored in thin-steel-walled tanks. If these hydrocarbons were not refrigerated, the storage tanks would have had to contain pressures of several hundred pounds per square inch, making the cost of storage prohibitive.

The condensate was stored at atmospheric pressure in a separate tank and did not have to be refrigerated. This product could be handled in an ordinary oil tanker so was shipped separately from the propane and butane. When the storage tanks were filled to a sufficient volume, the refrigerated propane and butane were loaded onto tankers for shipment to Japan. Separate tankers were used for each product as they were kept at different temperatures—propane at -45 to -50°F (-43 to -46°C), butane at -28°F (-33°C).

While in Houston in 1978–79, I made frequent trips to Calgary to try to line up people to operate our plant. I think this was one of my most difficult tasks during the whole project—convincing capable personnel to move to Dubai. Fortunately, I had many contacts in Calgary, where I had become well known as the chief engineer and vice-president of Mon-Max. Most of the people I tried to hire had never heard of Dubai, but when they found out I was moving there to live and work, it helped convince them that perhaps going there wouldn't be such a bad idea. It also didn't hurt that there was no income tax in Dubai, and we would be supplying housing and an excellent salary. These factors helped to tip the scale in my favour. Looking back, I think I did a tremendous job of persuading so many capable men to uproot their families and move to Dubai. The gratifying part is that not one of them regretted their decision, and all agreed that I had lived up to my promises.

Several of the men I recruited from Calgary had worked long enough that they could leave their jobs with a pension, even though they had not reached the compulsory retirement age of sixty-five. Two men from Imperial Oil who were in this position were Gerritt Van Haaften, who became my maintenance superintendent, and Warren Shaw, who became my safety supervisor. By coming to work for us, they ended up tripling the amount of pension they would have received from Imperial Oil. Another key employee was Kurt Wechselberger, who was retiring from Dresser Machinery at the time I recruited him. He became my compressor expert and without him I don't think we could have kept our compressors running with so few problems. The compressors, located on the platforms in the gulf, pumped the gas the 60 miles (100 km) to shore and were the heart of our operation. I had managed to get McDermott-Hudson to hire my former partner Wally Carlson as a construction superintendent, and as he was a very capable construction man, I felt more than confident that the plant would be built properly.

Most of the credit for our safety record in Dubai must go to Warren Shaw, our safety director. Warren had spent many years with Imperial Oil in Canada as a safety man. He was a vocal advocate of safety requirements and, because of this, probably didn't rise up the ranks as far as he should have at Imperial Oil. I can just imagine some of his meetings with superiors who didn't agree with him. One time, I had Warren give a course on safe driving, and you should have seen the Englishmen in the audience bridle when he said, "You English fellows are still in the last century with regard to driving." Warren always spoke his mind, no matter what the consequences. I appreciated his forthrightness and honesty and gave him my full backing, even though his proposals may have been unpopular.

At an early stage of the construction, the platforms were built onshore and then floated out to sea on barges for installation. Before the platforms were taken offshore, however, pilings had to be installed as their foundation. For this purpose, large-diameter pipes were driven some 70 feet (21 m) into the seabed—not an altogether simple undertaking as the water was approximately 100 feet (30 m) deep. The pilings had to be sited precisely, as they had to match the legs of the pre-built platforms that were to be placed on top of them. Two platforms had to be installed—a larger one at the main Fateh field and a slightly smaller one at the subsidiary Southwest Fateh field.

In sharp contrast to my experience with the McDermott-Hudson engineers in Houston, the offshore arm of the company excelled in installing offshore facilities and did an excellent job installing the platforms. A calm day was chosen for placing the platforms on their foundations. Each platform was towed into position so that two cranes, situated on other barges, could lift it onto the pilings. The lifting was done at dawn, the calmest period of the day. Everything went like clockwork and both platforms were installed without mishap or problems—much to everyone's relief. Simultaneously, a pipeline was laid from the Fateh field to shore, and another small pipeline was tied from the Southwest Fateh field into this main line. Construction proceeded on the onshore plant and the refrigerated storage tanks, and loading facilities were installed for the tankers, which were to berth at the new port of Jebel Ali adjacent to our onshore plant.

The Jebel Ali port, which was in the final phases of construction as our facilities were being built, was a huge undertaking and a tribute to the foresight of Dubai's ruler, Sheikh Rashid. It was, and still is, the largest man-made harbour in the world and reputedly ranked alongside the Great Wall of China and the Hoover Dam as being the only man-made objects that can be seen from space by the naked eye. The construction involved excavating several million cubic yards of sand and pouring huge amounts of concrete to form the wharves. When completed, it had berths for sixty-seven ocean-going ships, with 9 miles (15 km) of quayside.

The Dugas Gas Plant in Dubai, 1980.

After the liquid products were removed from the offshore gas, the remaining dry gas, primarily methane, was delivered free of charge via pipeline to the Dubal aluminum plant, located a short distance away, for use in its gas turbine engines. These engines drove the electrical generators that supplied power to produce aluminum. A valuable by-product of the plant's aluminum production was desalinated water, which was produced from the waste heat of the gas turbine engines that were driven by the dry methane gas—up to 150 million standard cubic feet of gas per day. The emirate was thus able to produce some 20 million gallons (91 million litres) of water per day to augment the water obtained from wells, which had previously been the only source of palatable water in Dubai. This new source of drinking water was welcomed by everyone in the country, since the well water—although drinkable—did not have a pleasant taste.

The completed plant was started up in midsummer of 1980. We had a grand opening, with Sheikh Rashid opening a valve to start the gas flowing. In the months that followed, we gradually got the bugs worked out and the plant operating smoothly, and we began to build up our stock of propane, butane, and condensate in our tanks. We had contracted to supply our products to the Japanese, with C. Itoh being our main customer. Our production became so steady that the Japanese said we were their favourite supplier as they could schedule their pickups with confidence. This was apparently in contrast to their experience with other producers in the gulf.

Soon after we began operating our plant, it became evident that we needed to increase its size, as we were unable to process all the gas being piped our way. McDermott-Hudson was eager to build the extension, but I knew they had charged us an exorbitant amount for building our original plant. For our plant expansion, I proposed that we do our own engineering design and construction, something unheard of in Dubai, as it was taken as a foregone conclusion that McDermott-Hudson would perform any engineering or construction work required in the emirate. This was, of course, predicated on the influence of Mahdi Al Tajir. However, the Dugas Project was under the

Sheikh Rashid bin Saeed Al Maktoum of Dubai opens a valve to
start gas flowing at the Dugas Plant opening in 1980.

auspices of Sheikh Hamdan Maktoum, one of Sheikh Rashid's sons, so
Mahdi Al Tajir would have no say in the matter if Sheikh Hamdan
allowed us to proceed. With our production going full blast and the
resultant monetary success we were enjoying, we proposed building the
extension out of our own revenues, without having to borrow money,
and so were given the go-ahead. Of course, I became very unpopular
with McDermott-Hudson—especially when I told them we knew more
than they did about designing and building gas plants.

Performing the engineering by ourselves was a formidable task, as
our engineering staff consisted of only two process engineers, one
instrumentation engineer, one electrical engineer, one civil engineer,
and three draftsmen. This was nothing compared to the much larger
number that would have been considered mandatory in Canada or the
United States. I could well understand why McDermott-Hudson

scoffed at the idea that a few Canadians could design and construct a large gas plant complex with such a limited staff. Fortunately, Harvey Wylie backed me to the hilt in all our proceedings. His faith in me was certainly appreciated.

To assist in our engineering, I called up Bob Pivoras, an old friend and colleague who lived in Calgary, and asked him to come to Dubai to work for us on a contract basis. It was gratifying to have him accept our offer—he could turn out the work of five routine draftsmen. With our team, we were able to complete our engineering with no major errors or conflicts, and construction began in 1981 under the capable leadership of Wally Carlson.

We had a very hazardous assignment before us, as we were preparing to perform construction within an operating gas plant that had very flammable materials flowing through it. The construction required welding with arc-welding machines, as well as cutting steel with oxyacetylene torches. There was a continual danger of igniting any gas or liquid hydrocarbon leak. The hazards were compounded by the unskilled Indian workmen we had to use (the only workers available at the time). The Philippine and European tradesmen were more knowledgeable about the risks that were involved, since they had previously been exposed to working in such environments. We were fortunate not to have even one serious accident or fatality during the whole project. We felt rather smug as we completed our construction on schedule, especially since we had heard that the McDermott-Hudson people had taken bets that we would fall flat on our faces and have to call on them to come to our rescue. We also patted ourselves on the back when the new facilities performed as we had calculated. The cost of construction was approximately a third of what we estimated McDermott-Hudson would have charged us, based on their charge for the original plant.

The throughput of the expanded facilities allowed us to double our production rate. The additional feed to the plant was augmented by gas from the new Rashid field, which produced natural gas and condensate. As we had been granted the right to the Rashid field's natural gas, as well as to the associated gas from DPC's oil production, we had to drill new wells and build a new pipeline to tie into our existing pipeline from the Fateh and Southwest Fateh fields.

When we opened up the new pipeline to bring in gas from the Rashid field, we waited several days for the gas to reach the shore. However, despite our anxious waiting, no gas appeared. We then inserted "pigs" into the line, thinking that something was blocking it.

One of our offshore platforms in the Persian Gulf off Dubai, ca. 1980.

("Pigs" are inflated rubber balls, similar in size to a soccer ball or basketball, used to remove accumulated debris.) Despite all our efforts, nothing happened. I then asked the construction superintendent, an American with many years of experience as a construction superintendent with Brown & Root, whether the check valve at the junction with the existing pipeline from Fateh had been installed correctly. Both he and his inspector stated unequivocally that the valve had been installed correctly, that they had both witnessed the installation, and that there was nothing wrong with the piping. Finally, after several days in which the gas didn't appear, I ordered a barge with a crane to lift the pipelines at the junction and cut the line open to examine it. The superintendent argued vehemently against taking this action, stating it was a waste of time and money. However, I insisted that we proceed with the inspection, and the necessary equipment was hired. When we inspected the line, we found that the check valve had been installed backward, and all the pigs we had sent from the Rashid field were stuck behind the valve. Needless to say, the superintendent and the inspector's days with us were numbered after this incident.

With the feed from the Rashid field augmenting the flow from the other fields, we soon began to produce in the order of 30,000 barrels a day of propane and butane, and 150 million standard cubic feet of dry gas. With production like this, we soon paid off all the debt from our foreign loan, and from then on the profits rolled in for the government and Scimitar Oils (Sunningdale Oils's new name). The Dugas Project and Scimitar Oils became the darlings of the financial world. ■

Living in Dubai

When I first saw Dubai in 1977, it was just beginning to awake from the somnolence it had been in since the nineteenth century, when its primary source of wealth was pearl diving. Before the introduction of oil into the economy, trading had been the main commercial activity, with dozens of dhows transporting goods up and down the gulf. Dhows, which can still be seen plying the waters of the gulf, are built of teak wood, with practically the same form as they have had for centuries, the only difference being the substitution of diesel- or gasoline-powered engines for the original sails. The dhows are built locally from pieces of gnarled teak, which are somehow shaped into boards suitable for forming the hull. In the 1950s, one of the primary activities in Dubai was smuggling gold into India. With gold at thirty-five U.S. dollars an ounce, but realizing much more in India, a thriving business had sprung up. Syndicates were formed with many of the prominent businessmen as participants, and perhaps leaders, in the venture. Each enterprise was quite hazardous as there was always the risk that the shipment would be seized as contraband. However, enough of the undertakings were successful that many Dubaians became quite wealthy, and it was generally accepted that most of the affluence of the eminent members of the business community was the result of successful gold smuggling.

As I have noted elsewhere, the Arab population of Dubai was quite small, with the majority of the residents being Indian or Pakistani and most of the army personnel being from Pakistan. In addition, there were perhaps a couple of thousand expats—mostly from Great Britain, although there were significant numbers of Europeans and Americans as well. Most of the expats lived in Jumaira, an area located a short distance from the "creek" downtown. Their homes were rented, as only local Dubaians were allowed to own property. With the building of our plant, we enhanced the North American flavour of the expat community by adding a few hundred Canadians to the group—this contingent being made up of seventy-or-so men, their wives, and their children.

The makeup of the local population varied between city dwellers and desert nomads. The desert people were Bedouins, who lived as their forbears had for centuries past—roaming the desert with their flocks of sheep and goats and, of course, camels. On the other hand, many of the city dwellers were of Iranian origin, although some had come from other Arab regions in the gulf, such as Bahrain. They were the businessmen who were responsible for the commerce in the region.

Some of the characters who had gravitated to Dubai could have come out of a work of fiction. One prominent businessman was alleged to have Mafia connections. He had built a large housing estate that rented houses to expatriates and owned a large offshore construction service, complete with tugs and other work boats. When he sold this company to a German firm for some thirty million dollars, his partner, who managed the operation, only received three million dollars, which he didn't consider his fair share. According to the story, when the disgruntled partner returned to the United States, he tried to hire a hit man to murder his former associate. However, the person whom he tried to recruit to do the killing was a "sting" FBI undercover operator, so he was apprehended and charged.

The man who installed the communication system that connected our offshore platform and the shore was a German whom we believed to be an agent of the Dubai government. He seemed to have a lot of power as he was able to have someone whom he suspected of trying to dally with his wife deported from the country. He always drove a Mercedes, which he said he had got as a cast-off from Sheikh Mohammed. He claimed to have the ear of Sheikh Mohammed and also claimed to have worked for the CIA in Germany. We suspected that he was still a CIA informant, as well as being a Dubai government agent.

Among the most interesting characters were the only two Arab lawyers with British legal training in Dubai. Since all court proceedings were in Arabic, none of the American or European lawyers in Dubai could argue cases before the Dubai courts, which made Fuad Barahim and his friend Mohammed Merjahn the pre-eminent barristers in the state. They were able to command very large fees from American and European corporations whenever they had legal problems in the country. I remember one instance in which Fuad demanded and received one million U.S. dollars before taking on a case.

Fuad was from Aden in Yemen and had obtained his legal training at the famous Inns of Court in London. He would jokingly remark that when he told any of the Arabs in Dubai that he had graduated from the Inns of Court, they thought he had taken a course in hotel management. Fuad, the most jovial person I knew, with a wonderful smile, became a true friend. He unfortunately died in 2004, and Kim and I sorely miss him. His widow, Elizabeth, now lives in England and remains one of our staunchest friends.

Life in Dubai was very pleasurable for expats—especially so for some of our operators and their wives who came from sleepy, small towns in western Canada. Most of them had never been away from North America, so living in a Middle Eastern state like Dubai was a real eye-opener for them. Their standard of living, in most cases, improved dramatically, as the men received much higher rates of pay than they would have earned in Canada. In addition to their wages, they received free housing and a generous living allowance—all this combined with fully paid fares back to Canada for a month's vacation each year. This arrangement allowed them to see parts of the world they would never have seen otherwise, as it was soon discovered that you could obtain a round-the-world ticket for less than the cost of a straight-return fare from Dubai to Canada. The round-the-world tickets allowed generous stopovers at various places, such as Hong

Kong and Singapore. Practically all the Canadian personnel made round-the-world flights at least once.

Certainly, Kim and I lived quite a glamorous existence in Dubai compared with our previous life in Canada. We had a year-round swimming pool installed in our yard, which was heated for use during the winter months and cooled by refrigeration during the summer months. Kim had two servants and didn't have to do any cooking or housecleaning. She also got to know several Arab women, with whom she became good friends. These women wore the most enormous diamonds, rubies, and emeralds that she had ever seen, an opulence that they carried over into their homes. Not content with sterling silverware, they sported gold-plated cutlery, as well as gold plate on every fixture in the house. I recall visiting the home of one of the Galadari brothers, who owned the Intercontinental Hotel, the Renault automobile agency, and many other businesses in town. I could hardly believe the amount of gold that was used throughout this dwelling— gold doorknobs, gold staircase railings, and gold bathroom fittings.

For entertainment, there were dinner-theatre nights at the Intercontinental Hotel, where theatre companies from London regularly put on performances. There were also appearances by well-known stars from the United States and England. The more adventurous types among us made forays into the desert on dune buggies or camels. Of course, you did not need to go far from the city to see the desert and herds of camels being driven somewhere. We also had access to the ocean. Sometimes we drove to Fujairah, the only emirate that borders the Indian Ocean. The waters off Fujairah have an abundance of shellfish and fish, and devotees of underwater diving took advantage of its beautiful water and natural life.

One of my favourite pastimes in Dubai was golf. When we were there, they had not yet built the luxurious grass courses that the emirate now boasts—we played on a sand course with oiled greens. The fairways were marked out, and as long as you were within the fairway boundaries, you could hit the ball off a piece of Astroturf that you carried with you. If you strayed off the fairway, however, the ball had to be struck off the sand. I used to play nine holes after work, even though the temperature was usually well above 100°F (38°C). At times, we had to contend with camels that refused to get out of the way and sometimes trampled the oiled greens.

Shopping was excellent in Dubai. You could purchase designer creations at much lower prices than in Paris, London, or New York, and there was an extensive selection available. Then there was the famous Soukh, a series of streets where dozens of merchants sold gold jewellery at the lowest prices in the world. The price of gold was the same worldwide, but the cost of the labour to create the jewellery, which was fashioned by Indian craftsmen, was very low. Since the higher the content of gold the more malleable it is, much of the jewellery was twenty- or twenty-two-karat gold, versus the fourteen- or eighteen-karat gold common to North America and Europe.

Before—and even after—the advent of the supermarket in Dubai, shopping for groceries was a major occupation for the Dubaian housewife. It was a fascinating operation, progressing from the vegetable market to the fish market to the meat market. In the vegetable market, almost anything grown anywhere in the world could be bought. We saw fruits and vegetables we had never heard of before. In the fish market, there was a huge variety of seafood available, all of it caught nearby in the gulf. A favourite was hamour, a grouper that was the tastiest fish you could wish to eat. The main problem for Westerners who were at all squeamish was the hordes of flies that descended upon all the food, and especially the dates. Ever since then, I have been leery of eating dates.

One of the boons of living in the gulf was the wonderful fishing. Although I was not a fisherman, some of our friends were, and they caught large marlin and other game fish. There must have been practically every type of fish in the gulf—some operators told of seeing sharks 20 feet (6 m) or so in length. The fishing I enjoyed was catching cigalees, a type of lobster or crayfish that is attracted to the water's surface by light at night. They only come to the surface in this manner during their spawning season in October, so we would wait for a moonless night in October and go offshore near the platforms, where the cigalees would come to the surface, drawn by the light of the flare. We would chase them in Zodiacs or other small boats, two to a boat, which were powered by outboard motors. While one man steered the boat, the other would kneel in the front with a net attached to a long pole and scoop up the cigalees. In this way, we would catch several hundred during the night. Immediately after boarding the larger mother boat, we would break off their triangular, fan-shaped heads, which left us with a lobster tail from 4 to 6 inches (10 to 15 cm) long. These were put on ice to take to shore. Each of us usually had as many as two hundred to freeze for later use. They are the tastiest and sweetest lobster tails that I have ever eaten.

There was quite a social whirl in Dubai. There seemed to be a continual round of company cocktail parties that I was obliged to attend because of my position as senior vice-president of our company, as well as many private house parties to which we were invited and felt we had to make an appearance. The round of festivities especially intensified in December before Christmas, when there seemed to be a function every night. It got so I dreaded the approach of Christmas. I especially disliked the late dinners. Dinners at these parties would usually be served just before midnight, and since we felt it would be impolite to leave before then, Kim and I would not get home until 2:00 AM at the earliest. Then I would have to get up to be at the office in Jebel Ali—a half-hour drive away—by 8:00 AM. After a week of this, I would be ready to drop.

We were also invited to several wedding celebrations, which were much different from our Western counterparts. Arab weddings are really extravagant affairs, and the local men seemed to compete with each other to see who could provide the most lavish wedding for their daughter. Some weddings cost hundreds of thousands of dollars and lasted for several days. For the men, the weddings were boring affairs—at least in my opinion—as the men were invited to a men-only party. The entertainment would be Arab music, which was not to my taste, and this would be followed by the dinner, which was quite sumptuous, but then everyone would soon leave to return home. The women, on the other hand, had their own celebrations that went on for several days. They were entertained by women dancers and had a much more gala time—the more affluent the parents the more sumptuous and elaborate the festivities. Very seldom were Westerners invited to these affairs, but Kim had become good friends with some of the Arab women and was invited to several of them.

One of the fringe benefits of living in Dubai that Kim and I enjoyed was being able to attend Royal Ascot in England every June for seven years. At that time, the three prime summer social events in England were, in chronological order, Ascot, Wimbledon, and Henley. Ascot is a week of horse racing that is attended by the Queen, who often has horses running in one of the races. Wimbledon is the world-famous tennis tournament played on grass courts, and Henley is a rowing event held on the Thames. Royal Ascot is probably the most prestigious of these events. The Queen and other members of the Royal Family drive from Windsor Castle in their horse-drawn coaches to the racetrack to make a grand entrance at the beginning of each day's racing. Along this route everyone lines up to get a glimpse of the Queen and her family as they make their way up to their box in the stadium, known as the Royal Enclosure. Tickets to the Royal Enclosure are difficult to obtain and are much prized, so we were fortunate to be able to attend each year. We were able to do so through our friendship with Omar Assi, the right-hand man of Sheikh Maktoum, the crown prince of Dubai. Omar was a very urbane and polished Palestinian who looked after the Sheikh's business affairs, especially matters concerned with racing. He had an English wife named Sandra, who resided in Sunningdale, near Ascot. Kim and I became very good friends with both Omar and Sandra, and thus Royal Ascot became an annual affair for us.

The Maktoum brothers—Maktoum (the crown prince), Hamdan, Mohammed, and Ahmed—between them owned some seven hundred racehorses and, as mentioned earlier, were then the foremost racehorse owners in Britain. Until their arrival on the British racing scene, Robert Sangster, the multi-millionaire owner of football pools in England, was the most successful racing owner. However, by the early 1980s he was eclipsed by the Maktoums, especially by Sheikh Mohammed, who in 1983 paid the highest-ever price for a yearling colt, some ten million U.S. dollars, at the annual Keeneland sales in Lexington, Kentucky. He paid this for an offspring of Northern Dancer, the famous Canadian racehorse, but unfortunately the colt failed to develop as anticipated and was never raced.

Because Royal Ascot was the highlight of social events in England during the summer, I had to get a top hat and tails and Kim had to shop for hats, as every woman had to wear a hat. There was, and still is, great competition amongst the women over who has the most beautiful millinery. Some of the hats we saw were outlandish creations, but some were gorgeous and it was delightful to see the ladies in their beautiful outfits. I felt a bit uncomfortable the first time I put on my tails and top hat, but when I got to Ascot and saw all the other men in Royal Enclosure in the same garb, it no longer bothered me. By this time Kim and I had purchased a flat in a building in Knightsbridge, London, that was occupied by several widows of titled men, who would therefore be referred to as Lady So and So. At first they were all rather aloof, but after seeing Sheikh Maktoum's limousine with a uniformed chauffeur pick us up each day to go Ascot, they became quite friendly—I suppose they thought we must be "somebodies."

The Maktoum family had two rooms at Ascot, which were dubbed "chalets." In these we could relax and were continually served with the best of food and drink. The highlight of each day was the visit to the paddock to await the arrival of the Queen and other members of the Royal Family. I enjoyed the racing as well, as I was fairly successful at betting on the races. I knew nothing about horses, but each racing day I would buy every newspaper and racing journal I could find and tabulate the ratings by each writer. In this way, I developed a handicapping system based on my analysis of the predictions of these "experts." My most successful day was when I asked Glenda Salyer if I could accompany her to the paddock where the horses paraded before going out onto the track. Glenda was an attractive veterinarian from Lexington, Kentucky, who served as an adviser to Sheikh Maktoum regarding the purchase of horses. She certainly knew her horseflesh, so I said to her: "Glenda, I have been fairly successful at handicapping, but I don't know anything about horses. Could you help me pick out the horses when they parade in the paddock?" She very kindly said, "Sure. Come with me." She asked me which horses I had picked and then gave me her opinion of them. That day, I won three "forecasts" at Ascot. A forecast is what we in Canada call an "exactor"—the bettor is required to pick the winner and the second-place horse. When the afternoon's racing was finished, Omar Assi, Glenda Salyer, and I drove to Lingfield for the evening racing there. There I won another forecast, so that made four in one day—a very profitable day's racing. ■

Afterword

Still Active

After leaving Dubai in 1987, I retired. Kim and I lived in England for several years, where we made some very good friends with whom I played golf. We now live in Kelowna, British Columbia. Of all the parts of the globe that Kim and I have seen, we knew Kelowna was the place where we wanted to retire. The climate is ideal, especially in the summer, and the winters are not too extreme. Besides, we usually retreat to Green Valley, south of Tucson, Arizona, for a few months in the winter. We feel more at home in Kelowna than in any other place in which we have lived or visited. Even if everything else came out even, Kelowna and the Okanagan Valley's fruits and vegetables would tip the balance. I don't think local residents realize that they are the best in the world.

In my retirement, I have kept busy with interests in various enterprises—including a gold and platinum property in Wyoming. I have also become involved in several other undertakings through my good friend David Coombs in Kelowna.

I have been very fortunate in being able to keep healthy—so healthy that when I went for my medical in Houston at the age of eighty-five in 2003, I astounded the staff at the Diagnostic Hospital when I took a stress test for my heart. Electrodes from an electrocardiogram apparatus were attached to my chest and with this equipment recording my pulse rate and other data, I began walking and then running on a treadmill. The treadmill was started at a slow rate, then the speed was increased and the slope was elevated every three minutes, six times for a total duration of eighteen minutes. To the amazement of the nurse attending me, I was able to do the whole eighteen minutes. She told me many thirty year olds couldn't do that. However, my cardiologist, whom I have known for several years, wasn't surprised—he had seen me do it before.

In 2002 Kim and I suffered a tragic loss with the death of our only son, Dana. He was living in Calgary while we were in Kelowna. He had complained of a pain in his back that he attributed to perhaps having hurt while playing golf. I had previously asked him if his heart was okay and he assured me that it was. I never suspected that his back problem was related to his heart, as I had always thought the symptom of a heart blockage was a pain in the arm. On the day before his death, he had gone to see our former family physician, who was now working part-time. I'm not sure what the doctor gave him but he did nothing else and sent him home. Dana died the next day from a one-hundred-percent blockage of a heart artery. Needless to say it was a terrible blow. In addition to being my son, he was a friend and an adviser whose advice I valued. His memory is kept alive by our two wonderful granddaughters, Ariel and Danielle, who were born in 1983 and 1985, respectively. Ariel has been a great help to me, arranging my golf tournaments and generally looking after some of my affairs.

Golf continues to be my favourite pastime. I have been fortunate enough to "shoot" my age in golf several times so far, and I am endeavouring to accomplish this on a regular basis. Theoretically, it should become easier to achieve this goal as I grow older—the score can go up a stroke each year! I have sponsored three golf tournaments—on my eightieth, eighty-fifth, and eighty-seventh birthdays. All were at the Dunes, a golf course in Kamloops, British Columbia, in which I used to own an interest. Several friends from England took part in the

It was truly a surprise to find out that Fort McMurray had named a street for my father. Here I am with my son, Dana, and my granddaughter, Ariel. (courtesy Duncan Brown)

My wife, Kim, and I continue to enjoy life, spending winters in Arizona
and spring and summer months in Kelowna, BC.

tournaments and enjoyed the experience. One of them remarked, "I've
never been on a three-day party before."

In 2001 most of my family and I attended the launch of Irwin
Huberman's book *A Place We Call Home*, a book about Fort
McMurray. The launch took place at the Fort McMurray Blueberry
Festival, which is held each September. To my surprise, we were
delighted and honoured to learn that the road in town that borders the
Snye had been designated "Morimoto Drive" in recognition of my

father, a pioneer resident of Fort McMurray.

I have been fortunate to live through a remarkable period in history. It should be remembered that in the early 1920s, especially in the North Country, life hadn't changed a great deal from the previous century. It was still mainly a horse-and-buggy era. Before the automobile age, most roads weren't paved, radio was in its infancy, movie films were silent, television was only a dream, and the airplane was still a novelty. The modern miracle drugs hadn't been invented— a person afflicted with an illness like pneumonia had only a fifty-fifty chance of surviving. In northern Canada where I grew up, winter travel was by dog team or snowshoes; in summer, travel was by canoe or boat on the lakes and rivers. Outdoor privies were the norm. Communications today like the Internet, which allow us to correspond almost immediately with someone continents away, would have been inconceivable.

I deem myself fortunate to have been an observer and a participant in the events of the twentieth century. I have also been favoured to have overcome the poverty and hardships of the Depression and to rise from humble beginnings to enjoy a life of comparative ease and comfort. I have been doubly blessed to have survived and escaped the fate of some of my comrades, to come through the war unscathed. Looking back, I'm proud of having had a part in conserving some of the earth's resources by recovering propane, butane, condensate, and natural gas—resources that oil companies had previously wasted. I think this was the crowning achievement of my professional career. ∎

Notes

Establishing Roots in Canada

1. Jim Darwish was an Arabic trader who had a trading post at Fort Rae in the Northwest Territories. It is remarkable how Arabs have penetrated areas of the globe such as inhospitable northern Canada. Other prominent Arab fur traders were Hamdon and Alley in Fort Chipewyan and Pete Baker, who later became a member of the Northwest Territories council.

Fort McMurray in the 1920s

1. J. G. MacGregor, *Paddle Wheels to Bucket-Wheels on the Athabasca* (Toronto: McClelland and Stewart, 1974).

Fort McMurray's Historic Roots

1. I have used the name Portage La Loche rather than the more commonly accepted Methye Portage. When I was a boy, this portage was called Portage La Loche by old-timers. It was also referred to by early writers as the Long Portage or Portage La Loche.

2. J. J. Hargrave, *Red River* (Montreal: John Lovell, 1871).

3. D. J. Comfort, *Ribbons of Water and Steamboats North* (Fort McMurray, AB: D. J. Comfort, 1974).

4. "Mr. William McMurray, an officer of the Hudson Bay Company, informed me that at a post established by him at latitude 56, longitude 111, he obtained a good crop of wheat, barley, oats, and all garden vegetables." Quoted in Comfort, *Ribbons of Water and Steamboats North*, 71.

5. MacGregor, *Paddle Wheels to Bucket-Wheels*.

6. It is worth noting that Mildred Lake is named after Mildred Terpening, the sister of my boyhood friend Rex Terpening, who has recently written the book *Bent Props and Blowpots* about his flying days in the North. Their father was the watchman at the Hudson's Bay Company shipyards just across the river from Mildred Lake near Tar Island. A sister lake near the Syncrude plant was named Ruth Lake after Rex and Mildred's mother.

7. According to my interpretation, Mr. McLeod's house, which was stated to be on the right bank of the Clearwater River, must have been on Macdonald Island. The HBC sketch on p. 41 erroneously shows the Clearwater flowing into the Athabasca at the west end of Macdonald Island. What is shown as the Clearwater is actually the Snye, which flowed in the opposite direction to join the Clearwater at the east end of the island.

The Rivermen

1. Inspector W. H. Routledge of the North-West Mounted Police, while on patrol by dog team from Fort Saskatchewan via Athabasca Landing to Fort McMurray and points north, arrived in Fort McMurray in January 1898. In his written account, he said, "I was informed by a man named John Macdonald, a servant of the Hudson's Bay who has resided in McMurray for 26 years." This would place John Macdonald as having resided at McMurray in 1872. In Comfort, *Ribbons of Water and Steamboats North*, 243.

2. Ernest Thompson Seton, *The Arctic Prairies: A Canoe-journey of 2,000 Miles in Search of the Caribou; Being the Account of a Voyage to the Region North of Alymer Lake* (New York: Scribner's, 1911).

3. I have never seen a reference to Billy being the first person to take a steamboat through the Grand Rapids, but both Billy and his widow claimed he had done just that. In an interview in 1937 with artist Kathleen Shackleton, sister of famous polar explorer Sir Ernest Shackleton, Loutit said he had taken the SS *Athabasca* down the Athabasca River through the Grand Rapids in 1914. Billy's widow, Jenny Loutit, also told me he had performed this feat. The idea

that someone could take a large steamboat through the Grand Rapids is almost unimaginable, as the rapids are actually a waterfall with a drop of several feet. In *Paddle Wheels to Bucket-Wheels on the Athabasca*, J. G. MacGregor states: "No one had ever taken a sternwheeler down the Grand Rapids but in 1914 the time had come to try that desperate venture. During high water that year the Hudson's Bay Company ran its ATHABASCA RIVER and the [Northern Trader Ltd.] took two of its steamers through the dangerous passage." However, he does not mention Billy Loutit as having been the first to do it.

4. Pete Baker, *Memoirs of an Arctic Arab* (Saskatoon: Yellowknife Publishing Company, c. 1976).

5. Joe Bird, who was the pilot for Jim Cornwall on their hazardous passage down the Athabasca River, came from pioneering stock. His father, James Bird, was an interpreter for the Honourable David Laird, the first lieutenant-governor of the Northwest Territories, when Laird negotiated Treaty No. 7 with the Blackfoot Nation in 1877. Joe remained the pilot of the *Northland Echo* on the Athabasca until his death in the early 1920s.

Early Residents and Characters

1. MacGregor, *Paddle Wheels to Bucket-Wheels*.

2. Ibid.

The Fort Chipewyan Families

1. Agnes Dean Cameron, *The New North* (New York and London: Appleton and Company, 1912).

2. Ibid.

3. Ibid.

The Coming of the Airplane

1. In my opinion, however, the real inception of commercial aviation in the North Country occurred in 1929. It was initiated, appropriately enough, by Wop May's Commercial Airways. As I have mentioned, Punch Dickins had made commercial flights in 1928, but Wop's Commercial Airways was the first airline with scheduled commercial flights, made possible because Wop obtained the government mail contract for locations as far north as Aklavik in the Northwest Territories, near the Arctic Ocean. Wop and his partner Cy Becker started Commercial Airways with financing from the stockbrokers Solloway and Mills.

2. Roy Brown, who founded General Airways, shot down the Red Baron, who was chasing Wop, still a green fledgling pilot.

Striking Out on My Own

1. William Rowan, "The Ten Year Cycle" (Edmonton, AB: University of Alberta, Department of Extension, July 1948). His paper includes a graph of 10-year cycles of HBC–lynx fur returns for 1821–1913 and 1915–34.

The Lure of Gold

1. John Michaels was a Damon Runyonesque character from New York. He had come to Edmonton in the early days and with his Alberta News Company had a stranglehold on distributing magazines and newspapers in northern Alberta. His expressions were as colourful as those of movie producer Samuel Goldwyn; for example, when Michaels wanted to emphasize how much he agreed with you, he'd say, "I'll say the world!"

2. Ray Price, *Yellowknife* (Toronto: Peter Marin Associates, 1974).

3. The liquor permit system was one of paternalistic regulations imposed on the people of the Northwest Territories by the federal government. The territories were ruled by a federally appointed commissioner and a four-member council, all of whom were civil servants in Ottawa. It wasn't until 1947 that a Northerner (J. G. McNiven) was appointed to the council and until 1951 that the Northwest Territories Act was amended to permit three elected representatives to join the five federally appointed members.

Into the Negus Mine

1. Many of the old miners contracted silicosis but wanted to keep on working underground, even when they were told they had the disease. They had such pride in their work, it was incredible.

Joining Up

1. I've often thought it is remarkable how uniform the Canadian accent is—the Maritimes and Newfoundland excepted—when you consider the size of our country. This is in contrast to a small country such as England, where the accent varies tremendously from one area to the next. Similarly, in the United States, there is a considerable difference between the accents of Easterners, Southerners, and Westerners.

The Invasion of Europe

1. Bailey bridges were light-steel temporary bridges designed by the British that could be speedily installed by the Royal Canadian Engineers (RCE). The bridges proved to be invaluable whenever river crossings were required in a hurry.

Back to Civvy Street

1. Although I didn't agree with the management's position on this issue, we were merely junior engineers who had received strict instructions from the general manager not to discuss the matter with anyone, let alone government investigators. We would have been fired immediately if we had. In the end, it didn't matter because of John Diefenbaker's ministrations, which had much more of an effect than anything we could have done.

The Mon-Max Years

1. Pearlite, also called perlite, is made by heating volcanic glass, a type of lava that expands to over twenty times its original volume when heated, which makes it an excellent insulator.

2. A fractionation plant uses distillation towers to separate propane, butane, and condensate (natural gasoline) from the gas that is separated from the oil.

Sunningdale Oils

1. A land man is a very important member of an oil company's staff. Once the leases are obtained, he is responsible for seeing that the company can drill on the property with no problems from landowners or other outside sources. He also attends to myriad details so that drilling can proceed smoothly.